AMERICAN PAGEANTRY

A Movement for Art & Democracy

Theatre and Dramatic Studies, No. 61

Oscar G. Brockett, Series Editor

Professor of Drama and Holder of the
Z. T. Scott Family Chair in Drama
The University of Texas at Austin

Other Titles in This Series

AMERICAN PAGEANTRY

A Movement for Art & Democracy

by
Naima
Prevots

U·M·I Research Press

Ann Arbor / London

Produced and distributed by
UMI Research Press
an imprint of
University Microfilms Inc.
Ann Arbor, Michigan 48106

Library of Congress Cataloging in Publication Data

Prevots, Naima, 1935-
    American pageantry : a movement for art and democracy
/ by Naima Prevots.
        p. cm.—(Theatre and dramatic studies ; no. 61)
    Includes bibliographical references and index.
    ISBN 0-8357-1991-X (alk. paper)
        1. Pageants—United States—History. I. Title. II. Series:
Theater and dramatic studies ; no. 61.
PN3209.P74   1990
791.6'2'0973—dc20   89-29255
                                                                CIP

British Library CIP data is available.

The paper used in this publication meets the minimum requirements of
American National Standard for Information Sciences—Permanence of Paper
for Printed Library Materials, ANSI Z39.48-1984. ♾ ™

In memory of my father, Reuben Wallenrod,
a gentle man for whom the beauty of art and life were intertwined

Contents

Preface

If anyone had told me ten years ago I would be writing a book about pageants I would have told them they were out of their mind. After all, wasn't it common knowledge that pageants were silly, trite productions, full of ridiculous poses and terrible dialogue?

What a surprise to discover that pageants during the period 1905 through 1925 were something totally different than I had ever imagined. I learned that these pageants embodied many of the social and artistic reforms of the early twentieth century and had a vital impact on the development of American theatre, dance, and music.

I am still amazed at how a phenomenon that was considered so important in its day has been forgotten and misunderstood. Those who created the pageants—social workers, civic leaders, and reformers in education, theatre, dance, and music—produced these huge spectacles as a way of changing society and making art an integral part of everyone's life. Their work gives an understanding of the various issues that troubled America during its first two decades, and shows how those in the performing arts were searching for new expressive forms.

My hope is that this book will introduce readers to a serious form of popular art and community ritual, designed to entertain and educate. My intent was not to write an interpretive social and cultural history of the Progressive Era. I wanted to provide a detailed examination of how and why a particular group of passionate people joined forces and what they hoped to achieve through the exciting social force of their dreams. I wanted to see pageantry restored to its rightful place in our history and the message of the pageant leaders spread—that the performing arts can play an important role in making the world a better place.

There are many people who helped make this book possible. Oscar Brockett planted the seed with a suggestion that pageantry should be looked into and provided valuable insights and encouragement during the many years of this research. A fellowship from The National Endowment for the

Humanities made it possible to go to various archives and do intensive writing and I am forever grateful for the honor and time afforded by the award. A faculty grant from the American University provided invaluable release time to work on the manuscript. Margaret Bucky gave emotional support and an enormous amount of editorial assistance. This book would not have been possible without her penetrating questions, her lively imagination and sense of humor, and her understanding of both style and substance. Judy Alter played an important role as friend and critic and offered assistance at many crucial points.

Barbara Filipac at Brown University Library was an amazing resource and helped me through the maze of the Langdon Collection. Mark Brown, curator of manuscripts at Brown University Library was also most helpful. Librarians at Dartmouth, Harvard, Wisconsin, Berkeley, UCLA, Columbia and Barnard, and the Boston and New York Public Libraries assisted greatly, as did Ellen Hughes and Craig Orr at the Smithsonian and Lance Bowling of Cambria Records. Cathie Zusy was wonderful in sharing material and with director Laura Lucky invited me to lecture on pageantry at the Bennington Museum. Ideas were tested and feedback offered when I presented two papers at meetings of dance history scholars.

Evelyn Davis Culbertson, Brice Farwell, Jim Heintze, Alan Kraut, and Michael Kazin and Karen Blair were most gracious in reading the manuscript and giving comments and suggestions. My husband, Martin Wallen, asked penetrating questions at various stages of the work. J. R. Glover came to my rescue in the final stage; in addition to the joy of having her in my house and as a graduate assistant, she pulled all the pieces together at the end. Additional thanks to Sandra Mitchell and Kay Neves for helping with the typing and document compilation. Sam and Frances Stern gave me a home and encouragement during various research trips.

Special thanks to Aaron and Becky for the joy they have given me and to Martin, Jeff, Ruth, and Albert for family caring and support.

Woman Suffrage Procession, Washington, D.C., March 3, 1913
Official program cover.
(Courtesy Brown University Library)

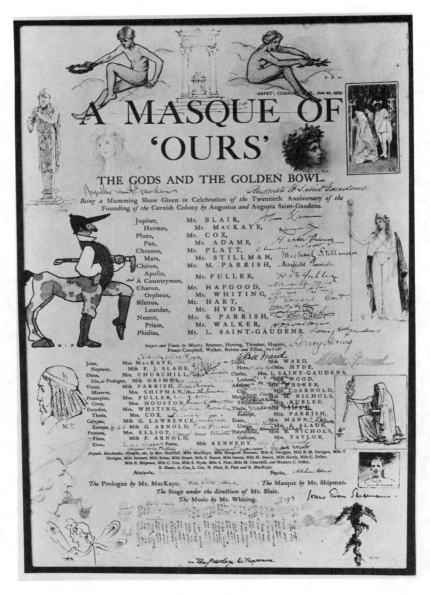

The Gods and the Golden Bowl, Cornish, New Hampshire, 1905
Autographed program. Also known as *The Saint-Gaudens Masque*, this
presentation, written by Percy MacKaye, is generally acknowledged as the first
important pageant to be held in the United States.
(Courtesy Dartmouth College Library)

1

Pageantry: Theatre of the People,
by the People, for the People

Across the vast open space the pilgrims convoyed forty-eight young women
bearing the state flags, as a replica of the Mayflower blazed with light in
Plymouth Harbor and the chorus sang to words by Robert Frost. . . . In a
New York armory women performed a "Dance of Steam" to symbolize
modern industry and their role as equal partners in shaping the world. . . .
On the sloping banks of a river in North Dakota the Spirit of Prophecy told
of the excitement and conflict of extending America's boundaries into the
Northwest. Sakakawea, also called Sacagawea and played by a full-blooded
Indian, sang in her native language about guiding Lewis and Clark over
dangerous mountain ranges. . . . In Boston's Arena, children and adults
danced portions of Swedish, Italian, Russian, Hungarian, and other traditional dances.

These were among the images audiences of thousands saw during the
years when American pageants flourished, from 1905 to 1925. The story of
American pageantry as it unfolded nationwide in dialogue, music, and
movement is told in this book through the writings and work of its leaders.
Their goal was a better America at a time when the country was severely
impacted by the industrial revolution, migration from farms to cities and
huge numbers of foreign immigrants. The pageants reflected the reform
efforts of various segments of the population.

The leaders of American pageantry were settlement-house workers,
civic leaders, playground organizers, suffrage activists, educational reformers, and innovators in theatre, dance, and music. Their premise was that a
better America was based on enlightened democracy—which meant educated participation by individuals in the life of the community. One of the
best ways to achieve democracy, they felt, was to create "art of the people,
by the people, for the people." It was the first time in American history
that such a diverse group of people had put forward the concept that art was
integral to, and a basic element of, the democratic process.

In 1905 when the first twentieth-century American pageant was created in a small town in New Hampshire, Theodore Roosevelt was in his second term as president and the Industrial Workers of the World (IWW) had just been organized.

America was trying to cope with urban congestion and poverty, economic and political control increasingly concentrated in the hands of large business corporations, and millions of new immigrants from foreign lands with different political and cultural traditions. Roosevelt represented those who wanted to bring order out of chaos by reforming existing institutions and putting forward new political initiatives. The IWW sought economic revolution—bread on the table for all and an overturn of the capitalist system. Those who developed American pageants did so as a response to the country's problems, by utilizing art as a way of bringing about change.

The pageant leaders wanted to develop popular art of quality in every community, to make dance, music, and theatre accessible to all and develop American thematic material; and in that they succeeded to a remarkable degree. They also wanted to use the pageants as part of the process of social reform. By bringing people together in their theatrical events they hoped to break down and eliminate ideological differences and barriers of race and class. Their record was mixed in this regard, although their attempt provides a provocative view of art as a political and economic tool.

They did gather together wide segments of the population during weeks of rehearsal and performance. They were sincere in their belief that their framework of art united with democracy would provide a mechanism for exchange of ideas leading to permanent improvements in society.

Ultimately their naive optimism became linked with a view of America skewed toward principles of unity fervently espoused by those who were predominantly white Anglo-Saxon natives. Many of their pageants did not recognize conflicting ideas of history, and their concept of democracy was not extended to include the American Indians or the Blacks, although their record as supporters of the suffrage movement is impressive. America, the land of the free, the home of the brave, was an image that became tarnished when juxtaposed with existing conditions.

The pageant leaders organized the American Pageant Association (APA) in 1913 as this new theatrical form became more widespread. A utopian spirit pervaded their first meeting as they talked about pageants—popular spectacles—an art form that involved entire communities. Pageants, they envisioned, would mobilize creative energy and provide a way of breaking down social, cultural, and economic barriers. The new technology had created cheap entertainment on a mass scale—nickelodeons, phonographs, pulp magazines, radios. These represented passive empty amusements which reinforced urban separation and false values. The pageant would be a new form of popular art that would educate and entertain.

Various members of the APA had their own agendas in creating pageants: the educators thought immigrants would absorb language and history while also learning democratic principles of cooperation and self-governance. They saw the pageant as symbolic of general educational reform which emphasized play, imagination, and experience as opposed to traditional rote methods of learning. Settlement-house workers found pageants to be a good vehicle for their constituents to take pride in their own customs while absorbing and participating in the customs and ideas of their new heritage. Since pageants were community based, settlement houses would become places where theatre was a part of daily life.

The artist members of the APA saw pageants as a catalyst to develop audiences and introduce dance, theatre, and music originating in American rhythms and energies. Civic leaders saw the productions as a way of bridging barriers between the rich and poor and also inculcating patriotic values. Others viewed the pageant form as a platform to make statements about child labor, women's suffrage, and the evils of capitalism.

The American pageant was a visual experience with many facets. It was a work of art, secular not religious, conceived on an enormous scale and called either pageant or *masque* (the name given to presentations that were more abstract and symbolic). It was an evening or afternoon of entertainment; an educational and moral vehicle for change.

Performances most often took place out of doors on a site that was in itself a symbol of the event being celebrated, but pageants also took place in armories and schools. Audiences numbered from 2,000 to 80,000. The participants on stage included as many as 5,000 performers and usually no fewer than 200 members of a community who were totally involved in the process of a pageant presentation.

The broad participatory aspect of pageant production helped define its nature as drama "of the people, by the people, and for the people." One of the leading pageant proponents, Percy MacKaye, summarized this democratic focus as a "new self-government in which political self-government must be rooted to have its flowering; self-government of those leisure hours which the vast movements of labor are fighting for and gradually attaining . . . from which our repressed generations have been too long divorced by the treadmills of machine industrialism."[1]

It was the community, organized into numerous committees, that democratically determined funding, costuming, publicity and even the pageant scripts themselves. The community members were the dancers, singers, actors, stage designers, prop makers, historical researchers, and the audience.

The pageant differed from a conventional piece of theatre in many respects. Instead of character and plot in a proscenium-arch setting, presented in a two- or three-act drama of conflict and resolution, a pageant was an epic-scale presentation, performed in a large open space, celebrating an occasion or a person important to a particular community. The pageant proceeded in a series of episodes, usually three to seven, that covered a span of 200 to 2,000 years. Each episode was self-contained. If an episode was eliminated it would mean no loss of continuity but simply that one facet of the theme would be unexplored, for a pageant was the story of an idea: Peace, Progress, Education, Brotherhood, Liberty, Freedom.

A spoken prologue introduced the pageant. Vocal and orchestral music were integrated into the presentation, as were expressive and symbolic movement, group pantomime, poetry, and dialogue. Much of the material originated in American history, folklore, and legends. Dance interludes or dialogue were used to separate one episode from the next and to illuminate the theme. A prologue provided a pageant summary and a "march past" created a heroic and colorful ending.

When a community decided on a pageant for an important celebration, a committee was established to hire a pageant master and develop a financial structure. The pageant master was an individual with experience in theatre, script writing, and organization. He or she would meet with the pageant committee many months in advance of the projected production to discuss ideas and finances. Most pageant masters believed that proceeds from ticket sales, publication of pageant scripts with paid advertisement, and donations and subscriptions from community members would pay the cost of production.

Budgets were large in the case of huge city-wide pageants, and modest when the pageants involved a smaller community or group of villages. Smaller pageants could cost $10,000 and larger ones over $100,000, but this was proportionate to the size of audience, the amount of advertising, and guaranteed subscriptions. Salaries were paid to the pageant masters, whose fees ranged from $1,000 to $2,000, and to dance directors, who received about $500. Expenses for the commission or performance of music could run from $2,000 to $6,000.

Often wealthy people in a community were asked to guarantee sums of money that would be utilized if the pageant was not self-sustaining. Sometimes a board of trade or some other central state, city, or local agency supplied start-up funds, enough to pay expenses for the several visits of a pageant master to meet the community, examine possible sites, and learn about the community's history and important events. Start-up money was also used to build stages, grandstands, or other pageant necessities.

The Pageant of Sherbourne in 1905, commemorating the twelve-hundredth anniversary of the founding of Sherbourne, England, is usually considered the model for the pageants that began emerging in the United States. It was conceived by Louis Napoleon Parker, an English dramatist, director, and composer, who is credited by American pageantry writers with being the father of the twentieth-century form.

As he was preparing this pageant, Parker explained to the community exactly what the pageant was not: "It is not a street procession. It is not a gala. It is not a wayzegoose. It is not a fete. It is not a beanfest. It is not done on trollies. It is not tableaux vivants."[2]

Parker was heavily influenced by Richard Wagner and in his autobiography, *Several of My Lives*, said he had an "epoch making experience" when Wagner came to London in 1877.[3] In Bayreuth, Parker missed only one performance, and when he created the pageant at Sherbourne, he wrote of Wagner's influence on his use of indigenous material and of uniting the people in a communal experience.[4]

Parker made it clear in his writing that there was a distinction between his use of the word *pageant* and the way it had been used historically to identify coronations, parades and processions. Although religious pageants such as Bavaria's Oberammergau Passion Play exhibited extensive community involvement, Parker identified his pageant as one that was distinctly secular, designed to emphasize historical development rather than religious spirit.

The first important American pageant, *The Gods and the Golden Bowl*, sometimes referred to as *The Saint-Gaudens Masque* was presented in June 1905 in celebration of the twentieth anniversary of the founding of an artists' colony in Cornish, New Hampshire, by Augustus and Augusta Saint-Gaudens.[5] The masque was written by Louis Evans Shipman and the prologue was created by Percy MacKaye. Along with the *Pageant of Sherbourne*, this presentation is credited as an influence on the development of pageantry in this country.

The performance took place in a pine grove on the Saint-Gaudens estate with more than seventy participants performing after several weeks of preparation. Maxfield Parrish designed a green-gray curtain on which hung green gilded masks. Members of the Boston Symphony Orchestra, artfully secreted behind evergreens, played under the baton of Arthur Whiting, who also composed the music. John Blair, the actor, was director of the production.

Although the characters were gods and goddesses (Jupiter, Hermes, and others) and not historical figures connected with either Cornish or New Hampshire, this masque made a deep impression on all those involved and marked a form of community celebration and participation that commemorated a place and a person, the person being the sculptor Augustus Saint-

Gaudens. It showed that a group of individuals could work together in a cooperative spirit, bringing music, dance, and poetry together in the creation of an original artistic presentation.

It was not until 1908–9 that the word *pageant* appeared in several community celebrations, all involving scripted productions, seated audiences, and episodic dramatic construction integrating dance, music, and the spoken word. *The Pageant of Education* produced in Boston in 1908 by Lotta Clark, a high-school teacher of American history, and *The Pageant of the Italian Renaissance,* presented by Thomas Wood Stevens in 1909 in the Statuary Hall of the Chicago Art Museum, were among the first two of note.

By 1911 there were pageants in Taunton, Deerfield, and Springfield, Massachusetts; Thetford and Bennington, Vermont; Peterborough, New Hampshire; New London, Connecticut; Milwaukee, Wisconsin; and St. Paul, Minnesota. In 1913 there were forty-six pageants produced in fifteen different states and in 1916 the state of Indiana alone produced forty-five pageants. The APA listed the pageants presented each year; numerous pageant scripts still exist in various libraries and special collections. Most of the pageants had historical themes of regional, national, or international importance and were produced by large and small communities, educational institutions, and various special interest groups.[6]

The increase in the number of pageants was directly related to the escalation of other unified coalition reform efforts that characterized the Progressive Era. "By around 1910, many of these crusading men and women were calling themselves progressives. Ever since, historians have used the term 'progressivism' to describe the many reform movements of the early twentieth century."[7] Reform efforts that had developed before the Civil War emphasized changing the individual. Post–Civil War reforms had as their focus changing society and identifying flaws in existing institutions. Numerous reform efforts had developed in the 1890s but before the turn of the century the groups involved were isolated from one another and "not until after 1900 would diverse dissatisfied Americans come together in support of progressive reforms. Until then they carried on separate and largely unsuccessful campaigns for change."[8] When Theodore Roosevelt ran for president in 1912 on the Progressive (Bull Moose) Party ticket national recognition was given to coalitions for change.

The early twentieth-century crusaders joined forces for a large variety of causes, such as forming the National Child Labor Committee (1904), organizing the radical Industrial Workers of the World (1905), and founding the Play-ground Association of America (1906). Other organizations for reform that came into being during this period were the National Association for Industrial Education (1909), the National Conference on City Planning and the National Association for the Advancement of Colored People (1909),

Historical Pageant of Bennington, Bennington, Vermont, 1911
Program cover.
(Courtesy Bennington Museum)

Scenes from Bennington Pageants, 1911 (*above*) and 1927 (*below*)
(*Courtesy Bennington Museum*)

and the National Women's Party (1913). Like the reformers of earlier periods those of the Progressive era spoke and wrote in strong moral tones reflecting primarily white, middle-class values rooted in patriotic allegiance to America.

When the American Pageant Association was formed in 1913, its members didn't agree about all facets of pageantry. They did agree, however, that pageant productions could be a powerful force for change in American life and they believed in pageants of quality. They were afraid that unless information was exchanged and professional control was exercised, pageants lacking in artistic and social import would flood the scene.

Eventually this did happen, but the decline of the American Pageantry Movement is also tied to the decline of optimism that shaped the reforms of the Progressive Era. "After the war, the balance tipped against organized ameliorative reform. A progressive movement which had been merely divided now became embattled. . . . Progressivism waned after 1917, not primarily because of the war, but more because of the revival of profound social divisions and growing malaise with reform."[9] The concerns about integrating immigrants had turned to distrust and fear. The Johnson-Reed Act was passed in 1924, limiting the number of immigrants allowed into the United States to the percentage of the group already here.

By the 1920s the character and intention of the American pageant had changed from the original artistic and visionary goals of the APA. The last important vestige of early American pageantry was Sidney Howard's 1925 *Pageant of Lexington* in Massachusetts, produced just after the author had won a Pulitzer Prize for his Broadway play *They Knew What They Wanted*.

Pageants became standardized, and model pageants were published and sold for use with elementary-school children, YWCAs, and commercial producing groups. Many of these pageants were written by individuals without professional theatre experience and the scripts had very little artistic merit. Gone was the original premise of the reformers who were the leaders of the APA that pageants could become a force for change by uniting art and democracy. No longer were groups interested in producing a pageant by mobilizing citizens for various tasks and encouraging them to participate in a secular community ritual.

The word pageant took on the connotation of a trite spectacle created and staged by amateurs. The bold idea of theatre "of the people, by the people, and for the people" was replaced by productions that had the superficial trappings of a popular spectacle without the vision and energy that originally defined American pageantry. The American Pageantry Movement was forgotten, barely mentioned in history books. Documents relating to its development and activities were stored in archives and for the most part were not easily accessible.

Pageantry deserves to be reevaluated, as it left a significant legacy in theatre, dance, and music and set a model for secular community celebrations. But it is the basic premise of the American Pageantry Movement that gives pageantry its greatest meaning for us today—that art can and should play a role in molding a better society.

The Pageant and Masque of Saint Louis, May 1914
Poster.
(Courtesy Brown University Library)

The Pageant Process:
Working Together by Playing Together

The key to an understanding of American pageantry is the way in which diverse reform groups sought democratic self-government through artistic enterprise. When a pageant was created the emphasis was as much on process as on product and citizens from all walks of life were mobilized to raise money, build stages, originate advertising campaigns, sew costumes, and rehearse their parts as members of a large cast. Implicit in the idea of presenting a pageant was involving as many people as possible and relating the content to the history and needs of the community. More often than not, the pageant reflected the efforts of different reformers to institute change that would culminate in what they perceived as a better self-image and improved living and working conditions.

The history of *The Pageant and Masque of St. Louis*, presented May 28–31, 1914, provides one example of the way pageant organization and process defined the form. The pageant leaders wrote about their venture as one that would show how art could facilitate and encourage democracy. They claimed that the pageant involved the whole city and broke down barriers. The documents show that for the most part this was true, but the involvement of Blacks was almost nonexistent and it is not clear whether organized labor or a multitude of the poorer working class played a significant role in the "democratic process."

Although the pageant was not presented until 1914, the first suggestion for a city-wide event came from Charlotte Rumbold in 1912. As secretary of the Public Recreation Commission of the St. Louis Park Department, she was active in the Playground Association of America. This organization saw the creation of new, defined play spaces as a solution for those who lived in poor, congested, urban environments—an important reform concept at the turn of the century. Rumbold was one of many civic leaders in St. Louis who felt the city was deteriorating because of poor political, social, and economic conditions brought on by the lack of ability to cope with new factories, immigrants, and business control of local government. The American writer Lincoln Steffens had published two articles in *McLure's Magazine* in 1902 and 1903 detailing political corruption in St. Louis.[1] In 1911, the St. Louis Civic League, concerned with the need for municipal reform, lost their campaign for a new city charter which would address some of the issues Steffens had raised. St. Louis had once been called "the gateway to the West," but as the fourth largest city in the United States it was rapidly gaining an image as a place inferior to the dynamic burgeoning industrial city of Chicago.

Charlotte Rumbold had become interested in pageants being held in other cities and towns, and she was a strong believer in the power of organized leisure to bring people together and set positive community goals. She succeeded in convincing the mayor, Henry Kiel, that a city-wide pageant should be planned for the one-hundred-fiftieth anniversary of St. Louis in 1914. On July 2, 1913, a group met at city hall to discuss the pageant project, and two representatives from each of seventy-five various local organizations formed the St. Louis Pageant Drama Association (SLPDA). They chose as officers two individuals who were also active in the St. Louis Civic League: John Gundlach, involved in real estate, became chair of the Pageant Executive Committee, and Luther Ely Smith, a lawyer, became secretary.

Charlotte Rumbold, in an article in *The Survey* (July 4, 1914), wrote of this meeting a year after the pageant had taken place:

> Last summer, a handful of people decided that the city was ripe for a new expression of its pride in past achievements and its hope for a solution of its present problems. Strong in the faith that if people play together, they will work together, and in the knowledge that a beautiful expression of an ideal increases many-fold the power of the ideal, they determined to put to the touch their faith in the city's inherent capacity for united action. . . . A call had been sent to every business, political, social, artistic, national, and religious organization in the city, explaining the purpose of their meeting and asking the appointment of delegates. The response was so unexpectedly large as to give assurance of the democracy of the undertaking from the very first. The organization of committees was taken in hand at once. Among them, of course, the committees on finance, on production, organization and publicity were the most important. On these committees and the others later appointed were persons, not only of every nationality, profession, trade, religion and social status, but from every ward and precinct of the city. With the idea of democracy continually in mind the executive organization took special care that no section of the city, no group of people should be omitted from the administrative committees, from the cast or from the financial campaign.[2]

The SLPDA Advisory Committee chose Percy MacKaye and Thomas Wood Stevens to write a masque and pageant depicting the history and development of St. Louis in both realistic and symbolic terms. By November 1913 the site for the pageant had been chosen and was described by Stevens in a letter to a colleague, Thomas H. Dickinson, as having "perfect sight lines."

The place chosen for the pageant was a natural amphitheatre and a semicircular hill which sloped down to a crescent-shaped lagoon approximately fifty feet wide by one hundred and twenty-five feet long. This location had served as the site of the Louisiana Purchase Centennial Exposition in 1904.

The program credited the park department with building the stage. "As many persons as are ordinarily employed in a big theatrical company will be at work for over two months."[3] When finally constructed the stage was semicircular: roughly 200 feet deep and about 500 feet wide in back and 800 feet wide in front. During the performance the stage and surrounding areas successfully accommodated about 7,500 participants and on some evenings over 100,000 audience members.

Casting for this enormous production was handled by a committee, which promised that it would be "as convenient to enroll for the cast of the Pageant and Masque as it is to go to a polling place and vote. In fact, it will be a great deal more so." Fifty registration places were established in all parts of the city, where "casting cards" were available for individuals to write their name, address, sex, occupation, national origin, age, weight, height, and name of employer. The card also had space for people to note whether they could dance, sing, ride a horse, or paddle a canoe.

Cast cards were placed in every public library, in downtown department stores, at all public and parochial schools, at universities, improvement associations, and social clubs. A representative of the casting committee was stationed at enrollment places at certain times to give information and answer questions. *The Pageant and Masque of St. Louis*, Bulletin No. 2, included a facsimile of the enrollment card which could be cut and mailed to the SLPDA headquarters (750 Century Building) and the format was explained:

> The reason our embryo stars are requested to give their age, as well as the color of their hair, their weight, height, etc. is that the committee, in selecting the performers, may be sure the actor possesses the natural qualifications for the particular part assigned. For example, old Indian chiefs will be required. The age, height, color of hair and weight of the persons selected for these roles will be important qualifications. So many actors and actresses are needed that the producing stage managers cannot hope to know them all, and a readily available index of each prospective member of the cast will be an invaluable aid in assigning the parts.[4]

"The cast was selected entirely on the basis of the answers to these questions, not in the least on social standing," noted Charlotte Rumbold.

I, THE UNDERSIGNED, HEREBY APPLY FOR AN ASSIGNMENT IN THE CAST OF THE SAINT LOUIS PAGEANT.

Name

Address

Sex   Age

Occupation

Nationality   Wt.   Ht.

Dancer ⎫
Singer ⎬   Employer
Horseman ⎪
Canoeist ⎭   Signature

Enlisting Participants
Enrollment card for the *Pageant and Masque of Saint Louis* (*above*)
and community speakers card for *Caliban* (*below*).
(*[above] Courtesy Brown University Library; [below] courtesy
Dartmouth College Library*)

COMMUNITY SPEAKERS REFERENCE CARD
(To be placed on file at the "Caliban" office)

Name
Address
                                    .   Tel.
School or College
Club
Occupation or Profession
Experience or training in speaking

Please mark X the time of day and days of the week most convenient for you to speak

Days of the week	Mornings	Afternoons	Evenings
Monday			
Tuesday			
Wednesday			
Thursday			
Friday			
Saturday			

Due notice will be given in regard to speaking dates

CALIBAN COMMITTEE OF GREATER BOSTON
420 Boylston Street

The enrollment places for cast members were identified as "polling places" and "women will not only be allowed to vote, they will be urged to do so. The fact that all applicants will be asked to give their age is not expected to have a depressing effect on the feminine vote for this occasion, in spite of dismal forebodings along this line from occasional humorists." Not all 7,500 performers to be enrolled would be needed at each performance, but the casting committee felt it necessary to have enough substitutes to cover contingencies of sickness or other unforeseen emergencies.

The casting committee solicited the participation of different ethnic and fraternal organizations as groups in particular episodes. Numerous immigrant groups were involved in specific episodes which had to do with their coming to St. Louis and becoming part of the city: Bavarians, Bohemians, Croations, Greeks, Italians, Poles, Hungarians, Serbians. One of the episodes required hunters and trappers for which the Swedish National Society recruited one hundred of its members.

> A group of Greeks who had not yet learned English appeared in their national costume. A group of Swedes endeared themselves to the costume and property committees by their wonderful helpfulness. Daughters of the American Revolution were costumed as ladies attending a ball in honor of Lafayette. The North-Western Improvement Association and the City Club, between them with their wives and children, made the great procession of pioneers that moved across the stage with ox-carts and prairie schooners and dogs and horses in the long, last lights of the sunset. And all these people knew their city as never before.[5]

The democratic thrust of the casting committee did not initially seem to include consideration of the large Black population of roughly 44,000 people. James L. Usher in a letter to Luther Ely Smith on April 17, 1914, complained that no Blacks had been appointed to the pageant executive committee, nor assigned any roles in the pageant. It appears that one Black did finally play in the pageant, and there were no stipulations in any of the publicity or notices about segregated seating, but there were clearly unfortunate limits in this notion of "democracy."

In July 1914 Smith presented a paper for a sociology conference, "Municipal Pageants as Destroyers of Race Prejudice." He noted that *The Pageant and Masque of St. Louis*, "a vast experiment in democracy," had broken down irrational artificial barriers between people of different races and created understanding and acceptance. He wrote that the keynote of the undertaking was this: "If we learn to play together, we shall work together." In working with all the different immigrant groups "we shall come to know them as they truly are and will like them and they will like us!" He felt the pageant "was like a transfiguration, like a vision of heaven— of the new earth that is to be . . . no race or natural apathy . . . destroyed not by logic or reason, but by playing together, working together." Blacks and Indians were not the focus of Smith's concerns for he was only interested with integration of the European immigrants to become "fine American citizens."[6]

The costume committee was a crucial part of the production: about 7,500 costumes had to be made and the pageant depended heavily on their beauty and visual effectiveness. This committee had its headquarters in an empty floor in a downtown office building. Hundreds of volunteers worked to meet the rehearsal and performance deadlines.

> The Mothers' Clubs of the public schools did wonders in completing the enormous task. There were committees from half a dozen other women's clubs who gave an afternoon regularly each week, and all sorts of individual volunteers—debutantes, matrons, school teachers, school girls and girls from the department store alteration rooms, gave their leisure time for weeks. Many of the properties were made in the manual training departments of the public schools.[7]

Another important committee provided publicity. One of its subcommittees was a lecture bureau that spread the word about the pageant, its purpose, meaning, and importance to the community. Speakers were sent to various organizations and parts of the city to explain the history of St. Louis and how the pageant was being developed, and to encourage participation. Rumbold reported that there were as many as four pageant speakers a night in different parts of the city. "City salesman from the great wholesale dry goods, hardware and other business houses made admirable speeches. In the public schools the larger boys and girls explained the Pageant and Masque to the children in the lower grades."

Many organizations expected the lecture to include a fund-raising request, and this did happen. But each lecturer was also requested to convince as many people as possible to fill out cast cards. "Many a tired business man, remembering that he had at one time been able to paddle a canoe, cheerfully agreed to come to all the rehearsals, wear a costume consisting chiefly of war paint, and do something for his city beside write a cheque."

Through a writers' bureau people were solicited to write articles about the forthcoming production and many of these were placed with newspapers in small towns throughout the state. Rumbold summed up the mission of the publicity committee:

> They understood and cordially agreed with the idea of the executive committee that the purpose of the great production and the production itself was the important thing, the thing that must be brought home to the community. The Pageant and Masque was not given to advertise St. Louis but to bring the people of St. Louis to an understanding of their city's possibilities. What the publicity committee had to present, therefore, was an ideal—which is much more difficult to work into advertising matter than a new breakfast food.

Community Involvement
Volunteerism was the critical element to the success of all pageants. Here, women
are shown sewing costumes for the *Philadelphia Pageant,* 1912.
(Courtesy Brown University Library)

The children in the public schools sold pageant buttons, about one hundred and thirty thousand, "and they did it, each one of them, with a pride in doing something for the city." A costume design contest offered a first prize of two-hundred dollars for at least five figures in one episode. There were five individual design prizes ranging from ten to fifty dollars. The St. Louis Public Library and the Mercantile Library were asked to assist the costume contestants by providing historical books, costume plates, and other material. The Missouri Historical Society and Jefferson Memorial Hall in Forest Park displayed collections of actual clothing, weapons, accessories, and portraits. Designs were displayed at the public library after the contest was over.

There was a design contest for program cover and postcards. The postcard contest was not successful, so the publicity committee hired a professional artist named Berminghaus. The city's largest firms enclosed 20,000 of his postcards for sale in their mailings. Many firms included St. Louis Pageant/Masque advertising circulars in parcels that they shipped, and salesmen carried brochures when they went on the road. The SLPDA opened rehearsals to the public and filmed the pageant.

Employers released workers for rehearsals—with a little pushing from pageant organizers. Thomas Wood Stevens divided his cast into twelve units and assigned each group a leader. Everyone in the cast was given a card with general instructions: a request for silence backstage, reporting times for the different units, how to turn in costumes, where to go for toilets and food, where to park, and so on. Performers for each episode assembled at designated places near the stage and remained there until a stage director with a megaphone had them assemble for entrances. Cues for the entrances of each group were given by stage directors seated in the towers on each side of the stage. The ninety-piece band and the five-hundred voice chorus "chosen from the best choirs . . . and from the singing societies and musical academies" performed from a sunken platform behind a low mound at center stage.

There was great concern that lack of money would prevent anyone from attending. In order to make seating as democratic as possible a central aisle running up the hill divided seats into two groups: those on the left were sold and those on the right were free. Reserved seats were in four price categories: $.25, $.50, $1.00 and $1.50. Individual box seats were $2.50 and boxes for six were $15.00. Various accounts indicate that for the opening performance the best of the free seats were gone by mid-afternoon and that many people came more than once.

During the four performances, at which attendance was estimated to be about half a million, volunteers assisted in crowd control. The police department detailed 235 people, including mounted men, captains, sergeants, and drill masters. They handled emergencies, dealt with parking 3,000 automobiles, and supervised the streetcar terminals and concessions. Several hundred boy scouts acted as ushers and general assistants. Rumbold proudly reported:

> But four times the number of police and boy scouts could not have handled that crowd. That crowd handled itself. St. Louis crowds are accustomed to self-government, and this was one more instance of what we call in St. Louis the "democratization of public recreational facilities."

As the pageant developed, one of the scenes showed "Saint" Louis calling upon the leading cities of the nation for help in the battle against the War Demon, the Elements, Ignorance, and Degradation. The publicity committee conceived the idea of having representatives from different cities appear in the pageant and holding a "Conference of Cities" during the day.

> The largest city in each State, as shown by the United States census of 1910, has been invited to send an envoy to take part in the drama, and . . . to represent the best things in the progress and development of your great city. The representative should also be

able to take part in the drama himself, to appear to advantage on horseback. . . . An important part of the programme of the Pageant and Masque of St. Louis will be a civic conference of the envoys from the various cities during Pageant week, to consider the municipal pageant, the civic theatre, the democratization of art in city life. Among those who are expected to take part are: Mr. John W. Alexander, Mr. Lorado Taft, Mr. Frederick Law Olmsted, Mr. Daniel Durham, Dr. Frederick Howe, Miss Jane Addams, Dr. Henry Bruere, Prof. George Pierce Baker, Prof. Richard Burton.[8]

The Conference of Cities took place during the days of the performances and was very successful. It is not clear how many people in St. Louis attended the conference speeches, which covered an array of topics: "The Development of Folk Dancing in America," Luther Gulick; "Music and the Pageant," Arthur Farwell; "People's Choral and Musical Societies," Frank Damrosch; "People's Orchestra," F. X. Arens; "Municipal Recreation: A School of Democracy," Charlotte Rumbold; "Humanizing City Government," Henry Bruere. In his address, "City Government," Bruere played an advocacy role for pageantry and the arts, saying, "You cannot win the people to an active interest in government until you begin to dramatize and humanize government acts."

The conference agenda included "suggestion for an Immediate Program for St. Louis: retention of open-air theatre on pageant site; use of school auditorium, rooms and gymnasiums for musical and dramatic clubs for physical culture, dancing and recreation; development of civic spirit among existing choral societies and clubs (in conjunction with Symphony Orchestra) looking to great Public Musical Festivals." After the performances, the St. Louis Municipal Theatre was constructed with the balance of funds and the St. Louis Pageant Drama Association and the Pageant Choral Society remained active.

The Pageant of St. Louis by Thomas Wood Stevens began at 6:30 P.M. There was an intermission of thirty minutes after which the audience assembled for Percy MacKaye's *The Masque of St. Louis.* Stevens and MacKaye worked closely together from the beginning to make sure the pageant would be realistic, the masque symbolic. The creation of an outdoor structure was important for both; it was a democratic environment for large audiences which recaptured the ancient Greek theatre's sense of art as community ritual.

As the audiences settled into their seats they could see the set of the pageant: trees and a few dwellings; a partially constructed mound on top of which a fire burned low. Suggestion rather than literal realism was the key visually, as it was in all other pageants of that era. The ancient past was imaginatively portrayed to the audience as the "mound-builders," the first settlers of St. Louis, appeared, led by their priest.

A young chief arrived and told the high priest that "the mounds, at the end of this hunting shall lift their heads no higher." The priest fell in a heap at the feet of the young chief, as people came, according to the pageant script, "bringing earth, which they cast over the body of the dead man."

Then the audience watched a long pantomime scene depicting the daily activities, dances, and songs of the next group to settle in St. Louis, the Plains Indians. Also in pantomime was the arrival of the explorer de Soto, his search for gold and disappointment in not finding it. The arrival and departure of Joliet, Marquette, and La Salle were depicted in dialogue. An Indian "Prophet" appeared and foretold of "strong pale men with thunder in their hands . . . who will make new trails." The Indian prophet further foresaw "into the west our nations trooping slow" as they were made to move from their own lands.

The pageant then covered the period 1763 to 1803—from the coming of the French to the time when Americans took possession of the city. While the shift in ownership was depicted almost completely in dialogue, a lengthy pantomime showed the Lewis and Clark expedition setting out in boats and the arrival of new settlers in "covered wagons drawn by oxen. . . . Up stage considerable parties of hunters and trappers, Kentucky pioneers, pass, stopping for various goods." The scene began to change dramatically: "The old French type of dress is rapidly disappearing, the various American types taking its place. . . . New buildings are erected, until the stage assumes the look of a square surrounded by business structures. . . . The settlers who pass now . . . represent various European nationalities as well as the eastern and southern states."

The Civil War and the ensuing victory were enacted as the final pantomime of the pageant.

> Enter a torchlight procession, bearing banners and transparencies, and toward the end, a picture of Lincoln. . . . The procession passes from sight. The music changes, and the people crowd to the left, where a newspaper bulletin, illuminated by torchlight, is seen. From this focal point spreads through the crowd and the city the tidings from Fort Sumter; and when the action of the crowd permits, groups of young men are seen departing from the two sides of the stage—northward and southward. The music changes to the Battle Hymn of the Republic, and bodies of Union troops are seen marching across and to the South, singing. There is a pause in the music as they pass from sight, and women's voices are heard in the distance, at the right, singing Dixie. They cease, and the sad lines of wounded and prisoners are brought in, nurses and the men of the Sanitary Commission working among them. Again the mood of the music changes, and the people gather by the newspaper offices. An exultant note creeps in, and then the news of peace is sounded, and the people, with flags and flowers, make momentary festival. The music ceases, the lights disappear.

Percy MacKaye commissioned Frederick S. Converse to write music and Joseph Lindon Smith to be the stage director of *The Masque of St. Louis*. The masque opened with "The Prelude," subtitled "Cahókia's

Dream," and the program description shows how the opening set the tone for the entire masque.

THE PRELUDE

Out of complete darkness mysterious music rises, prelusive to the appearance of a visionary scene on the plaza. There, before the central mound (as the music continues, descriptive) Spirits of the Mound-Builders perform the ceremonies of a prehistoric ritual. Dimly seen, in the darkness of the vast stage, is an ancient temple of the Maya civilization—a concrete expression of the religion of the great race of red men of Yucatan and Central America. The temple is to some extent a replica of the famous CHICHEN ITZA, one of the great masterpieces of architecture of this wonderful period of art in the Western World. Into the scene comes a great procession, suggesting the symbolism and imagery of the race: Heroes and gods—priests and priestesses (dancers) and musicians walk solemnly across the great plaza before the temple—a brilliant spectacle, exotic and unique, flooded in the warm glow of sunset light. While priests perform a ceremony at the altar in front of a great mound, above which towers the shrine of the temple, groups of men, boys and girls give expression in dance to religious inspiration and embodiment of strength and grace; and when the climax of the dance is reached, the vision fades—the lights grow dim, night steals on, and only the glow of the altar fire remains.

MacKaye then presented Cahókia, who symbolized "the pinnacle of the social aspirations of the Indian race." Soon from above the wall of the temple appeared the Spirits of the Stars. They were "grouped in their constellations: Orion, the Pleiades, the Scorpion, etc. Highest over all—a vast, silhouetted bulk on the sky, twinkling with the seven lights of the 'Dipper'— looms Wásapédan, the Great Bear." This dialogue ensued between Wásapédan and Cahókia:

WÁSAPÉDAN	Hope I behold, Cahókia.
CAHÓKIA	What is the hope you behold there?
WÁSAPÉDAN	Life and new labor.
CAHÓKIA	Who brings me Life out of death?
WÁSAPÉDAN	Mississippi.
CAHÓKIA	How shall his spirit restore me Seed for new harvest?
WÁSAPÉDAN	He wanders To ends of the earth
CAHÓKIA	But what token Has he attained there?
WÁSAPÉDAN	A child
CAHÓKIA	Ha! Child of my loins—of my red race Shall he restore me, to build now Mounds for my temples once more?
WÁSAPÉDAN	Nay! Child of a new race he brings you Pale as a star—child, and starry

CAHÓKIA	Now Speak, Wásapédan! What means his Sword and its mission?
WÁSAPÉDAN	He brings it To fight for the rights of the star-born— Freedom and brotherhood
CAHÓKIA	So, then, He shall inherit my battles Bolder to wage them, and nobler Temples to build on my mound-tops. O Wásapédan, my heart beats Higher to welcome him. When, ah, When shall I greet him?
WÁSAPÉDAN	Behold him! Lo, where the Father of Waters Brings now the white child!

(From the sky region of the Bear, a shooting-star flies trailing across the dark and falls beyond the bend of the waters on the south. Filling it with his gaze, Cahókia gives a long, joyous cry!)

MacKaye established a continuous sense of mystery, excitement, and suspense through the integrated use of music, dance, choral speaking, singing, lighting, and stage setting. The audience was helped through the difficult symbolism by MacKaye's supreme theatricality and was prepared for the next series of events and symbols. As in many of the pageants and masques, water was used in the St. Louis masque as a dramatic and symbolic device: as Cahókia cried "El-a-ho,"

Round the far bend of the waters appears the prow of an immense canoe, fantastic with totem carvings and ancient Mayan symbols. In the painted prow stands Mississippi—masked figure of great stature, murky yellow, with huge flowing beard of yellow, and body adorned with river-reeds. The canoe is manned by his River Spirits, of whom the central group bear upraised on their heads and bended arms a litter of rushes. On this stands a little child—a strong-limbed boy—with golden hair. Beside him, perpendicular, shines a colossal sword.

Mississippi moved toward Cahókia with the child, preceded by the chanting of the River Spirits. As he gave the child to Cahókia and prepared to depart once again on the waters, Mississippi proclaimed: "Here on your ancient / Mound—here I leave them: / Cherish the child: / Guard well his token."

This was immediately followed by a dramatic scene as "With loud yelling, the Wild Nature Forces leap up from their places of shadow . . . forms masked with heads of wolves, bears, and horned antelopes . . . rush forward tumultuous, in live rhythmic waves, and surround the mound. There, mingled with feathered Indians, they dance wildly to the war-beat of tom-toms." They are confronted by the child who holds his sword, and finally "they rush into the darkness and vanish." Wásapédan reappeared and heralded the coming of ships carrying additional symbolic figures clothed in brilliant and fantastic garb to the accompaniment of a male chorus singing the "Veni Creator." Among the groups emerging from the boats were monks and priests, "men and women of the Latin nations, Elves, Dryands and Fauns." The main point of this grand entry was to prepare the way for "three male figures, masked." One was a knight with the standard of lions who had come "to do homage . . . to the white child." Another was a figure called "the One with the Lillies," who had also come to honor the child. The main figure was "the One with the Cross," who had come to christen the child "St. Louis."

The second part of *The Masque of St. Louis* was the symbolic story of a boy named St. Louis growing up, fulfilling the promise of a "new world," and overcoming all evils in the process. After a chorus sang "Where shall we camp—camp—camp," large groups of pioneers dressed as miners and rangers carrying picks, scythes, and rifles arrived. They saluted St. Louis, but their joy was disrupted by the entrance of Gold. He was accompanied by "Earth Spirits" who responded to his call as "the ground, opening now in various places, belches forth green, blue, yellow and silver fire." After a dramatic fight, which was accompanied by mass action, dialogue, and a good deal of sword clanging, Gold was vanquished. St. Louis proclaimed, "Now freedom and strong brotherhood prevail." After Gold left "there enters now a multitude of men and women, garbed in native costumes of all nations." Preeminent among them, on horseback, ride five masked figures, symbolic of Europe, Africa, Asia, Australia, and the Ocean Islands. The "Chorus of the World Adventurers" merged with the pioneers and spoke of America as a star in the west.

But there is no rest for St. Louis and the forces of good. The entire space is soon swarming with war demons, poverty, and once again Gold. St. Louis calls on the other cities to form in league with him and conquer Gold, and figures on horseback in medieval garb, each representing an American city, come to his aid. St. Louis tells them to "shape the sordid world to the likeness of our dreams." Wásapédan then calls to St. Louis, "Behold the wings! . . . Eagle's wings! . . . America! Your league rides on his wings, and rises towards the stars!" MacKaye wrote a spectacular finale: as they all cry out "St. Louis! The League of Cities," an airplane flies across the sky with fireworks in its wake, symbolizing the American eagle: power, strength, beauty. Finally, a large chorus sings the words and theme stated earlier in the masque:

The Masque of Saint Louis, 1914
"Gold" being deposed by "Love" and "Imagination."
(From Ralph Davol, A Handbook of American Pageantry *[Taunton, Mass.: Davol Publishing Company, 1915])*

The Masque of Saint Louis, 1914
"World Adventurers" and the "League of Cities" come to the aid of Saint Louis.
(Courtesy Smithsonian Institution, Washington, D.C.)

Out of the formless void
Beauty and order are born:
One for the all, all in one,
We wheel in the joy of our dance.

Brother with brother
Sharing our light,
Build we new worlds
With ancient fire!

In her article in *The Survey* Charlotte Rumbold summarized what for her was the true definition and meaning of both pageant and masque.

To readers of *The Survey*, the significance of the Pageant and Masque of St. Louis is that a group of citizens tried a daring experiment and succeeded. Citizens first and artists secondarily, they are not the type to stage "Big Shows" just for the show's sake. They tried to arouse a city of 800,000 people to a sense of its solidarity, to a sense of the possibility of infinite achievement by a community under the spell of a unifying idealism. And they succeeded. They proved that though democracy may never have been tried, it is not an academic abstraction but a workable hypothesis, and they proved it through the age-long appeal of Art.

Cave Life to City Life, Boston, 1910
(Courtesy Brown University Library)

3

Pageantry and the Mandate for Social Reform

One of the first examples of a pageant specifically oriented toward social reform was *Cave Life to City Life*, presented in 1910 as an outgrowth of Boston's concerns about the future of its city. There were serious problems related to immigration, housing, transportation, education, recreation, political corruption, and public health.

The schools, accustomed to teaching English-speaking natives through a classical curriculum, were no longer adequately serving the new immigrants and the rising numbers of urban workers. Educators were proposing drastic changes: industrial and vocational schools; adult education; broadened learning possibilities for young girls and women; the substitution of Greek and Latin for geography, civic studies, and even art. Urban planners and social workers, concerned about keeping people off the streets and out of the bars and dance halls, created playgrounds and settlement houses to improve the physical, social, and intellectual environment. The staid, homogenous city of Boston was changing as new powerful business interests attempted to control the political process. Nickelodeons were capturing the attention of young and old, and civic leaders wanted new facilities where theatre of a higher order would inculcate values and educate as well as entertain.

A year before the pageant was performed, in 1909, a group of Boston's leading citizens decided the only way of instituting any of the necessary reform was to bring all segments of the population together in a cooperative effort. They began by grouping over 1,200 organizations into thirteen categories: Business, Charity and Correctional, Educational, Health, Labor, Religious, Fine Arts, City Planning, Civic, Women's Clubs, Neighborhood, Youth, and Co-Operative. Next, representatives from each category were chosen to sit on a central committee called "Boston-1915" whose mandate was to set change in motion with the goal of significant improvements by the year 1915. The Boston-1915 Committee was to operate as a "single federated, co-ordinated organization, giving to each project for city better-ment the concerted strength of the whole citizen body."[1]

Out of the multitude of social and economic concerns came the decision by Boston-1915 to dramatize, in a city-wide pageant, the city's history and problems and to present a glowing vision for the future. *Cave Life to City Life* was an attempt by the pageant organizers to mirror, as they saw it, the heart and mind of Boston during the Progressive Era. The pageant was meant to be an instrument that would bring reform groups together while dramatizing many of their concerns. An in-depth analysis of the pageant from the perspective of those who did not participate, who were more militant in their rejection of evolutionary change and establishment leader-ship, would probably illuminate the diverse ideological framework of the city, but that is not the focus here. The point of view for the pageant leaders was clear—if they led the way their vision would take hold and soon all would follow. They wanted settlement-house workers, civic leaders, labor union members, educators, politicians, city planners, transportation special-ists, and religious leaders to join forces in a spectacle that would convey the history of Boston and the potential the city had for a bright future.

It was hoped that weeks of rehearsal and several performances would accomplish a variety of goals: facilitate a unified outlet and sharing process for different cultural traditions and values; show that education through active learning was a powerful tool for all ages and classes of society; help in the creation of an environment which would break down socio-economic barriers and allow for the practice of the democratic process.

There was a strong belief on the part of the organizers that as the pageant was planned, rehearsed, and performed, various groups in Boston would get to know each other and understand the problems facing the city they all shared. Protestants, Jews, and Catholics who might have prejudices based on lack of familiarity would laugh, sing, and dance together. Indeed middle-class young people from the Curry School of Expression performed as Dust Clouds and Disease Germs alongside immigrants from Hale House, who depicted Flames. Sons of Veterans were listed on the program in the role of War. They stood side by side with workers from the Central Labor Union who depicted Strife, Slavery, and Serfdom. The elite students from the Latin Girls School, as "the Greek element in the Athens of America," danced next to Russian immigrants from the Elizabeth Peabody House. The Allston Women's Club participated in a minuet and the Boston Teachers' Club dramatized The City of the Future. Industry was represented by spinners from the Girls' High School of Practical Arts. "Women colonists" were members of the Old South Historical Society and the Young Women's Christian Union and "colonial workmen" were students from English High School and Mechanical Arts High School. One reviewer wrote about the pageant, "Commonwealth Avenue and Beacon Street met with the North and West End."

Cave Life to City Life was meant to inform the people of Boston, excite their imaginations, and create what the Boston-1915 Committee called the proper "state of mind." If the right "state of mind" could be achieved for the city, then reform would be a natural occurrence, as explained in "The Significance of Boston-1915" in *New Boston:*

> Outsiders used to jeer at Boston by calling her a "state of mind." Some hustling Western-ers have even dared to call her a "state of talk." The joke, however, is now on them; for we Americans are finding out that every city is a "state of mind," and that to bring a municipality to the right "state of mind," there is required a vast amount of repeated and reiterated talk. If its state of mind is quarrelsome, a city will be an armed camp. . . . If one man, or even ten men, of intellect, having also the vision, resourcefulness and perseverance, can accomplish such seeming miracles in city building, what might not all the minds of a modern city do in these days of science, inventiveness and skill, were those minds instructed, united and determined to succeed? . . . There is no reason except bad habits to the contrary, why a municipality should not be planned . . . why its affairs should not be conducted economically. . . . To secure a city which is properly planned, decently ordered and economically administered, its citizens have only to get into a "state of mind" where they not only want these things but also believe them to be possible. One of the fundamentals of Boston-1915 is to help to create that state of mind.[2]

Cave Life to City Life was an important aspect of the "state of mind" required by the Boston-1915 Committee as a framework for its reform campaign. As the first pageant in America to be part of a reform effort, it set a precedent for many others in the next few years.

> I show the progress of the human race;
> From darksome caves man's spirit led him up,
> By slow degrees, unto a high estate,
> Through storm and stress and struggle unto peace—
>   Time works for good.[3]

These were the stirring words delivered by Father Time in the beginning prologue of the pageant as he invited "Labor, Progress, Success, Prosperity, Peace and Happiness to assist man in his work." The first stanza of the prologue immediately set the tone for the pageant by establishing the idea that, given time and effort, society could be improved.

The pageant was divided into four episodes, and rather than depicting history through the heroic actions of individuals, the emphasis was on progress through community interaction and cooperation. The caveman in Episode I was shown with his family "cooking their meal over the first hearthstone."[4] The Indians in the second episode, Iroquois from reservations in

Cave Life to City Life, Episode I—"Caveman's Dwelling"
(Brown University Library)

western New York and Canada, were seen in group activities—pitching tents, dancing, and singing—and in the third episode colonists were introduced "who sought freedom in the new land." They settled the land with the help of friendly Indians who joined them in repelling the "enemy" Indians.

Early colonists were portrayed working together and establishing homes in the wilderness while overcoming hardship through group effort. In one scene a harvest festival is in progress. An oxen team draws a load of corn as villagers dance old-fashioned reels to the tune of "Pop Goes the Weasel." In the last section of Episode III the colonists have an elaborate celebration in honor of Governor Wentworth's wedding. Guests are dressed in silk and satin and arrive in fancy carriages.

Episode IV was the longest and most important part of *Cave Life to City Life*. Its opening scene was "Contrasts of the Past and Present in Communication, Travel, Education and Industry." A Colonial town crier carried his candle lantern, followed by a group of Boston newsboys "during whose progress across the floor the stereopticon pictures the wireless telegraph . . . symbolizing the history and development of communication." The colonists reappeared as if going to the governor's wedding in their coaches; juxtaposed against that was the latest model of an electric automobile, while "the stereopticon displays an aeroplane overhead." An old-fashioned school where pupils recited catechism and the three Rs was contrasted with a group of seventy-five high-school girls "who went through the gymnastic work of the school of today." A group of spinners was shown against a picture of a modern factory "and suggests something of the improvement possible in these same conditions so far as they have been made up to the present year."

Episode IV continued as groups of dancers impersonating Dust Clouds and Disease Germs attacked "Boston and Her Neighbors" and were repelled by the Knights of Economy. The Boy Scouts were shown driving out Crime and Insanity. A figure representing Peace advanced to give her banner to War; Labor and Capital were brought together "by means of blind Justice, led by Progress." The last scene of this episode was called "The Assimilation of the Nations (Sweden, Russia, Southern Europe, Holland, Hungary, Italy, Scotland, England, Ireland, Greece)." Each group danced a few measures "of their national or symbolic dances," followed by an American dance. The pageant closed with a symbolic dance, "Aspiration," followed by "Patriotic Hymns by audience, chorus and pageanters."

The process of change adopted by Boston-1915 had four aspects: the use of conferences during 1910 for problem identification; the use of a central committee for review of recommendations developed by the conferences; the use of existing agencies for implementation and where necessary creation of new institutions; and the use of the civic pageant *Cave Life to City Life* as an artistic expression, community ritual, and didactic tool for unity and cooperation.

If *Cave Life to City Life* had been created as an isolated event it could be seen as a simplistic overview of history related only superficially to diverse issues of reform. What must be kept in mind is that many of those who participated in and saw the pageant had been involved in numerous committees, subcommittees and conferences developed by the directors of Boston-1915. It is likely that they were stirred and moved by the symbolism, which was simple and direct, and understood that underlying each symbol lay a multitude of problems which were being addressed in the reform effort. The power of the pageant lay in its ability to compress into a few dynamic images the complex process of change that all the organizations involved in Boston-1915 were trying to set in motion. The pageant was also an attempt to validate the basic underlying premise of the entire reform effort, that cooperation and education would create the necessary positive environmental conditions for overcoming obstacles.

Education Conference

The Education Conference convened as part of the Boston-1915 effort on March 3, 1910, became a permanent organization on March 10, and a mass meeting was held on April 29. In addition to a general survey of the education needs of the city, the conference addressed specific concerns: education of immigrant children; construction of schoolhouses; industrial and vocational education; the encouragement of a "Saner Fourth" celebration, stressing constructive activity as opposed to dangerous fireworks and unorganized festivities.

The Education Conference was addressing the impact of foreign immigrants on Boston. Prior to the Civil War, immigrants had come to America but they were mostly from northern and western Europe and assimilation had occurred over a period of time. Between 1880 and 1921 more people came to this country than ever before, over 23,500,000 from a large number of countries. The majority were from southern and eastern Europe, primarily Russia, Italy, Greece, Lithuania, Latvia, and smaller Balkan states, with significantly distinct customs of eating, family organization, dress, education, and working habits which identified each particular group. They were all distinct from one another and differed vastly from the majority of older settlers of Protestant Anglo-Saxon heritage.

Boston and other cities were also experiencing internal immigration. Individuals from rural areas and farms were seeking greater economic opportunity in large urban factories. Small farmers were losing their land and becoming tenants, as they were at the mercy of banks and railroads run by conglomerates, ruthless tycoons, and an international market system.

The influx of foreign and native immigrants into cities such as Boston created a variety of problems which affected housing, transportation, and recreation. The natives of Boston watched new political alliances develop and experienced cultural and economic clashes with the new inhabitants. The immigrants spoke different languages and had what seemed to many strange values and customs. They often lacked economic skills necessary for survival in their new homeland and were also lacking in knowledge of American history and the democratic way of life.

The Boston-1915 organizers believed that environmental conditions could be an instrument of positive social, economic, and moral change. Traditional methods of education, operative during the nineteenth century, would not serve the needs of this vast new population. Education became the focal point for assimilating the rural and foreign immigrants and providing opportunities that would secure jobs and make them better citizens.

Three scenes in *Cave Life to City Life* effectively symbolized the major concerns of the Education Conference. Episode III showed the way young women were taught in the era of the colonists, both in a spinning school and a dame school, where the three Rs and catechism were recited by rote. Episode IV pictured high-school girls engaged in gymnastics and people working in a modern factory. The message was clear—educating the women of the twentieth century to simply spin and sing would not make it possible for them to live in today's society. In the last scene of Episode IV the educational problem was presented in terms of accepting and assimilating the foreign immigrants: groups from each country performed small sections of their native dances. After this a large group did an American dance, followed by the symbolic dance "Aspiration" and patriotic hymns.

For all those involved in Boston-1915's Education Conference the goals were clear. Their mandate was to reform the traditional schoolhouse from a purely academic institution for the few to one serving the entire community of diverse populations. Education had to include training individuals of both sexes and all ages for work and leisure. Memorizing the three Rs was not enough; creative play and artistic expression had to be included.

The reforms on the agenda of the Education Conference that made pageantry an integral part of Boston-1915 had their bases in the work and writings of the philosopher John Dewey. He was one of the major educational reformers of the twentieth century and had a significant impact on many involved in the Boston-1915 effort. Dewey put forward new ideas on the relationship of the schools to the community, learning through doing, and the importance of expressive play in the learning process. The influence of Dewey was at the core of many reform ideas about curriculum, extended use of schoolhouses, industrial and vocational education, and the importance of pageantry.

John Dewey's first major treatise on education, *The School and Society*, was a series of three lectures regarding an experimental laboratory school he established at the University of Chicago in 1899. He questioned traditional nineteenth-century methods and goals of teaching and learning. He felt these were inappropriate to the diverse population and industrial situation of his time. Rote learning in large inflexible groups, emphasis on the classics, and elimination of play, experience, and environment would not prepare youth for the contemporary world or enable them to enter into democratic relations with their peers. School was not just a place to teach basic skills. "New education" had to be part of "the whole social evolution."[5] Schools did not exist in a vacuum, and must respond to current needs. "The modification going on in the method and curriculum of education is as much a product of the changed social situation, and as much an effort to meet the needs of the new society that is forming, as are changes in modes of industry and commerce."

In critical moments we all realize that the only discipline that stands by us . . . is that got through life itself. That we learn from experience, and from books or the sayings of others only as they are related to experience, and not mere phrases. . . . The great thing to keep in mind, then, regarding the introduction into the school of various forms of active occupation, is that through them the entire spirit of the school is renewed. It has a chance to affiliate itself with life, to become the child's habitat, where he learns through directed living; instead of being only a place to learn lessons having an abstract and remote reference to some possible living to be done in the future. It gets a chance to be a miniature community, an embryonic society.[6]

Dewey believed a crucial element of school and society to be the cultivation of the basic impulse and "natural resource" of artistic expression. Artistic expression allows the individual to understand the world and cultivate the imagination. Only when creative play is part of education will we have "a larger society which is worthy, lovely, and harmonious."[7] What better way to understand the past and the present than through doing— storytelling, painting, constructing, moving, and exploring through creative means the ideas of the world.

Cave Life to City Life was the ideal of John Dewey realized on a massive scale. "When nature and society can live in the schoolroom, the forms of learning are subordinated to the substance of experience, then shall there be an opportunity for this identification, and culture shall be the democratic password."[8]

Imagination and creative play became a way of teaching American history, economics, and politics. The schools were not closed elitist institutions but rather institutions that formed an integral part of a larger community framework. Life itself was the subject of the pageant, and "the school was affiliated with life." The total education of the student was encompassed: democratic cooperation, knowledge of today's problems, emotional well-being, and artistic expression. Discipline came from within and was learned through completing a task and working with others.

The program for the pageant indicates that schools and youth organizations from all over the city participated in *Cave Life to City Life*. "The American Dance" in the last scene was performed by Posse Gymnasium, Boston Normal School, and Milton, Waltham, Charlestown, South Boston and West Roxbury High Schools. The "Hungarian Dance" near the end was performed by students from Braintree, Stoneham, and Dedham High Schools. The school became the community and the community the school as Boy Scouts and the Boston Newsboys' Club took their places in the pageant along with the South End Industrial School and the North Bennet Street Industrial School.

Fine and Industrial Arts Conference

When Boston-1915 sponsored *Cave Life to City Life* it was strong propaganda for the reform efforts of this conference. The pageant was living proof of the need for a civic assembly hall and enterprises where the arts could benefit each individual and the whole city.

The conference was organized February 25, 1910, and several committees were created to consider specific issues: the advisability of enlarging the powers of the Boston Art Commission; the assessment of educational needs in the realms of art, music, and drama; and the need for securing a great assembly hall for Boston.

The leaders of the Fine and Industrial Arts Conference felt that existing attitudes in Boston toward art and leisure were negative and elitist. Many still influenced by harsh puritan attitudes believed the arts could be dangerous; others saw them as playful pastimes for the highly educated or well-to-do.

The agenda of the conference was to integrate the arts with education and leisure, creating programmed leisure activities to replace time spent aimlessly in bars, dance halls, and movie theatres. Constructive leisure could help prevent crime, restlessness, and wasted energies. An assembly hall built as a civic enterprise would provide a place "relieved from the baneful influences of pure commercialism . . . of interest to every kind of worker in Boston."

Health Conference

The members of the Health Conference must have been very pleased as they watched *Cave Life to City Life*. Several groups of dancers representing the evils of Disease, Dust, and Germs were shown surrounding the city of Boston from all directions. According to the pageant text, "Boston and her Suburbs are next shown defending themselves by modern methods of preparation" from these evils. It is not quite clear in any of the reviews or the pageant script how this was accomplished, but it is certain that Disease, Dust, and Germs were depicted as properly destroyed in Boston's city of the future.

In colorful symbolic visualization the pageant successfully portrayed some of the by-products of twentieth-century industrialization and immigration. Overcrowding, low wages, and different customs would cause health and social problems unless attention was paid through new government agencies, legislation, and education.

The Health Conference was organized on March 8 and held meetings on April 15, May 16, and June 24. Major concerns were birth, morbidity, and mortality statistics and the conference recommended the establishment of a Bureau of Child Hygiene. Several leaders of the Health Conference were also involved in the hearings that took place at Boston City Hall regarding disposal of garbage and refuse.

Neighborhood Work Conference

The settlement houses were a crucial part of all aspects of Boston-1915's reform efforts, and they played a pivotal role in the creation of *Cave Life to City Life*. In 1910 there were thirty-three settlement houses in Boston, mostly located in the slum area of the South End. The better known of these houses were Elizabeth Peabody, Denison, Lincoln, South End, and Hull Street. The Neighborhood Work Conference, composed of the various settlement-house reformers, met February 23, April 8, and May 11.

At the core of the settlement houses were idealists who addressed the problems of industrialization and immigration by going to live in working-class neighborhoods. They would take over bleak old tenement houses and establish a wide range of services from these headquarters, including classes, lectures, health services, and entertainments.

The basic premise was that change in environment would help the individuals and the community overcome poverty, ignorance, poor housing, and problems of assimilation. Settlement-house workers became active in politics and neighborhood institutions. They sought understanding of the cultural traditions in the immigrant groups while encouraging knowledge of American history and customs.

The first such institution in the United States was established in New York in 1886 as the Neighborhood Guild. Probably two of the most famous were Hull House in Chicago, founded in 1889 by Jane Addams and Ellen Gates Starr, and Henry Street Settlement House, founded by Lillian Wald and Mary Brewster in 1893. In 1897 there were seventy-four such neighborhood establishments and by 1910 there were more than four hundred. The founders of the settlement houses felt they were creating an instrument of social, educational, civic, and humanitarian reform. Jane Addams, in an 1892 article in *Forum* wrote that she wanted "to make social intercourse express the growing sense of economic unity of society and to add to the social functions of society."[9]

When Boston-1915's pageant was presented in the Arena, several settlement houses participated in the fourth scene of Episode IV, "the Assimilation of the Nations." When different nationalities presented their native dances, the program listing was as follows: Scotch, Lincoln House; Irish, South End House; Dutch, Denison House; Russian, Elizabeth Peabody House; Italian, Hull Street House.

The pageants were a natural outlet for the expressive needs of individual ethnically isolated neighborhoods, as they allowed for expression of personal heritage and exposure to American history and traditions. As the American Pageantry Movement picked up momentum, many settlement houses produced their own pageants, in Boston and in other cities. Often these pageants led to the formation of local theatre groups.

The settlement houses were strong in their arts classes, and these local theatre groups were of more than average caliber. Participants were encouraged to develop professional careers in the arts. After the first pageant at Henry Street Settlement House in 1913, that institution developed a professional training school and theatre group which became the Neighborhood Playhouse.

Youth Conference

This conference first convened in Boston on February 24, and met again April 12, June 9, and June 29. A major concern was development of proper recreational opportunities and facilities. Dirty overcrowded streets and tenements made poor play space. Parents overburdened with many children, heavy work schedules, and low wages had little spare time. Immigrant children from American rural areas or small villages in other countries needed leadership in the use of leisure time in a foreign environment and teenagers working long hours in routine factory jobs needed outlets for their energies.

Boston-1915's Youth Conference was closely linked with the work of the Playground Association of America, which had its first national meeting in 1906. At the philosophical core of this association were the ideas of the psychologist G. Stanley Hall (1844–1924), who saw organized physical activity as an essential element in human development. A healthy society had to be based on healthy bodies. An essential aspect of reforming society related to creating the proper environment and opportunities for developing morality through body conditioning. Hall believed

> that few realize what physical vigor is in man or woman, or how dangerously near weakness often is to wickedness, how impossible healthful energy of will is without strong muscles, or how endurance and self-control, no less than great achievements depend on muscle-habits. Good moral and physical development are more than analogous; and where intelligence is separated from action the former becomes mystic, abstract, and desiccated, and the latter formal routine.[10]

During the 1890s Hall wrote many articles and in 1904 published his ideas in his first book, *Adolescence*.[11] When he became president of Clark University in 1889 his influence in the area of child development became widespread. The idea for a National Playground Association came from Henry S. Curtis, one of Hall's students. The first president of the organization was Luther H. Gulick who counted Hall as one of his major influences.

The Russell Sage Foundation provided Gulick with funding for the new association, whose members soon joined settlement-house workers and educational reformers in coordinating urban reform efforts.

Gulick summed up the philosophy of the Playground Association in an article published in 1910.

> Dependency is reduced by giving men more for which to live. Delinquency is reduced by providing a wholesome outlet for youthful energy. Industrial efficiency is increased by giving individuals a play life which will develop greater resourcefulness and adaptability. Good citizenship is promoted by forming habits of cooperation in play. People who play together find it easier to live together and are more loyal as well as more efficient citizens. Democracy rests on the most firm basis when a community has formed the habit of playing together.[12]

It is interesting that in a review of *Cave Life to City Life* the writer made an analogy between team sports and the pageant efforts. He wrote that Harvard won a football game because of "better team work" and the pageant was a success "because the 'pageant team' played together and caught the spirit of the game as did the football team." The American Playground Association became an active champion of the American Pageantry Movement following the success of *Cave Life to City Life*. Luther Gulick was the person at the Russell Sage Foundation who supported William Chauncy Langdon's request for funding for both a Bureau of Pageantry and for his *Pageant of Thetford*. Langdon himself was on the general advisory committee of the Boston pageant. By the time Langdon became president of the American Pageant Association, pageants were encouraged on playgrounds not only in Boston but in all major cities.

Charities and Correction Conference and Civic Conference

On March 18 the Charities and Correction Conference was organized as part of Boston-1915 and a full meeting took place on May 5. The leaders saw an urgent need for a civic building to house agencies aimed at charities and correction, civic improvement, and general public welfare. Two sub-committees were formed, one to work on the issue of delays in court procedure related to criminal and civil cases and the other for the purpose of pursuing the Workmen's Compensation Act. The conference also commissioned a survey to outline the overall civic needs of Boston.

The work of this conference was integrated with that of the Civic Conference, which was organized on February 21. Members of both conferences served on joint committees related to workmen's compensation and delays in court procedure. The Civic Conference also had separate concerns: establishing a plan for a Bureau of Municipal Research; participating in the Saner

Fourth Committee; coordinating metropolitan districts; and abolishing preferential voting. The Civic Conference was also active in defeat of the Treadway Bill, which was designed to hinder the abolition of illegal billboards.

Other Conferences

Several other conferences integrated their work with that of the conferences described as part of the general Boston-1915 planning process. The Women's Club Conference worked on the construction of schoolhouses, a "Saner Fourth," and on the disposal of garbage and refuse. The Industrial Conditions Conference worked with other groups in several areas: delays in court procedure, Workmen's Compensation Act, construction and location of schoolhouses, a saner Fourth, and education of immigrant children. This conference also worked with the Powers of the Art Commission, whose mandate was "to draft a bill amending the present statute in such a way as to put public buildings under jurisdiction of the Boston Art Commission and in other respects enlarge its powers."

The mandate of the City Planning and Housing Conference was in the direction of reports leading to specific actions. Various phases of city planning were assigned to members for preparation of special reports. A committee was appointed to take up the matter of intelligent and useful numbering of streetcar routes.

The work of the Religious Conference is a little vague and all that can be gathered is that Protestant, Jewish, and Catholic groups met together and formed separate federations. A separate Construction of Schoolhouses Conference was established to study the use of school buildings "with reference to their more extended use as social and civic centers." There is no mention of separate conferences dealing with mass transit, but the magazine *New Boston* presented readers with various plans to relieve the subway problem. *New Boston* also kept its readers informed of Boston elevated improvements—well-designed stations, viaducts, and other improvements that were important for "realizing the ideals of a better city."

Boston-1915 epitomized the spiritual quality of the Progressive Era—an optimistic belief in change through democratic cooperation. An article in *New Boston* (1910), "The Significance of Boston-1915," was a clear statement of belief in progress achieved only through mutual support.

> The citizens of Boston or of any other place can have everything, within reason, that makes for health, comfort, beauty and efficiency if only they will work for it. To be successful, however, they must work not as individuals, not through isolated clubs or societies, not as divided communities or sections—they must work as a single federated, co-ordinated organization, giving to each project for city betterment the concerted

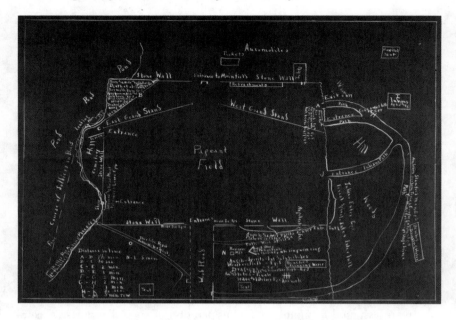

Blueprint of Pageant Field for the *Pageant of Thetford*
Designed by William Chauncy Langdon.
(*Courtesy Brown University Library*)

strength of the whole citizen body. The purpose of Boston-1915 is to stimulate and
organize this spirit of co-operation by studying through conferences of experts the city's
immediate and future needs, by deciding through a representative directorate which of
these needs should enlist immediate attention and by bringing, through its effective
organization, intelligent and widespread support to the projects thus endorsed. The aim
of Boston-1915 is constructive work, carried out through democratic methods and in a
spirit of unfaltering optimism.[13]

Additional Social Reform Pageants

William Chauncy Langdon's *The Pageant of Thetford* addressed issues of
change related to the Country Life Movement, a movement concerned with
the quality of life in rural areas, and an outgrowth of President Theodore
Roosevelt's 1908 Commission on Country Life.

When Langdon created his pageant in 1911 he saw it as "a study of the
rural problem in dramatic form, and it is hoped, a contribution toward
solving the question of how to make the country town an ideal place to
live."[14] Farmers were leaving the land, as new machinery and corporate
marketing techniques made it difficult for them to compete and survive.

Traditional rural values were perceived as important to the overall spiritual health of America, and it was necessary to help families stay together. The Country Life Movement sought ways for farmers to cooperate in marketing and obtain secure income, and encouraged retraining for industrialized agricultural tools and methods.

Langdon brought together six small towns in Vermont and created an advisory committee of people from many different fields: Professor Marshall Cummings, horticulturist from the University of Vermont; Ray Stannard Baker, writer; Bruce Crane, painter; Arthur Farwell, composer; A. F. Hawes, John M. Glenn, and Luther H. Gulick, Russell Sage Foundation; Willet M. Hays, Assistant Secretary of Agriculture; L. G. Dodge, Bureau of Farm Management; Milton Whitney, Chief of Bureau of Soils; John M. Thomas, State Commission of Conservation member and President of Middlebury College; and Mary Schenck Woolman, Director of Household Arts of Teachers College, Columbia University. A letter from Theodore Roosevelt gave the project a special seal of approval.

The Pageant of Thetford, presented for the one-hundred-fiftieth anniversary of the town charter, was performed August 12, 14, and 15, 1911. Three professionals were employed: William Chauncy Langdon, master of the pageant serving as writer and director, and James T. Sleeper and Virginia Tanner, directors of music and dance, respectively. The six small towns which participated were East Thetford, Thetford Center, Thetford Hill, North Thetford, Post Mills, and Union Village. The pageant grounds were on the banks of the Connecticut River. A grandstand was built facing toward a large grove of pine trees. A low vine-covered fence divided the grounds into two parts, one for individual and the other for group action.

The outline of the pageant was as follows:

Introduction	The Nature Spirits and the Indians
Episode 1	The Coming of the First Settler, "Old Quail John"
Episode 2	Richard Wallace and Burgoyne's Invasion
Episode 3	The Building of the Church on Thetford Hill, and the Musical Society in Thetford and Lyme
Interlude I	The Spirit of Home
Episode 4	The Founding of Thetford Academy
Episode 5	The Country Fair
Episode 6	The Coming of the Railroad
Interlude II	The Age of Homespun
Episode 7	The Civil War
Episode 8	The Introduction of Machinery
Episode 9	The Rural Problem
Interlude III	The Spirit of Pageantry

Episode 10	The New Agriculture
Episode 11	The New Education
Episode 12	The New Life
Finale	Thetford Presents her Six Villages and the past, the present and the future to Vermont and America

The pageant opened with an introduction which created an air of mystery and visual beauty. The first image the audience saw was the Spirit of the Mountain emerging from the pine grove. Clothed in green, her movements were "slow and stately." Soon she was joined from the river bank by the Spirit of the River in blue draperies with a shimmer of white. Her dance was "swift and smooth, sweeping up to the Spirit of the Mountain and away from her." Next came the Spirit of the Intervale "in pale gold, the color of grain" and her movements were "rich, opulent and votive." All three were joined by a group pantomiming the daily activities of Indian braves, squaws and children and they danced "in and out among the Nature Spirits with no conflict." During this dance a Puritan man appeared, gazing at the scene, and then all withdrew to their entrance places. Each spirit had an original musical motif and the Indian dance was accompanied by native melodies.

Episode 1 provided a contrasting visual and dramatic experience, although it also had no dialogue. John Chamberlain, the first white settler, was shown coming to an agreement with the Indians. The incident was based on a portion of verse about John Chamberlain from local folklore:

> Old Quail John
> Was the first to come on,
>   As poor as a calf in the spring;
> But now he's as rich
> As Governor Fitch
>   And lives like a lord or a king.

A feeling of suspense was created as the Indian braves, squaws, children, and babies arrived in canoes. After beaching their canoes the women hung the babies on trees, then gathered berries as children played and men hunted game. An Indian melody, "Canoe Song," accompanied the action. John Chamberlain arrived in a boat after the Indians had moved from center stage and could only be seen through the trees. Chamberlain disembarked, the Indians reappeared, and he covered all the Indians "with a sweep of his gun." A pantomimed sequence showed a desire for amicable encounter, and all sat together, smoked a peace pipe, and shared the quail. The agreement between Chamberlain and the Indians followed, showing that each would live on a separate side of the river—and then all exited.

Scenes from the *Pageant of Thetford*, Thetford, Vermont, 1911
Directed by William Chauncy Langdon.
(Courtesy Brown University Library)

Episodes 2 and 3 continued the early history of Thetford, with dialogue among several main characters, group scenes, and accompanying music. Two popular songs were part of Episode 2 and the fight against the British— "The British Grenadier" and "Yankee Doodle." Three old hymns—"Invitation," "Bridgewater," and "New Jerusalem"—were integrated into Episode 3 and the building of a new church. Interlude I followed, bringing back the Nature Spirits with the addition of the Spirit of Home—all with original music. Episodes 4, 5, and 6 took the story of Thetford to 1848.

The Civil War was the subject of Episode 7, and in Episodes 8 and 9 Langdon dramatized the contemporary issues for the town: the coming of new types of farm machinery making old methods obsolete and eliminating some manpower needs; the attraction of life away from rural communities along with excitement about the city and new jobs; and the conflict within families responding to these changes. In Episode 8, "The Introduction of Machinery," there were four characters symbolizing the old and the new. A short scene presented the conflict surrounding the changes occurring in society and in Thetford. Richard Towne symbolized those dissatisfied with rural life who saw the town (that is, the city) and new industries as offering greater opportunities. Benjamin Farmer embodied the individuals who sought to bring new machinery to their farms, replacing old ways but staying in Thetford. Sam and Sally Small represented a family whose labors were no longer needed with the coming of new machinery, and who were faced with decisions about their future.

RICHARD TOWNE	The City's the place. I tell you this is the age of machinery. Everything in the city is done by machinery nowadays. Even in your home.
BENJAMIN FARMER	Well, we're introducing machinery a bit here on the farm, too.
SAMUEL SMALL	Yes, it's a case of machinery in both places—in the country and in the town. Well, we'll settle this thing up tonight. (Sam and his wife go off with the child between them.)

Episode 9, "The Rural Problem," provided another perspective on issues raised in the previous episode. The theme became personalized through dialogue between George Edwards (father), Joe Edwards (son), Mrs. Edwards (wife and mother), and Lettie Davis (girlfriend of Joe). We see the Edwards parents and the girlfriend trying to stop the son from leaving in order to learn new farming ideas. We see the caring of the family, the classic situation of parents loving their son enough to allow him to find his own ways. In the end, young Joe does leave and the Spirit of Thetford appears "stretching out her arms in compassion to them."

The pageant ended on a note of optimism and hope for the future. The third and last interlude, to music of Bach, Dvořák, and Sleeper, showed the Spirit of Pageantry convincing the Spirit of Thetford to accept the joy of play, the joy of work, and the future. Episodes 10, 11, and 12 actually constituted one short scene with two major characters, Henry West and Master of the Grange. The Master of the Grange convinced Henry that he should return to Thetford from the west. The dialogue showed that Thetford had resolved problems of machinery and the rural issue by adopting new methods of farming, selling, and buying. The additional inducement for Henry to return was that there is no place like home. The last part showed the importance of family and community staying together in work and play as the people of Thetford, boys, girls, and adults, came back for a picnic. James Sleeper wrote a song for this section, "Come, with a Cheer, Good Neighbors Come."

William Chauncy Langdon felt that his pageant was an integral element in the exposition and solution of the problems facing the citizens of rural communities. It could create a "state of mind" about change, he believed, and it could help bring about reform:

> The Pageant of Thetford will not however be merely a picture of the work done for the development of the town and a prophecy of its results. It is not merely a reflection of it, which may be more or less accurate in regard to the past and present and rather more than less fantastically optimistic in regard to the future. The Pageant is itself a part of the development work. The principles at the base of the work are that no aspect of life can prosper by itself, and that joy is a creative factor of economic value in the life of the community. The preparation of the pageant is itself a social movement. . . . Thetford is boldly undertaking to solve the hard problems of the country town for itself and for others and the Pageant tells the story from beginning to end, raises the standard of the ideal country, and predicts the realization of the hopes that the people of the town have set before them.[15]

In a letter to the Russell Sage Foundation, dated February 24, 1911, Langdon proudly reported the reforms that had taken place as a result of *The Pageant of Thetford.*

1. The Masters of the two Granges in the town have taken up together the matter of uniting their Granges to interest all the farmers in the town in a movement of all the farmers of the country to secure from the Department of Agriculture a soil survey and also the farmers' cooperative demonstration work which has been carried on in the south. The end in view is a request for these two kinds of assistance that shall come from literally the whole agricultural community; they are doing it not merely for themselves but for the other towns in their county; they are working vigorously and will succeed.
2. A desire has been spontaneously expressed for similar expert help and direction in forestry. This will be secured if possible.
3. A similar desire has also been expressed for help and direction in the sheep indus-

try; one man has started to make sheep a profitable industry in connection with his farm.

4. In three of the villages a start has been made with the Boy Scouts. The plan is to get every boy in the town into the Boy Scouts, and to have the organization centre at the Academy, thus helping to give the Academy the hold on all the boys of the town that it ought to have. The boys are taking this up.

5. In connection with the Boy Scouts the Corn Growing Contest which the Department of Agriculture has been conducting in the South will be introduced. In one village a beginning has already been made. Success in corn growing will be one of the honors for the boys to work for in the Boy Scouts. The great result of this will be that the boys will gain an instinctive appreciation of their soil and the promise of a career in their own town.

6. A group for girls at one of the villages have expressed a desire for girls similar to the Boy Scouts. Consultation has been begun to arrange something of the kind locally, if a national organization, a Camp Fire Girls of America, cannot be formed to fill this need.

7. So also the same girls want something similar to the Corn Growing Contest. This is being taken up.

8. There is a Choral Union composed of the choirs of a number of towns in the upper Connecticut River Valley. From this the local singers are being gathered as a nucleus for a Thetford Chorus which will sing the choral music arranged and written for them in the pageant, and which will continue as a centre of musical culture permanently.

9. Similarly an Orchestra is being formed of the people in Thetford who play instruments, which will play the orchestral music that is being arranged and written for the pageant, and which will continue afterward with the Chorus as a centre of musical culture.

10. Interest in local history is increasing. Material quite complete for an important episode was supplied to me by a lumberman and a cobbler, for instance. The ministers of the town are uniting to help get a thorough canvas of the people for facts and information of the history of the town.

11. The ministers of the town have united, and have been appointed a committee by the Pageant Committee, to make of Sunday, August 13, a day of town-wide religious celebration. Special services in all the churches of the six villages in the morning will have the same music, etc. In the afternoon there will be a great service for the whole town on the Pageant grounds, with music by the Pageant Orchestra and Chorus and a sermon by some prominent preacher to be invited for the occasion.

12. All six villages of the town have united to put through this pageant along the lines of town development and of the working out of the rural problem so that other country towns may benefit by their experience and success. The altruistic purpose is consciously part of their motive. In one evening at the town hall they raised between $400 and $500 for their expenses; and they have put into the warning for their town meeting as early in March the proposal that the town appropriate $500 a as a guarantee fund for their pageant.[16]

Suffrage and the Role of Women in Pageantry

Other American pageants during the period 1910–21 reflected diverse reform issues and became an integral part of the Progressive Era's mandate for change. One of the major reform issues of the era was the role of women in society, and suffragettes campaigned all over the country for the right to vote and have an equal share in the country's political and economic concerns. American pageantry reflected the issue of women's rights in two ways: through the vigorous leadership of women in the entire pageantry movement, and through the creation of numerous suffrage pageants.

The American Pageantry Movement legitimized leadership of women in the community and in the theatre in an unprecedented way. Women were writers, directors, producers, and heads of civic committees. Women as pageant masters were highly respected professionals who often traveled to different cities, paid to organize and create productions that would have otherwise been delegated to men. Women served as leaders in the American Pageant Association and achieved remarkable authority alongside the men in everything having to do with pageantry.

One of the many suffrage pageants[17] was Mary Porter Beegle's *The Romance of Work*, produced for the National League of Women Workers Convention and presented May 15, 1914, at the 69 Regiment Armory, Lexington Avenue and 26 Street, New York. According to the program, "The Pageant will illustrate the Evolution of Woman's Work; its past development; its present fields; and its future promises."

Episode I	Indian scene showing the work of the primitive women around the fire.
Interlude for Episode I	The Fire Dance.
Episode II	This Episode is set for the purely domestic phase in a Colonial household.
Interlude for Episode II	The Minuet. This dance will show the traditional dignity and conventionality of the times.
Episode III	The South before the Civil War, showing work supervised by the woman of the home, with the Southern woman conducting the home life and supervising the work of the slaves.
Interlude for Episode III	Military Dance, suggesting the spirit of 1860.
Episode IV	Modern Industrial Period, showing work taken out of the home into the commu-

Woman Suffrage Allegory, Washington, D.C., March 3, 1913
Directed by Hazel MacKaye and performed on the Treasury Building steps.
(Courtesy Brown University Library)

	nity, with men and women in pursuit of it. In this is also shown the inequality of the division of labor.
Interlude for Episode IV	Dance of Steam. This dance symbolizes the spirit of modern industry, showing the power and energy under control.
Episode V	In this is shown the future with work evenly divided, men and women sharing the division of responsibility in the home and the community.
Interlude for Episode V	The Dance of Happiness. Symbolizing the Freedom and the Joy of the future. Garland Dance of the children. Dance of the Maidens.
Finale	Procession of all groups to the altar and The Song of Work.[18]

The Indian scene was similar to the ones depicted in many other pageants, with the women seen grinding corn and setting up tepees while the men shoot arrows. The difference is that Beegle made a dance of squaws and braves an important part of the scene. "The Fire Dance" interlude carried on the importance of dance as expressing the basic concepts of the pageant. Beegle wrote in the program, "Fire is used as the key-note of the interlude to symbolize the element around which the industries of the primitive women were grouped. The dance will show the small fire of each clan, then the larger fire and its power, and finally fire uncontrolled which at last burns itself out."

The second episode, set in a colonial household, showed the women involved in various activities: knitting, weaving, preparing flax, setting up a quilting frame. When the spinning wheel was brought in and the grandmother took her place at the wheel, the young girls gathered around her and "join with her in singing the Song of the Spinning Wheel. At the end of the Song the young girls run out and dance the Dance of the Home Industries."

The Civil War episode was constructed in similar fashion; women were shown working and then dancing "to the fiddler's music." They end the scene singing. Episode IV, the Modern Industrial Period, was dramatic in its visual presentation. Beegle started with a street scene, a factory whistle, and the early morning workers—laborers and scrubwomen. Then came clerks, factory workers, businessmen, employers, professional men and women, and children on their way to school. These were followed by the women of leisure with "little interest in real work and humanity." Beegle

Scenes from *The Romance of Work*, New York City, 1914
(Courtesy Brown University Library)

ended the scene with women of leisure who "have employed their time for the betterment of others," and then looked ahead.

> The Future. . . . An altar representing the fire of the home and the community is the center to which a procession of organized Industrial and Social Activities bring their gifts. The groups enter from opposite sides and march majestically toward the altar where they join hands to signify co-operation between all classes. Then they group themselves in a semi-circle around the altar. A woman enters from one side, and a man from the other, advancing together they light the fire.

Other Pageants of Social Reform

Specific reform issues were addressed in other pageants. Constance D'Arcy MacKay's *Pageant of Sunshine and Shadow* (May 2, 1916), commissioned by the National Child Labor Committee, was presented at the City College of New York. The various episodes showed the plight of child laborers and the overall theme was the exploitation of youth. Renamed *The Child Labor Pageant*, it was produced in several cities from 1916 to 1918.

Although only performed once, on June 7, 1913, in Madison Square Garden, *The Paterson Strike Pageant* became one of the landmark public statements against capitalist oppression, and called for major reforms in our political and economic system. John Reed organized and directed the pageant and Robert Edmond Jones designed the set and program cover. An executive committee for the pageant consisted of William D. Haywood, Margaret H. Sanger, Jessie Ashley, Mabel Dodge, John Reed, and F. Summer Boyd. Over 1,000 people participated, and more than 15,000 made up the audience.

This pageant recreated events of the strike that had begun in February, organized by the IWW for the workers from silk factories in Paterson, New Jersey, against the mill owners. The strike had been fraught with violence. Police and private detectives had been hired by mill owners; by June two workers had been killed because of random gunfire and nearly 1,500 strikers and sympathizers had been arrested. The introduction to the pageant provided a summary and overview:

> The Pageant represents a battle between the working class and the capitalist class conducted by the Industrial Workers of the World (IWW) making use of the General Strike as the chief weapon. It is a conflict between two social forces—the force of labor and the force of capital.
>
> While the workers are clubbed and shot by detectives and policemen, the mills remain dead. While the workers are sent to jail by hundreds, the mills remain dead. While organizers are persecuted, the strike continues, and still the mills are dead. While the pulpit thunders denunciation and the press screams lies, the mills remain dead. No

Paterson Strike Pageant, New York City, 1913
Poster.
(Courtesy Smithsonian Institution, Division of Community Life, Washington, D.C.)

Scene from the *Paterson Strike Pageant*
Directed by John Reed, this pageant, in support of the Paterson silk workers strike, was
controversial for its revolutionary sympathies.
(*Courtesy Smithsonian Institution, Division of Community Life, Washington, D.C.*)

violence can make the mills alive—no legal process can resurrect them from the dead.
Bayonets and clubs, injunctions and court orders are equally futile.

Only the return of the workers to the mills can give the dead things life. The mills
remain dead throughout the enactment of the following episodes.

The strikers themselves were the actors and the actresses. In Episode
I we see the workers coming to the mill "in the bitter cold of dawn." As
they begin the strike, they sing the "Marseillaise" and the entire audience
is "invited to join in the song of revolt." In Episode II we see mass picketing
and police brutality. Valentino Modestino, who was neither a striker nor a
silk-mill worker, is hit by a bullet and killed as he stands on the porch of his
home with one of his children in his arms. Episode III shows Modestino's
funeral, with the striking workers putting red carnations and ribbons upon
the coffin until it is buried beneath the crimson symbol of the workers'
blood. We are told the funeral procession is accompanied by the Dead
March.

In Episode IV we see a great mass meeting of strikers, at which IWW
organizers speak and "songs by the strike composers are sung by the strik-

ers." They also sing the "International," the "Marseillaise," and "The Red Flag," and the audience is invited to join in. Episode V shows the May Day Parade and the celebration of the international revolutionary labor day. The strikers give their children to the "strike mothers" from other cities to be cared for "during the war in the silk industry." Speeches are made by Elizabeth Gurley Flynn and William D. Haywood. The pageant ends with the sixth episode. "The strikers, men and women, legislate for themselves. They pass a law for the eight-hour day. No court can declare the law thus made unconstitutional. Elizabeth Gurley Flynn, Carlo Tresca, and William D. Haywood make typical strike speeches."

The Paterson Strike Pageant engendered enormous controversy among participants, organizers, and members of the press—all amply documented by Martin Green in his book *New York 1913*.[19] The controversies centered around the reasons for the pageant, its impact on the strike and the IWW, and the political and economic message of revolt.

There were those who felt the event had been successful in calling attention to the strike and the plight of the workers, while some felt it had taken energy and time away from the picket lines. The strikers themselves may have had the most positive response to the pageant. When the organizing committee considered dropping the project, the workers themselves pushed to continue and more volunteered to take part than had originally planned to.

The pageant form was open-ended and flexible, making it a vehicle for militant strikers and more moderate social workers, educators, and settlement-house workers. The pageants had the ability to bring people together in an expressive experience about their hopes and dreams. Intangible elements of self-awareness and pride are involved in performance, as well as the ability to work with other people. A work of art cannot enact political legislation or give people better wages, but the convergence of reform forces in the pageants gave additional impact to various agendas for change.

This brings us back to the goals of the pageant leaders—to unite art and democracy. It is interesting that the organizers of the Paterson strike chose a pageant as opposed to a mass meeting with political speeches to bring the strikers together. The pageant allowed for participation and catharsis in a way that sitting at a meeting would not. Although the goals of social reform were different in each pageant, the act and process of joining forces in a symbolic event achieved through hours of rehearsal and the intimate act of singing and laughing together had a power nothing else could have.

Caliban, Cambridge, Massachusetts, 1917
Directed by Percy MacKaye as part of the Shakespeare tercentennial observances.
(Courtesy Dartmouth College Library)

4

Pageantry and Twentieth-Century Artistic Reform

From Thetford, Vermont, to Grand Forks, North Dakota, pageant masters saw themselves as pioneers on a new frontier where artistic reform would take its place alongside social reform. Every pageant was seen as one step in the direction of a theatre where new forms of expression would be integrated with agendas to improve society. Every pageant was produced with the idea of supplementing existing commercial presentations with spectacles supported by the community and integrated with its life.

The American Pageantry Movement was deeply influenced by the reforms suggested in the writings of three men, Romain Rolland, Gordon Craig, and Percy MacKaye, all of whom had utopian visions for the theatre, seeking to change it from what they felt was a stalemated aristocratic medium to a vital democratic art form.

The books written by Rolland, Craig, and MacKaye that influenced the American Pageantry Movement were published during the period 1903 through 1915. All three authors made it clear that they considered theatre to be in a wretched state, and nothing but serious reform would change existing conditions. They proposed eliminating theatre as a commercial enterprise governed by profit, and establishing endowed theatres for public benefit.

Gordon Craig likened his task of creating the "Theatre of the Future" to that of an Arctic explorer setting out to discover everything there is to know about the North Pole: it is a long and difficult journey toward an idea rather than a concrete object. Many routes are possible and only the adventurous will leave what is comfortable and go toward the unknown. Along the way, there are many observations and experiments, a good deal of trial and error. For those involved in American pageantry, Rolland, MacKaye, and Craig were companions and guides on their own North Pole journey—aiming to reach the idea of a new and vital institution of theatre in America.

Romain Rolland: The People's Theatre

Romain Rolland's contribution to American pageantry lies in his book *Le Théatre du peuple* published in France in 1903 and in an English edition as *The People's Theatre* in 1918. Rolland (1866–1944) achieved international fame with his Nobel Prize winning novel, *Jean-Christophe* (1904–12), and made his living as a professor of art history and later musicology at the Sorbonne. His first interest, however, was in the theatre and by 1895 he had written several plays. From 1895 to 1904 he completed ten full-length dramas, including a trilogy, *The Tragedies of Faith*, and the first three volumes of a projected twelve-part dramatic cycle, *The Theatre of the Revolution*.

The chapters in *The People's Theatre* originally appeared as articles in the *Revue d'art dramatique* between 1900 and 1903. The essays formed an impassioned argument for new types of productions and presentational formats providing recreation and enlightenment for the masses of working people in both city and country.

Rolland felt the theatres of his time were inadequate because they blindly sought "to impose upon the people of the twentieth century the art and thought of the aristocratic society of the past."[1] He wrote that "among those who claim to represent the aims of the people's theatre, there are two diametrically opposed ideals: the adherents of the first seek to give the people the theatre as it now exists . . . those of the second attempt to extract from this new force, the people, an entirely new theatre." The art of the past was created from the needs and energies of particular historical events and currents in society and does not speak to the facts of the twentieth century. "I do not know whether the society of today will create its own art, but I am sure that if it fails to do so, we shall have no living art, only a museum, a mausoleum wherein sleep the embalmed mummies of the past."

The People's Theatre was divided into two sections. In Part I Rolland included seven essays on various aspects of "The Theatre of the Past," and showed why the plays of Molière, Racine, Corneille, and others were not suitable for the majority of contemporary audiences. Rolland wrote that the classical masterpieces of Molière left the people "unmoved." "I have seen them sit, politely bored, through a performance of *Le Misanthrope*."

In Part II, Rolland placed five essays in which he discussed different aspects of the people's future theatre—types of presentations, physical spaces, and funding. Before addressing what he contemplated as the theatre of the future, Rolland showed that "Bourgeois Drama" and "Foreign Plays" were also of the past. "Bourgeois Drama," as exemplified in the work of Emile Augier and Alexandre Dumas fils, speaks to the nineteenth century. Sophocles, Shakespeare, Lope de Vega, Calderón, and Schiller "have all been dramatists of the people in their day—at least in some of their plays. But differences of time and of race are most unfortunate." These "foreign dramas" do not address the needs of the French people in the twentieth century. After surveying the past, Rolland declared his belief in the power of the theatre, for which he had "an unbounded admiration. . . . It is man's statue, shaped by himself out of his own imagination, a flaming image of the universe, itself a greater universe."

Rolland then outlined the basic requisites of his people's theatre and it is here that we see the ideas that appear continuously in the writings of those involved in American pageantry.

> The first requisite of the People's Theatre is that it must be a recreation. The theatre should be a source of energy: this is the second requisite. . . . Let the theatre be an arena of action. Let the people make of their dramatist a congenial traveling-companion, alert, jovial, heroic if need be. . . . It is the duty of this companion to take the people straight to their destination—without of course neglecting to teach them to observe along the road. This, it seems to me, is the third requisite of our People's Theatre.

There were many recommendations in Rolland's book related to types of people's drama, the physical environment in which these should be presented, and the lessons that could be learned from the past. He strongly urged the development of historical drama. He considered that history teaches not just about the past, but about the present and future. The stories of great heroes and heroines tell of moral battles fought and won; of ideas and actions that fuel the imagination and the soul and give greater meaning to daily life. Historical drama shapes "the conscience and the intelligence of the people" and provides a perspective for actions that encompass a broader framework for rules and relationships in a democratic society.

Four other kinds of people's drama were discussed by Rolland: the social play, rustic drama, legends and tales, and the circus. He favored the social drama, as it intensified life. Social drama can gather the people together in understanding the evil forces that must be abolished and changed and provides an important mechanism for creating awareness. The rural drama is that which focuses on individual small communities and "preserves what is poetic and records for posterity their vanishing individuality." He called the rural drama "the poem of Earth" and felt it was "a precious mine" for the people's theatre, "impregnated with the odor of fields and overflowing with peasant humor and rich language."

His discussion of the use of historical, social, and rural drama was translated by American writers into a need for developing material based on the history and legends of our country. There were lessons to be learned from the American Revolution, the Civil War, the exploits of George Wash-

Pageants as Recreation
Rolland's ideal of the people's theatre as a source of "energy" is echoed
in these scenes from the *Philadelphia Pageant* (1912, *above*) and the
Pageant of Indiana (1916, *below*).
(Courtesy Brown University Library)

ington and Abraham Lincoln. The legends of Hiawatha, Old Quail John, Cahókia, and Sakakawea[2] were important parts of our history and in retelling the stories we were restoring our heritage and creating a bond among people. For those involved in American pageantry Rolland's rejection of past masterpieces validated a need to break away from the traditions of Europe.

In *The People's Theatre* Rolland supported the notion of large numbers of people involved as audience and performers. He favored outdoor theaters, as they provided the most democratic environment and were most adaptable to large numbers of participants.[3] The natural environment provided more powerful scenery than artificial sets.

Rolland felt that indoor spaces could be used if they were constructed so that all the seats were "equally good, eliminating the stupid system of orchestra-seats and boxes, and the resultant antagonism between classes." The stage should be large enough to "allow masses of people to act on it," and the auditorium should also allow for huge numbers of spectators.

In the beginning this new kind of theatre would demand suitable large-scale methods of presentation; effect and meaning are created in broad strokes that communicate to thousands in the natural environment of an outdoor space. Dialogue must be short and simple, gestures large and meaningful, and concentration on totality of impression rather than specificity of detail and intimate psychology. To achieve "great mass effects . . . you must paint with a broom." He made two references to useful examples: the theatre of the Greeks and the people's festivals of Switzerland.

In his book Rolland discussed historical precedents for a people's theater, starting with the work of the eighteenth-century philosophers Jean-Jacques Rousseau and Diderot, "the first men who appear to have conceived the idea of a new dramatic art for the new society." He cited the pioneering work of eighteenth-century Louis-Sébastien Mercier, who "demanded the establishment of a people's theatre," and the French writer Michelet, who wrote in the mid-nineteenth century, the next important figure in the development of a people's theatre.

In the late nineteenth century there were developments in the people's theatre movement which engaged Rolland's imagination and energies for several years. Among his models were a *Volks-Theater* established in Vienna (1889); the *Schiller-Theater* in Berlin (1894); the revival of numerous people's theatres in Switzerland (1880s); the founding by Maurice Pottecher of *Le Théâtre du peuple* in Bussang, a little village in the Vosges (1892); and other experiments in Nancy, Lille, Flanders, and at the People's Universities in Paris.

As a result of all this activity, Rolland and other young writers on the staff of the *Revue d'art dramatique* tried to organize, in 1899, "an interna-

Pageants as Historical Drama
Rolland's concept of historical drama within the people's theatre seems
borne out in American pageants focusing on historical events, such as
the jousting tournament from the *Philadelphia Pageant* (*above*) and the
young Benjamin Franklin scene from the *Pageant of Patriots* (*below*).
(*[above] Courtesy Brown University Library; [below] from Ralph
Davol*, A Handbook of American Pageantry *[Taunton, Mass.: Davol
Publishing Company, 1915]*)

tional congress for the purpose of uniting the efforts of the world toward a true democracy of art." Their efforts proved too ambitious and in 1900 they decided instead to meet on the subject of the people's theatre of Paris.

Romain Rolland provided important historical background for those involved in American pageantry. He placed before them not only ideas of reform but the fact that there were many individuals who had attempted to put these ideas into practice. He never used the word *pageantry* in his book, but all of his ideas were an important part of the American Pageantry Movement. His message was loud and clear—reform the theatre and you reform the world. Reject the past and create new productions that will inform the thoughts and actions of the great mass of people with a new energy and moral insights.

Gordon Craig: Towards a New Theatre

Gordon Craig (1872–1966) designed and produced about a dozen plays and operas from 1900 through the 1920s, all of which were radical in their concepts of lighting, stage, design, visualization of the script's meaning, and emphasis on the director as unifying mastermind. His ideas were embodied in three books written between 1905 and 1913 in which he rejected the theatre as it existed and proposed a series of reforms: *The Art of the Theatre* (1905), *On the Art of the Theatre* (1911), and *Towards a New Theatre* (1913).[4] American pageant leaders referred often to Craig's writings and found that many of his ideas were important to their work—ideas such as noncommercial theatre endowed by the state and run by artists, outdoor theatre as a festival for the people; and theatre of "sound, light and motion"—visual spectacles that captured the "spiritual universe of the imagination."

The leaders of American pageantry were challenged to action by the broad sweep of Gordon Craig's vision. His notion of an endowed theatre where there would be room for experimentation and study was appealing. The need for laboratories in theatre coincided with the work of pageantry leaders such as Thomas Wood Stevens, George Pierce Baker, Frederick Koch, and Mary Porter Beegle, who were working in the universities. In addition, the pageants themselves were seen as productions where trial and error were possible and where professionals could work in a somewhat exploratory environment.

The fluidity of the pageants and the masques and the open-ended possibilities of these forms also coincided with Craig's ideas of the possibilities of the theatre in the future. The American Pageantry Movement found Craig's concepts of endowed theatres, where instruction and amusement are side by side, important in their own work.

Craig's ideas of a theatre of "Sound, Light and Motion" proved to be a controversial but stimulating guideline in the work of the American Pageantry Movement. All those involved in pageantry believed in Craig's ideas of a theatre where seeing was more important than hearing. They all wanted to integrate and emphasize movement, mass, color, and sound, but the question became one of degree.

The pageants were often a mix of symbolism and realism and Craig's concept of a visual theatre proved extremely influential in the development of American pageantry. Craig equated sound, light, and motion with "action, scene and voice," which he explained as follows:

> When I say *action* I mean both gesture and dancing, the prose and poetry of action. . . .
> When I say *scene* I mean all of which comes before the eye, such as the lighting, costume, as well as the scenery. When I say *voice*, I mean the spoken word or the word which is sung, in contradiction to the word which is read, for the word written to be spoken and the word written to be read are two entirely different things.

Craig's concept of a symbolic theatre integrating sound, light, and motion led him to feel that outdoor theatres were the ultimate physical environment for presentation. Craig's comment that "when Drama went indoors, it died"[5] was often quoted by those involved in American pageantry. He believed that the natural light of the sun created the most powerful ambiance for the stage. He also believed that only outdoors could that sense of community and religious feeling be part of the theatrical experience for the audience.

One of the most visionary aspects of Gordon Craig's writing is contained in "The Second Dialogue" in *On the Art of the Theatre*. In a fascinating imaginary conversation between a playgoer and a stage director Craig gradually leads the reader into a vision of theatre, revolutionary and far-reaching. He cautions us that he "cannot alter the theatre in a day" but with patience and time he can create the "Theatre of the Future."

Gordon Craig had a vision of a theatre of the future which must pursue the "ideal" and this can only be achieved if the artist advances "towards that which he has seen in his imagination." This means a shifting point—an ideal that is always open to change and flux, dependent on trial and error and the vision of those farsighted and strong in their passion. Given that "no one can see farther than the vanishing point at any time" Craig points out that "with each advancing step the position of the vanishing point alters and we are thus enabled continually to see farther than before."

Craig saw the journey toward achievement of the ideal theatre as analogous to exploration of the North Pole. He felt there is never any question about the need for scientists to have the necessary time and money for their task. This should be true for those seeking the beauty and mystery of the theatre. He proposed that the State guarantee 5,000 pounds a year for five years. With this money he would build and equip a college which would contain two theatres, one open-air and one roofed-in.

> These two stages, closed and open, are necessary for our experiments, and on one or on the other, sometimes on both, every theory shall be tested and records made of the results. These records will be written, drawn, photographed or registered on the cinematograph or gramophone for future reference, but they will not be made public and will be only for the use of members of the college. Other instruments for the study of natural sound and light will be purchased, together with the instruments for producing these artificially, and will lead us to the better knowledge of both sound and light, and also to the invention of yet better instruments through which the purer beauty of both sound and light may be passed. In addition, instruments will be purchased for the study of motion, and some will be especially invented for this purpose.

Other equipment would be purchased or invented—a printing press, carpenter's tools—and there would be a well-stocked library. "With these materials and instruments we shall pursue the study of the Stage as it is to-day with the intention of finding out those weaknesses which have brought it to its present unfortunate condition."

Craig made the analogy with the North Pole clearer. He pointed out that by creating a college and two theatres he would create

> a centre from which search-parties shall be sent in different directions, our object being to explore within reason any part of the theatrical world which is unknown to us. We shall at the same time go over much old ground in the belief that it has never been thoroughly examined. No great hopes are entertained of finding there anything of great value, but an examination is necessary. As soon as possible we shall push forward in the direction of the unknown. Just as search-parties are sent in a certain direction with instructions to sound and make observations and then to return to the point selected as a base, so will our investigators push forward their studies into certain regions from which, when they have fully explored them and collected sufficient evidence, they will return to the point where they had separated from us to make known the result of their observations.

For the sum of 25,000 pounds over five years Craig proposed that the college and its two theatres be supported by the State. The experiments, observations, and findings would eventually create a theatre that would both "amuse and instruct." Such a theatre would be of great benefit to the State because it would produce that which is noble and beautiful. The State supports Arctic expeditions, as well as experiments in scientific laboratories, because it stands to gain from the knowledge and beauty of the discoveries. In the same way the State should support experiments in theatre. Craig presented the following dialogue between a stage director and a playgoer, and showed the linkage between theatre that "amuses and instructs" and that which is "noblest and most beautiful."

PLAYGOER	If we seek for instruction it is easier to comprehend the beautiful and the noble, for it is that which we are searching for; if we seek for amusement the ignoble and ugly is possibly more immediate in its effect.
STAGE-DIRECTOR	And is the beautiful and the noble more amusing?
PLAYGOER	I think it is not.
STAGE-DIRECTOR	And yet what is that which, when you see and hear it, causes you to feel smilingly from top to toe?
PLAYGOER	The beautiful—truth—oh, something which it is quite beyond us to explain.
STAGE-DIRECTOR	I think so too. Yet is there not something of amusement in it? For we smile; and a smile is the whisper of laughter. . . . Perhaps we may call it the very best part of amusement. . . . And this is connected, as we have seen, with the beautiful and the noble; therefore the very best part of amusement is akin to the best part of instruction. . . . Now, we have said that the Theatre either instructs or amuses. Yet we see that sometimes it acts in both ways; in short, it both instructs and amuses when it is noblest and most beautiful.

If theatre can "both instruct and amuse" it produces a "state of mental and physical ease in the people." When theatre serves this purpose it not only benefits each individual, but also the State—or society as a whole. It remained for Craig to prove to readers that if the State is to support such a theatre "the gain exceeds the expense." So he argued that £25,000 in a five-year period was not a great deal of expenditure, as the same sum would be spent by the State on one picture in the National Gallery or three-to-five productions in His Majesty's Theatre or Drury Lane, and less than half the sum on enlarging and improving the Lyceum Theatre in London in 1881.

Gordon Craig wanted to bring the life of the imagination to every individual—rich and poor, man, woman, and child—and American pageantry took this mission seriously. One last phrase of Craig's sums up the belief in the possibilities of theatre that he passed on to the pageant leaders: "You want to fly; you want to exist in some other state, to be intoxicated with the air, and to create this state in others."[6]

Percy MacKaye: Art and Democracy

Percy MacKaye (1875–1956), poet, playwright, social commentator, was the first American to write about pageants as a new form and place them in the

Pageants as Education
Gordon Craig's view of a theatre of the future sought drama which
could instruct as well as entertain. Pageants in Deerfield,
Massachusetts (*above*) and Boston (*below*) stressed the involvement of
children and educational institutions in recreating historical events.
(*[above] Courtesy Brown University Library; [below] from Ralph
Davol*, A Handbook of American Pageantry *[Taunton, Mass.: Davol
Publishing Company, 1915])*

larger context of reforming all aspects of theatre in our country. MacKaye's two books, *The Playhouse and the Play: And Other Addresses Concerning the Theatre and Democracy in America* (1909) and *The Civic Theatre in Relation to the Redemption of Leisure: A Book of Suggestions* (1912)[7] contain revolutionary ideas related to the purpose of theatre, its place in society, and the role of the arts in people's lives.

Percy MacKaye practiced what he preached. MacKaye's pageant/masques and his involvement with the American Pageant Association made him an active leader in reforming the American theatre. The three large pageant/masques MacKaye produced in St. Louis (1914), New York (1916), and Boston (1917) stimulated the civic theatre movement in those three cities. One example is MacKaye's transformation of the outdoor athletic stadium at New York's City College into a theatrical facility for his *Caliban by the Yellow Sands*. The success of this great pageant/masque convinced the city bureaucracy that an outdoor performance space for the people of New York was a viable option. What had been used for athletics became Lewisohn Stadium, and for over forty years this functioned as an endowed civic theatre where tickets were inexpensive and great art was available for the masses.

In an essay in *The Civic Theatre*, "American Pageants and Their Promise," MacKaye described pageantry as a crucial component in his reform proposals. Pageantry, he wrote, has the potential of fulfilling all the needs of art as a partner with democracy: extensive participation by the people in every community; productions which educate as well as amuse; themes rooted in the American experience; endowment from within the community; constructive use of leisure time for the masses; creation of a mechanism for grass-roots civic theatres; and development of a form that unites popular art with public benefit.

MacKaye called pageantry "poetry for the masses." He felt it could make "an elemental appeal to every man in the street" for it is a form that can reveal to many "the mystery and meaning of life" through "sensuous form." "Pageantry satisfies an elemental instinct for art, a popular demand for poetry. This instinct and this demand, like other human instincts and demands, are capable of being educated, refined, developed into a mighty agency of civilization." The art of pageantry is a form of drama that can bring together painting, dancing, music, and sculpture (the latter as applied to plastic groupings).

MacKaye also advocated pageant competitions between cities that would stimulate industry, trade, education, and creative work on a high level. A professional master of pageants would be appointed to public service in every city, assuring the quality of pageants and their production on a regular basis. The additional benefit of a master of pageants was the

Percy MacKaye
(Courtesy Dartmouth College Library)

placement of such a person in a position of authority as part of a community's leadership. Civic leaders and leaders in the fine arts would then create an ongoing association that could "enlarge the horizons of both."

"The form of pageantry most popular and impressive in appeal as a fine art is that of the dramatic pageant, or masque," wrote MacKaye. His definition of pageantry was not limited to historic themes. "All vital modern forces and institutions of our nation—the press, the law, the railroads, the public-school system, athletics, the universities, the trades unions in all their variety, the vast industries of steel and copper and wheat and fisheries and agriculture, and hundreds more—might appropriately find symbolic expression in majestic masques, educative and entertaining to all the people."

According to MacKaye, the pageant fulfilled all the functions of art in democracy and could initiate great national art that would promote the development of numerous civic theatres. "For true democracy is vitally concerned with beauty, and true art is vitally concerned with citizenship." MacKaye seemed to indicate that American pageantry had the potential to become an art form that would remain fresh and vital as long as it remained close to the people and was controlled by great artists.

One of the central issues raised by MacKaye was what purpose the theatre had historically in different periods and countries. He identified three distinctive European traditions of theatre—Anglo-Saxon, Continental, and Greek—and asked which could serve as a model for twentieth-century America.

Although not specific about what countries fostered the Continental tradition, he mentioned as examples France and Germany. The Continental tradition placed theatre in a "position of strong influence and high regard in society, but less influence in the state proper. . . . Artists have long been leaders in social taste but not in civic strategy."

In contrast to both Anglo-Saxon and Continental traditions MacKaye believed the Greeks had a better model. In Greece "the theatre—being concerned with art—held a position of double vantage, due to the special genius of that people—a people whose artists were also soldiers and statesmen. The theatre in Athens exerted a guiding influence both upon society and the state, and thereby rose to the full dignity of its proper status and function."

MacKaye wanted to extend the Greek ideal to twentieth-century America, "an ideal which shall establish the art of the dramatist as a permanent civic agency in the structure of American communities; an agency of guidance and liberation to the people . . . an ideal which tends to reconcile the traditions of art and democracy." One of his key ideas was the concept of a "civic theatre," by which he meant a theatre endowed with public and private funds that did not depend on profit motives or the lowest levels of public taste. He envisioned a civic theatre in every community, supported by people of that community who would call on all individuals to participate in its activities. He also wanted a national civic theatre supported by the country as a whole.

In the civic theatre funding is allocated for artists, who are considered workers who make important contributions to daily life. Artists become leaders in society by producing work that contributes to excellence of thought and action. theatre becomes an institution integrated with other democratic institutions of our country. "It is frequently asserted that the ideas of art and democracy are irreconcilable; that art differentiates and uplifts, whereas democracy assimilates and levels. To this I venture the opinion that in such an assertion, the ideals of democracy and commercialism are confused. Commercialism always levels; true democracy never."

MacKaye felt the time had come for the country to realize that theatre is an important civic institution which has the power to reach the masses and create in them a desire for the values of democracy—cooperation, clear thinking, and true moral action. The time had come for artists to function as leaders of our society—central in the daily process of making a better society. He was optimistic, and felt that although he was suggesting long-term "reformative conditions" the future held great promise. He wrote, with hope:

> The true causes for the unique promise and the encouraging achievement of our drama to-day arise not from any conducive qualifications of the existing theatrical system as a private speculative business, but from that great reawakening of our national consciousness which everywhere to-day is increasingly alive to deeper significance in our life and institutions. In brief, our national life now claims the theatre to express itself, and to that end the theatre, sooner or later, must be overhauled and reconstituted to meet the larger needs of national life.

"Enlightened public opinion" is the key to all activities in a democracy and to the power of theatre in our society. MacKaye talked about "the Law of Dramatic Deterioration" which is created by "public demand." He proposed that we govern our playhouses with "the Law of Dramatic Regeneration" in which we "set in motion a law of aesthetic demand and supply." "By this means, the skilled judgement of acknowledged masters in dramatic art will select, from among competing dramatists, the fittest to survive; and in turn this selection, through artistic competition, will by its supply create a responsive demand in the public, who will thus, for the first time, acquire unconsciously self-discipline in taste, and cultivate for themselves in the playhouse a joy which does not pall."

In the minds of many, theatre is associated only with entertainment. An assumption is made that an evening in the playhouse passes the time away before we go on to more important things. MacKaye put this notion to rest. "In theatrical amusement we are concerned with public happiness. Real happiness is education; real education means happiness." It is only when we endow our theatres and recognize their power will they "be free to become an institution of leadership in public service."

MacKaye developed the idea of theatre's role in "constructive leisure." Rather than thinking of leisure hours as killing time MacKaye suggested that leisure time be put to constructive use. Time spent in public parks, churches, schools, and libraries is constructive use of leisure time, and time spent in the theatre must also fall into that category.

The theatre can "fill time" rather than "kill time," can "refill it to overflowing with that quality of charmed eternity which it always possesses in normal childhood—when a summer's afternoon may pass like an instant, yet seem an eon of joy in retrospection. For to unfettered childhood, the age of imaginative play, all time is a garden of leisure for the transplanting of wild flowers from Elysian pastures."

In reforming the playhouse by creating endowed civic theatres it would be possible to wrest control of leisure from "the amusement business" where profit is the motive. "The use of a nation's leisure is the test of its civilization."

MacKaye suggested a bureau in Washington in connection with the American Federation of Arts which would organize civic theatre committees and coordinate activities all over America. Another suggestion was that the Playground Association include special committees for the organization of civic theatres in all playgrounds and public spaces. Theatre as an element of constructive leisure has the ability to substitute "the imaginative ritual of play" for "languor, social decay, alcoholism, morbidity and joyless individualism."

MacKaye called on city planners, local and state governments' architects, politicians, and all leaders in the community to make the civic theatre a focal part of urban and country life. He recommended physical structure be given great thought and theatre facilities be placed in central locations. Related to his concern about physical space was MacKaye's interest in outdoor theatres. Outdoor theatre is a natural environment where "dramatic art becomes convincing to the people." These kinds of facilities should exist in every town and city and in as many public parks and universities as possible. "In direct relation to the redeeming of country and industrial districts through constructive leisure, is the founding of outdoor theatres for the people."

Given the need for endowed civic theatres which would create constructive use of leisure time, who would create the productions, what form will they take, and what would be their themes? For MacKaye the answer rested in the development of American dramatists, poets, dancers, musicians, and visual artists, who would create popular spectacles bringing our history, folklore and legends to life. "The American Drama still lies fallow for we have listened too long to the courtly muses of Europe," wrote MacKaye, and continued:

> In America, therefore, where our Cyclopean industries of iron and gold and brass and blazing ores sit on our Appalachians and our Rockies and, like so many Polyphemi, gaze down with fiery eyes upon their smoking hearth-stones-ten thousand cities with their consumed humanity; in America where again the silent forests range, solitude after solitude, millions of acres, and you shall hear nothing but the water-falls and the wind, and behold nothing but far peaks and endless pines shadowing their twilight . . . surely in this America we shall discover, in riches, more than the raw stuff of our bank accounts; in art, more than a mere standing place . . . in prophecy more than the bourgeois hope of imitation and self-disguise.

MacKaye published a short essay in 1915 in which he further extended the reform ideas stated in *The Playhouse and the Play* and *The Civic Theatre*. In *A Substitute for War*[8] he discussed the potential for theatrical enterprises that would marshall people's energies toward peace and not war.

He felt the act of war was a pageant with stirring symbols—flags, uniforms, marches, fighting hymns. The act of peace was symbolized by the dove—a symbol he termed weak and ineffective. Peace had to be as attractive a community venture as war, and theatre had the power to create the "moral equivalent of war" with equally stirring symbols and organized group activity.

MacKaye noted that "the fighting armies of peace are not properly organized; and secondly, their functions are not properly symbolized." He suggested a new twentieth-century profession—civic engineering—"for the problems involved are so large and various that their solution takes on the dignity and efficiency of an expert science." The role of organizing "the armies of peace" "will require the directive insight of one who may aptly be called the Political Engineer." The person who would be responsible for organizing the symbolism involved in creating armies of peace would be called the dramatic engineer. MacKaye gave *The Pageant and Masque of St. Louis* as an example of how a dramatic engineer would use theatre to create symbolism for peace and brotherhood that would be as powerful as symbolism for war and destruction.

In the essay *A Substitute for War* MacKaye developed his ideas to the point where the art of the theatre could be transformed to save all of society from destruction. The artist is not only at the service of local communities and the nation but at the service of the world. "This potential science of dramatic engineering" is MacKaye's final vision of the arts as the most

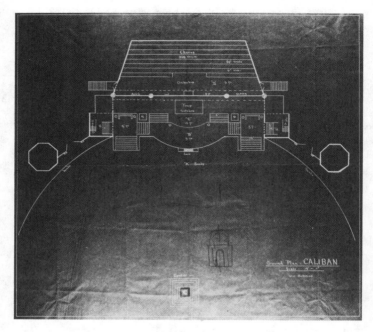

Plans (*above*) and Set (*below*) for New York Performances of *Caliban*, 1916
(*Courtesy Dartmouth College Library*)

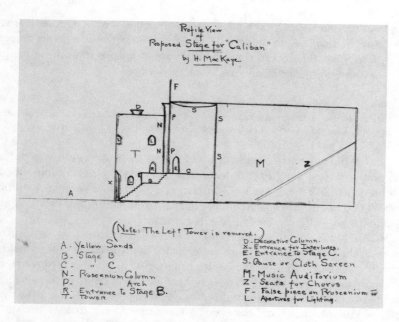

Profile View of Stage (*above*) and Ground Plan of Stage (*below*) for New
York Performances of *Caliban*, 1916
Designed by Hazel MacKaye.
(*Courtesy Dartmouth College Library*)

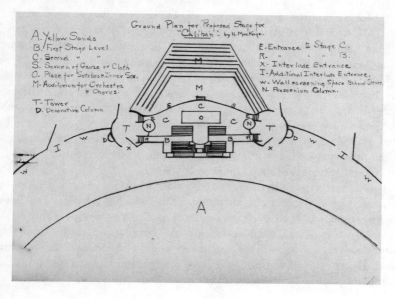

complete weapon society has against destruction and decay. Dramatic engineering is the final key to unlock the successful interplay of art and democracy, where civic theatres in their creative use of leisure time bring people together in harmony and peace. In MacKaye's words:

> In brief, our national life now claims the theatre to express itself, and to that end the theatre, sooner or later, must be overhauled and reconstructed to meet the larger needs of national life. In America itself lies the assured renaissance of American drama.

One of the most striking examples of Percy MacKaye's ability to put his ideas into practice was his production of *Caliban by the Yellow Sands,* presented July 2 through 18, 1917, at Harvard Stadium. There were nightly about 20,000 people in the audience, 1,400 amateur actors and dancers, and 600 singers from all over Boston and its suburbs.[9]

When MacKaye produced *Caliban* in 1917 he instituted an unusual feature in the organizational structure in order to achieve his goal of making pageantry a truly democratic enterprise. He hired his sister Hazel MacKaye,[10] a trained actress, dancer, writer, and avid believer in pageantry herself, to serve as community director. A formal contract was drawn up between Miss MacKaye and the Caliban Executive Committee. For a salary of $1,500 she was responsible for the development of community spirit with the potential audience as well as the performers.

Hazel MacKaye submitted two reports on her work, in April and May 1917. In the first report she announced the successful arrangements for a series of "community speakers classes." These were to be held at Bates Hall, YMCA Building, 316 Huntington Avenue, at 4:30 P.M. On April 30 and May 2 and 4, the topic was to be "The Community and the Masque," and on May 1, 3, and 5, "The Story and Production of the Masque." She provided an accounting of the thirteen organizations she had contacted regarding classes for community speakers: The Protestant Churches of Greater Boston and environs within a radius of twenty-five miles; Massachusetts Federation of Teachers; Greater Boston Teachers; College Club; Young Women's Christian Association; Young Men's Christian Association and the following colleges: Radcliffe, Simmons, Emerson, and Burdett colleges; Curry School; Catholic and Jewish Clergy.

Hazel MacKaye also reported she was working with the recruiting department of the Caliban organization. "Miss MacKaye has spoken before clubs, organizations and mass meetings in connection with recruiting and will continue to speak until recruiting has been completed. Among the organizations where Miss MacKaye has spoken are the following: The Curry School, Dorchester Community Centre, Cantabrigia Club, Teachers' Club, Fabian Club, Municipal Gymnasiums of Dorchester and Jamaica Plain."

Hazel MacKaye, ca. 1915
(Courtesy Dartmouth College Library)

Miss MacKaye seems to have had a real talent for bringing people together and allowing individuals to help her in a variety of capacities. She created the Community Committee which in turn formed subcommittees to promote community spirit at rehearsals and provide help in recruitment. In her April report she announced that several community and recruiting meetings had been held. These involved the cast of a particular scene and were in addition to regular rehearsals. She listed recruiting meetings as follows: April 5, Armenians; April 11, Egyptian Dancers; April 12, Roman Dancers; April 18, Powers of Setebos. The Community Committee eventually included several people who were put specifically in charge of various sections of *Caliban,* and the final program lists subcommittees for "the Powers of Setebos," "the Egyptian Interlude," "the Greek Interlude," "the Roman Interlude," "the Germanic Interlude," "the French-English Interlude," "the Spanish-Italian Interlude," "the English Interlude," and "the Chorus." It was common in most pageants to have volunteer community leaders placed in charge of casting and rehearsing individual episodes and interludes.

MacKaye evolved a staff and a structure in her role as community director for *Caliban.* Listed as community staff were the following: assembly director, Percy J. Burrell; community director, Hazel MacKaye; organizer of community speakers, Hannah London; recruiting director, Margaret Wilson Shipman; assistant recruiting director, Mrs. Joseph Bedlow. There is no record of payment of salary to anyone except Miss MacKaye and it can be safely assumed that all the others worked on a volunteer basis. She also established a subcommittee on chaperons, a subcommittee on Assembly, a subcommittee on entertainment, an overall Advisory Board; an Executive Recruiting Committee; an Advisory Recruiting Committee; and a District Recruiting Committee.

Percy J. Burrell, whose official role was assembly director, made the following revealing notes in his attempt to carry forward the complexities of community organization:

I. Shall different groups participate on different nights?
    1. Probable response to appeal
    2. Time for rehearsals
II. *Initial Work*
    1. Numerical requirements of production for volunteers. Three general divisions
       a. Actors (speaking parts)
       b. Masses (non-speaking parts)
          1. mobs
          2. professionals

      3. dancers
      4. soldiers
      5. gymnasts
   c. Choir
      1. visible
      2. invisible
What is the minimum and maximum number that can be used?
Determined by
      1. number of present costumes
      2. means to purchase more
  2. Survey of Greater Boston for organized units
   a.   public schools
   b.   private schools
   c.   churches
   d.   settlement houses
   e.   civic clubs
   f.   social clubs
   g.   military organizations
   h.   special schools
      1. dancing
      2. music
      3. physical culture
      4. art
III. The call for Volunteers (participants)
    1. How?
    2. When?
    3. Where?
IV. The Enrollment of Volunteers (participants)
    1. What Method
     a.   Ticket
     b.   Badge
V. Committee on Enrollment
    1. General committee selected from survey groups
    2. Sub-committees on
     a.   music
     b.   dancing

These notes were translated into action over the next few weeks. A small booklet was widely circulated, titled "Some Questions and Answers about CALIBAN BY THE YELLOW SANDS." Another small booklet, "What Is CALIBAN," which carried a summary of the plot and meaning of *Caliban,* was also circulated. Enrollment and rehearsal cards were given

HOW TO WIN
— A —
Caliban Emblem of Service

TO ALL CALIBAN PARTICIPANTS

WE have promised the people of New England the greatest out-of-door spectacle ever given in this part of the country. Caliban is making good our promise.

IT is really **your** Caliban and your continued service is needed for next week. The committee will reward each loyal participant and to those faithful in attendance it will give a CALIBAN EMBLEM OF SERVICE (an enamelled badge-pin). You will take increasing pride in this emblem as the years go by.

EVERY effort and sacrifice you can make for Caliban next week will be greatly appreciated by both the Governor of the Commonwealth and the Caliban Committee of Greater Boston.

Gratefully yours,

E. F. CULLEN,
For the Caliban Committee of Greater Boston.

COUNT ON ME!

To the Caliban Committee of Greater Boston :

1. I want Caliban to be a great success.
2. I will stand by Caliban.
3. I will come on my assigned nights for Caliban.
4. I will come RAIN or SHINE to Caliban to make sure if a performance is to be given.
5. I wish to earn a Caliban Emblem of Service.

Please fill in on proper line

INTERLUDE No.

CHORUS No.

SHAKESPEAREAN SCENE No.

MASQUE PROPER No.

Name

Address

(Please leave this at Information Office.)

Caliban Emblem of Service Requirements
(*Courtesy Dartmouth College Library*)

out all over the Greater Boston area and a Caliban Emblem of Service (an enameled badge pin) was created to reward those who were "faithful in attendance." A variety of advance ticket-order forms were printed and made available all over the city and surrounding districts.

All those involved were given a complimentary ticket and were required to attend from three to ten rehearsals. Rehearsals were conducted by directors in local districts and were meant to be "socially and dramatically interesting." Participants were enrolled in five general groups: district, town, nationality, school and college, clubs and organizations.

There were several issues of the *Caliban News* published during and right after the performances (July 9, 12, 16, and 20) which featured articles by and about various participants and important people involved with the production. These were in the format of a mini-newspaper and, in addition to personality features, often reviewed the content and purpose of the script and production.

The *Caliban* production in Boston had originally been planned for performances that would end on July 14, but the July 12, 1917, issue of *Caliban News* reported "the tremendous public appeal for a continuance of 'Caliban' has met with response, and 'Caliban' will positively be given Monday, Tuesday and Wednesday of next week, July 16, 17 and 18."

On July 14, 1917, a group of people met in Boston to organize a league that would continue the spirit of cooperation and the community interaction through the following months and years. They gave themselves the name The Caliban Community League of Greater Boston and their object was "to encourage and foster the community ideals exemplified in 'Caliban' by developing and practicing community drama, community singing and music and other community activities in which all citizens may cooperate." The league was to be composed of no fewer than ten clubs: the Caliban Chorus Club, the Caliban Masque Club (inner scenes, powers of Setebos, muses, spirits of Ariel); the Caliban Interlude Clubs (Egyptian, Greek, Roman, Germanic, French-English, Spanish-Italian, English); and the Caliban Junior Club (Roman Fauns, Roman Nymphs, Renaissance Fauns, Merry Elves, Fairies, Germanic Children).

The last issue of the *Caliban News* was October 15, 1917, and an article calling for more meetings of the Caliban League noted that "by building Community Drama—this young and brave democracy of art—we are helping to build the democracy of the world." The article called for a big rally, which may or may not have taken place. There is no indication of any further *Caliban* activities past October 15. It is likely that the war effort began to assume the energies of civic leaders and shifted focus to a larger effort for peace.

Percy MacKaye worked closely with his sister to make sure the production would indeed be "a drama for democracy." He wanted to make sure participation was widespread and that everyone understood the script's message and its loose relationship to Shakespeare's *The Tempest*. He issued a one-page information sheet designed to explain the symbolism and meaning of *Caliban*.

What is Percy MacKaye's masque about?
    About Caliban, by the Yellow Sands.
What are the Yellow Sands?
    The Sands of Prospero's magic Isle.
What Isle is that?
    The world of time—where we all live.
What is Caliban like?
    He is something like you and me—sometimes good and sometimes bad.
Who was his father?
    Setebos, a fierce god, half tiger and half toad.
Who was his mother?
    Sycorax, a gigantic witch, a kind of earth-spirit.
How was Caliban brought up?
    By three wicked teachers.
What were their names?
    Lust, Death and War.
Did he do what they told him?
    Yes, until he met Miranda.
How did she help him?
    She brought her father, Prospero.
Who is Prospero?
    A great Enchanter, whose servant is Ariel.
What do these do to help Caliban?
    They try to make him better.
How do they try to make him better?
    They show him beautiful things.
What beautiful things?
    They show him scenes from plays.
What plays?
    Shakespeare's.
Is Caliban made good at once?
    No, he is still influenced by his old teachers.
Lust, Death and War?
    Yes.
Do they win in the end?
    No, the Magic of Prospero wins, with the help of a great Spirit.
What great Spirit?
    The Spirit of Time?
What is the Magic of Prospero?
    The same as that of Shakespeare.
What is that Magic?
    The old and beautiful Art of the Theatre.

Percy MacKaye used Shakespeare as a jumping-off point, as explained in his preface to the published script:

> It is, I think, incumbent on me to point out . . . the characters, derived—but re-imagined from . . . 'The Tempest' . . . are my own conception. Their words (save for a very few song-snatches and sentences) and their actions are those which I have given them; the development of their characters accords with the theme—not of Shakespeare's play but of this Masque, in which Caliban's nature is developed to become the protagonist of aspiring humanity, not simply its butt of shame and ridicule.

MacKaye designed the action to take place on three separate planes: the yellow sands, which constituted the ground-circle, designed to resemble the orchestra of a Greek theatre; a middle stage; and an inner stage. The yellow sands was the largest area, in which participants played out the history of the theatre through dance, pantomime, procession, and choral singing. It was here that the three major interludes and the epilogue were presented. The middle stage was designed to represent the cave of Setebos and much of the dialogue took place here, with leading roles taken by professional actors: Caliban was Lionel Braham; Ariel, Gareth Hughes; Prospero, Howard Kyle; and Miranda, Alexandra Carlisle.[11] The inner stage, "the mind of Prospero," was where the Shakespearean vision scenes were performed.

The last scene of *Caliban* provided a summary of MacKaye's theme and a sense of what the audience saw. The Spirit of Time, whom MacKaye described as "a serene female Figure," opened the action with the following words:

> Children of men, my passionate children, hark!
> To-day and Yesterday I am To-morrow:
>   Out of my primal dark
>   You dawn—my joy, my sorrow.
>
> Lovers of life, you rapturous lovers, lo
> The lives you clutch are by my lightnings riven:
>   Yea, on my flux and flow,
>   Like sea-birds tempest driven.
>
> Yet from my founts of life, fecund, divine,
> Still dauntless lovers dare my dark tribunal,
>   Building a common shrine
>   To hold their love communal.
>
> So out of War up looms unconquered Art:
> Blind forces rage, but masters rise to mould them.
>   Soldiers and kings depart;
>   Time's artists—still behold them!

As the Spirit of Time finished her speech the yellow sands became the focus of all activity. "From either side enters a Pageant of the great Theatres of the world—from the ancient Theatre of Dionysius to the Comédie Française—in symbolic groups, with their distinctive banners and insignia . . . announced from either end of the high balcony above the inner stage by two spirit Trumpeters, the one beneath a glowing disk of the sun, the other beneath a sickle moon." The groups of War, Lust, and Death that had fought with the Spirits of Ariel and captured Miranda, Prospero, and Ariel in the previous scene now "dwindled away in the background darkness."

MacKaye unfolded his pageant of great theatres with grand fanfare and used a striking visual image as famous dramatists were portrayed coming through the mouths of two colossal masks on either side of the stage—the mask of tragedy and the mask of comedy. Finally, after all appeared, from Thespis to Ibsen, Shakespeare himself came on stage. He approached Prospero and they exchanged places so that Shakespeare was center stage and Prospero was standing silently with all the others. Shakespeare was joined by Ariel and Miranda. Then, out of the dimness, came forth Caliban. Groping, dazed, he reached toward the dark circle, where the stately Spirit has vanished. Caliban spoke, "in a voice hoarse with feeling."

> Lady of the Yellow Sands! O Life! O Time!
> Thy tempest blindedth me; Thy beauty baffleth.—
> A little have I crawled, a little only
> Out of mine ancient cave. All that I build
> I botch; all that I do destroyeth my dream.
> Yet—yet I yearn to build, to be thine Artist
> And stablish this thine Earth among the stars—
> Beautiful!
>   —O bright Beings, help me still!
> Move visions—visions, Master!

With those words Caliban crouched at Shakespeare's feet "gazing up in his face, which looks on him with tenderness." Miranda also approached Shakespeare and said to him "Master?" MacKaye noted in the script that Shakespeare then spoke (as Prospero):

> Child
> Our revels now are ended. These our actors,
> As I foretold you, were all spirits and
> Are melted into air, into thin air:
> And, like the baseless fabric of this vision,
> The cloud-capp'd towers, the gorgeous palaces,
> The solemn temples, the great globe itself,
> Yea, all of which it inherit, shall dissolve,
> And like this unsubstantial pageant faded,

Percy MacKaye, New York, 1916
*(Photo by Paul Thompson. Courtesy Dartmouth
College Library)*

> Leave not a rack behind. We are such stuff
> As dreams are made on, and our little life
> Is rounded with a sleep. [12]

At the end of this speech, "the light focuses and fades in darkness on the pensive form of Shakespeare." As the production ended softly, hidden from view the choirs of Ariel's Spirits repeated:

> We are such stuff
> As dreams are made on, and our little life
> Is rounded with a sleep.

MacKaye summed up the meaning of the production in his preface:

I have called this work a Masque, because—like other works so named in the past—it is a dramatic work of symbolism involving, in its structure, pageantry, poetry, and the dance. Yet I have by no means sought to relate its structure to an historic form; I have simply sought by its structure to solve a modern (and a future) problem of the art of the theatre. That problem is the new one of creating a focussed dramatic technique for the growing but groping movement vaguely called "pageantry" which is itself a vital sign of social evolution—the half-desire of the people not merely to remain receptive to a popular art created by specialists, but to take part themselves in creating it; the desire, that is, of democracy consistently to seek expression through a drama and the people, not merely *for* the people.

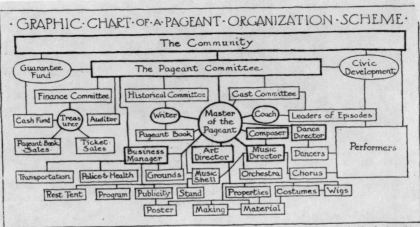

Pageant Organization
From American Pageantry Handbook, No. 11.
(*Courtesy Brown University Library*)

5

The American Pageant Association

About eight hundred people attended a conference of pageant masters in Boston on January 31 and February 1, 1913.[1] Never before had there been a conference of this kind and a great deal of enthusiasm was generated for a continued sharing of information about pageants.

The idea for a permanent organization was strongly supported and the Boston conference gave birth to the American Pageant Association. William Chauncy Langdon was elected president, Lotta A. Clark became secretary, and a board of directors was chosen.[2] "The American Pageant Association— A New Force Working for the Future of Pageantry in America" was an article written to explain the necessity for founding the APA.

> It became evident how important a matter it was to educate the public as to the knowledge of pageantry, so as to prevent their being misled by so-called "pageants" announced in connection with ice carnivals, political picnics, military organizations, parades and other like celebrations, as otherwise it would be a matter of a few years before the pageant would become entirely discredited by that very community for whose benefit and inspiration it is a most effective and logical instrument.[3]

The APA issued its first bulletin on May 15, 1913.[4] An art-deco-like logo appeared at the top of the one-page publication, featuring a strong likeness of the goddess Athena holding a spear posed against the background of the American flag. Half of the page was taken up with a "list of announced pageants, 1913," featuring productions from all over the United States— California, Wisconsin, Illinois, South Carolina, Maine, New York, New Jersey, and others. The other half contained a discussion of pageantry:

> In a recent article John Collier says, "Pageantry—the new Pageantry—is not only the birth of a new art, or the rebirth of a lost art. It is the birth of a new educational idea. It is the forerunner of a distinctly different and a distinctly higher civic and social life. . . . Incidentally, Pageantry is the form of art which comes nearest to expressing the new social idea which is already moving through a hundred million minds, and which is destined to make the world over during the next century or so; and the most general

definition of the new social idea might be that it believes in freedom through cooperation,—and in the possibility of higher and intenser personal life, which waits to be built
on through new social arrangements. The historical definition of Pageantry means merely
a pompous and evanescent ceremonial parade, with vaudeville features. But the Pageantry developed in recent years is anything but a meaningless parade. It is community
drama, as distinct from individual drama. It symbolizes, in a thousand possible ways, the
growing and striving community, depicted through a course of long time, gathering up
into its soul the growing tradition and idealism, the strivings and hopes of its generations
of men and women. Pageantry, viewed by this idea, is the great modern art, just being
discovered, and is made possible only through the existence of imminent potentiality of
the new social idea. It rests on community consciousness and brotherhood."

The 1913 Boston conference of pageant masters created an organization
arising from several years of concern about potential corruption of pageant
goals and ideals.

William Chauncy Langdon, Lotta Clark, and George Pierce Baker were
each involved prior to 1913 in trying to establish an organizational base for
pageantry, and their early efforts are important in the creation of the APA.[5]
The three perspectives they brought to bear represent various forces that
brought agreement as well as dissension in the APA.

William Chauncy Langdon's role as first president of the APA was a
logical progression from his early attempt at founding a bureau of American
pageantry. This occurred in 1910 when he was employed in the Department
of Child Hygiene of the Russell Sage Foundation in New York. The Russell
Sage Foundation had been founded in 1907 "for the improvement of social
and living conditions in the United States."[6] Langdon found a strong sup-
porter for a bureau of pageantry in Luther Gulick, who headed the Department of Child Hygiene for the Sage Foundation.

Gulick was the first president of the Playground Association of America,
founded in 1906. Gulick's philosophy that "democracy rests on the most firm
basis when a community has formed the habit of playing together" was key
in his support of Langdon. Pageants were an extension of creative play and
Gulick agreed with Langdon that they could have an important role in social
reform.

In October 1910 Langdon wrote to George Pierce Baker asking him to
become a member of the pageantry bureau he was forming. Baker's *Peterborough Memorial Pageant* had been a great success that summer and he
agreed to work with Langdon. By March 1911 the situation had changed.
John Glenn, the director of the Sage Foundation, was not willing to give
money for a bureau.

Langdon wrote to Baker that all was not lost. "The Russell Sage Foundation, however, has said that the question of whether the pageant is as
great a civic force as I claim it to be is worthy of demonstration and has

William Chauncy Langdon, 1913
(Courtesy Brown University Library)

made me a grant to enable me this summer to prove my contention if I can."[7] Langdon received $2,500 from the foundation to create a pageant at Thetford, Vermont, and the idea for a pageant organization was temporarily dropped.

Lotta Clark's attempts to create a clearing house of information about pageantry also date from 1910. Clark, chair of the History Department at Charlestown High School in Massachusetts had created her first pageant for the Boston Normal School in 1908. In 1910 she staged a pageant in Charlestown in addition to *Cave Life to City Life—The Pageant of a Perfect City*.

Lotta Clark was a member of the Twentieth Century Club, one of the organizations involved in Boston-1915. Founded in 1894, the purpose of the club was to create a forum for discussions about all aspects of social reform. Frank Chouteau Brown, who became extremely active in the Drama League of America and in the APA, was chairman of the Drama Committee of the Twentieth Century Club, and on October 31, 1910, the club sponsored a free public conference on pageantry.

A notice about the meeting informed the public that "an episode from the coming municipal pageant will be rehearsed"—the enticement being a preview of the November performances of *Cave Life to City Life*. The notice continued: "William Chauncy Langdon, of the Russell Sage Foundation, will preside, and Miss Lotta Clark and Professor George P. Baker will speak."[8]

In 1912 both Clark and Langdon, separately and together, became concerned once again about organizing pageantry. Clark was by that time chair of the Twentieth Century Club's Drama Committee and with the assistance of Frank Chouteau Brown was interested in sponsoring a pageant conference.

Langdon, on January 26, 1912, wrote to George Pierce Baker, "Do you think it might be well to get together a Conference of Pageant Workers sometime soon for the discussion of questions affecting the best development of this new type of drama? I have been thinking the matter over and I should like to talk it over first with you, Miss Clark and Mr. Brown. After we four have talked the matter over, if it seems wise, we can go ahead to bring others into the plan." The 1913 pageant conference that took place on January 31 and February 1 was hosted by the Twentieth Century Club and proved a satisfying culmination of the efforts initiated in 1910.

After issuing their first bulletin in May 1913, the APA leaders planned a conference on February 21, 22, and 23, 1914, in connection with the Columbia University Institute of Arts and Sciences in New York. On Saturday, February 21, a business meeting was held at which a constitution was adopted and two new officers were elected; Frank Chouteau Brown, president, and Mary Porter Beegle, secretary. Three kinds of membership were designated: active, guild, and associate. Active members had to be approved by the board of directors, "*only* on proof of their meritorious services in an executive position in connection with one or more pageants" and their dues were set at $2.00 per year. Guild members were "those who have taken, or are taking, part in pageantry" and their dues were also $2.00. Associate membership was open to anyone "merely upon payment of the fee of $1.00 the year." Provision was also made for "supporting membership at $5.00" and "life membership at $50.00 or more."

Another order of business was the establishment of a committee to publish a "Who's Who in Pageantry." This committee was authorized "to request all pageant directors, whether members of the Association or not, to immediately communicate with them, giving briefly full data in regard to their experience and abilities in pageant work, with references and information as to work done or in contemplation."

The "Who's Who" was published in May 1914 "for the express purpose of supplying information for all those contemplating undertaking a pageant; and especially to be used, so far as is possible, in answering all requests or inquiry coming to the Association." The booklet listed nineteen people as officers and members of the board of directors and a score more as members. A committee on finance was also established to support an active membership campaign with the hopes of having at least 1,000 paid individuals involved with the APA by the end of the second year.

The first public meeting of the conference took place on February 21 in Havermeyer Hall of Columbia University at 2:30 P.M. Approximately 125 were in the audience for the session which lasted until around 5:00 P.M. William Chauncy Langdon delivered the president's address, "Will the Pageant Last?" Five other speakers presented a variety of topics: William Bohn, "The Status of the School Festival"; Charles H. Farnsworth, "Educational Value of Festival Music"; Percy MacKaye, "The Form and Value of the Masque"; George F. Kunz, "Municipal Celebrations"; and Frank Chouteau Brown, "The Pageant Book." The next event was a dinner for members only in the National Arts Club in Gramercy Park and "proved to be one of the most successful meetings of the Conference, being especially successful in making the various members acquainted and giving them opportunities for comparison of their various problems."

The members of the APA must have been a very intense and patient group, for after the dinner they listened to eight more speeches: John W. Alexander, "The Opportunity of Art in American Pageantry"; Thomas Wood Stevens, "The Pageant in the Middle West"; Margaret MacLaren Eager, "Pageant Reminiscences"; Percy MacKaye, "The Civic Theatre"; Ellis P. Oberholzer, "The Large Pageant"; Constance D'Arcy MacKay, "The Pageantry of the Child"; George P. Baker, "The Relation of the Pageant to the

Regular Drama"; and Will H. Irwin, "The Grove Plays of the Bohemian Club of San Francisco." Certainly at the end of the first day of the conference, the general public and members of the association must have had a great deal to think about in relationship to pageants.

The second day of the APA conference began at 2:30 P.M. with a pageant service at the Church of the Messiah, 34th Street and Fourth Avenue, attended by about 300 people. In reporting on the Sunday events, Bulletin No. 3 of the APA (March 1, 1914) noted that "pageant hymns and other pageant music were rendered on the organ, and addresses were made bearing on the significance of the pageant and festival movements." The minister of the Church of the Messiah spoke on "The Social Need for Festival Expression" and the organist of St. Thomas Church played and spoke about the music from *The Pageant of York*. Arthur Farwell, who had composed music for pageants in New Hampshire and Connecticut gave a lecture entitled "Pageant Music."

The rest of the afternoon featured other topics and speakers: Lotta Clark on "The Educational Significance of Pageantry," John Collier on "The New People and the New Festival," Miss Langdon on "An Indian Christmas Mystery Play in the Interior of Alaska," and Reverend Arthur Ketcham on "The Religious Significance of Dramatic Festivals."[9]

The third and last day of the APA Conference, February 23, attracted about 200 people and was devoted to design, costume, and dance as related to pageants. Beginning at 10:30 in the morning the following presentations were given: Vesper Lincoln George, "Design and Color in Pageantry"; Durr Friedly, "Costume Materials"; La Mont Warner, "Pageant Properties"; John P. Cambell, "Armory Technique in Pageantry"; Mary Porter Beegle, "Out Door Festival Dancing"; Florence Fleming Noyes, "The Idea in Festival Dancing"; and Virginia Tanner, "Dancing in the Pageant."

The conference concluded with a "Lantern Slide Symposium, consisting of brief addresses by a number of pageant-directors in regard to their work with illustrations from their pageants and festivals." In conjunction with the conference, there was an exhibit of pageant material at Columbia's Avery Library which "in twenty-four cases and on a number of screens, proved to be of such high merit and general interest that, at the request of the Librarian, the exhibit has been left in place for a public showing of several additional weeks."

The APA's second conference had been well attended, the events stimulating and diverse, and public interest positive. A major concern was to bring in more members and create a stronger financial base. Imposing a tax on each pageant was suggested but rejected, and the conference report gave the reason: "If instead of imposing a tax upon pageant performance, each Active member of the Association can bring in from twenty-five to fifty new members during the next six months, its influence will be increased by from 1000 to 2000 additional members; which will enable the officers and directors to give their attention to collating and supplying members with much timely and valuable information, through increasing the issuance of bulletins, thus keeping them fully and completely informed."

The APA flourished over the next years. Bulletins were issued with greater frequency and more conferences were held. The bulletins issued in 1914 and 1915 expressed a sense of excitement, discovery, and messianic zeal. The APA was trying to define and control a new form that was by its nature experimental and unwieldy. In general there was agreement that the organization was involved in furthering community drama in the form of pageants, masques, and festivals—and "mere parades, of all types, are eliminated." Mary Porter Beegle wrote in Bulletin No. 7 (September 1914), "The promiscuous use of the word 'Pageant' has caused a great deal of confusion in the minds of the general public."[10] She felt the organization should consider only those productions that met the following three criteria: social service, artistic merit, and institutional change. Beegle's article makes it very clear that none of these criteria would be met unless a professional and highly skilled pageant master was involved.

Beegle explained that social service "in its broadest sense, means bringing to the people the opportunity to organize, cooperate and unite in a form of art production readily accessible to them all." Beegle wanted to make it understood that social value alone would not create a good pageant. "If the Pageant is lacking either in artistic or dramatic qualities it is a failure, for the reason that such a pageant does not establish a true standard."

Equally important to Beegle was the possibility for the pageant to create institutional change. "It may be the beautifying of the town, the formation of a local orchestra, classes in dancing or organizations for serious dramatic study." Participation in a pageant should not only change the community, but change the individual as well, creating "a desire for a more intimate expression in an art form."

Lotta Clark, in "The Development of American Pageantry" (Bulletin No. 9, November 1914) emphasized other aspects of pageantry. She was less concerned with artistic merit and placed more importance on the process of people "playing and working together." She underplayed the role of the pageant master and self-expression, and wrote about community identity and the development of shared values through understanding of past history and consideration of future goals.

Clark made the community the hero of the pageant, and wanted to present an idealistic notion of a noble America where all was possible. Clark's view of history as presented in the pageant did not include conflict—class differences, racial or religious strife. Any incidents of radical change to create a more equal society were not within her definition of pageant material. There is a feeling in Clark's writing that magic is at work in pageantry, and differences among people will be erased through the process of coming together in a joint effort.

William Chauncy Langdon shared Clark's views on pageantry. In the December 1914 APA Bulletin he wrote, "The Pageant is the drama of the history and life of a community, showing how the character of that community as a community has developed. . . . [T]he Pageant is drama in which the place is the hero and the development of the community is the plot." Clark and Langdon's views were challenged in 1915 by two fellow APA members—Percy and Hazel MacKaye.

Percy MacKaye was listed in the 1914 "Who's Who" as a "writer of pageants, masques and plays." His sister, Hazel MacKaye, was listed as a "writer and director of pageants." Both had been founding members of the APA and were prolific proselytizers for the movement. In 1915 Hazel MacKaye produced *The Pageant of Susan B. Anthony*, a suffrage pageant commissioned by the National Women's Party "in order to impress upon the congressmen the imperativeness of our demand for the vote."[11]

It was an indoor production in Washington's Convention Hall and utilized over four-hundred actors, an orchestra of twenty-five, and a chorus of sixty female voices. It was the first pageant that departed from the notion of the community as the hero. Instead, it dealt with the life of Susan B. Anthony as an individual, and through the biographical presentation of her life explored the idea of women's rights.

Hazel MacKaye submitted this pageant for inclusion in the 1915 list of pageants published in the APA Bulletin. Much to her surprise she found the legitimacy of her presentation being questioned by the APA in a letter she received from the president, Frank Chouteau Brown, on October 1, 1915.

> Your "Pageant of Susan B. Anthony" has excited some comment. What or how do you make the definition, which has now practically been adopted and which will very likely be in one of the early bulletins, apply to an individual? So far the limitation does not extend beyond the "drama expressing the character of a community" or based upon "the development of a social idea." Is this not more properly a Masque or something else; or a straight-a-way drama, as the pageant also transcends the bounds of an ordinary lifetime. As this is the first indication of that kind of pageant, I would be glad to have a little more information about it, if you have defined the scheme enough to provide it.

It is hard to know whether Brown was upset by MacKaye's deviation from his idea of a pageant in the formal sense, or whether he strenuously objected to her political stance and the suffrage theme. It is possible that he saw both as threatening experimental directions that could destroy the harmonious operation of the APA.

Pageant Susan B. Anthony By Hazel MacKaye

DEC. 13th, WASHINGTON, D. C.

Pageant of Susan B. Anthony, Washington, D.C., December 1915
Official program cover. Directed by Hazel MacKaye.
(Courtesy Brown University Library)

MacKaye was not about to be intimidated and responded promptly and with determination to Brown's letter.

> In your letter you say that "so far the limitation (of a pageant) does not extend beyond the 'drama expressing the character of a community' or based upon 'the development of a social idea.'" I am glad you said "so far," for I think that phrase pittily expresses the whole situation. Pageantry is still in its infancy, and if we attempt to lay down the rules for it too arbitrarily, I believe we shall be doing this growing form of art an irreparable injury. It seems to me we cannot this early in its development limit the subject matter of a Pageant. Perhaps my Susan B. Anthony Pageant has come in the nick of time to prove the truth of this, for there is no name save a "Pageant" which can fittingly describe the dramatic form I have used to interpret my subject. A Pageant is distinctly a type of dramatic technique; the subject matter, it seems to me, should be left to the choice and the free will of those desiring to use that form.

Percy MacKaye was quick in responding to Brown's communication with his sister. In a letter dated October 6 MacKaye left no doubt as to his stand on the matter.

> I learn for the first time from a letter from my sister Hazel that a bulletin of the American Pageant Association is soon to appear in which the precise definition of a pageant is to be settled and standardized by the Association "for the good of all." As one of the directors of the Association, I want to say as emphatically as possible that I do not believe at all in such definitions and that I shall surely count upon having the bulletin submitted to me, as one of the directors, before it is printed and sent forth so that I may know whether it is a thing which I wish to stand for or not.

Hazel MacKaye had the last word in a letter to Brown dated December 18, for her *Pageant of Susan B. Anthony* did eventually appear on one of the APA bulletin lists.

> I do not question that the American Pageant Association should stand for the Pageant as a form of community expression, but this does not necessarily imply that the theme of a community pageant should be a community theme. It implies solely (and essentially) that the production of the Pageant should involve some form of community participation with some civic or community purpose in view. In these respects my Susan B. Anthony Pageant is eminently qualified.

The controversy engendered by Hazel MacKaye's pageant had a marked influence on the development of the APA and helped usher in a new phase of activity for the organization.

William Chauncy Langdon expressed the prevailing philosophy when he wrote in the December 1914 Bulletin, that "the Pageant is the dramatic portrait of the community. No two communities are alike any more than two individual men and women are alike. Consequently no two pageants can be alike."

MacKaye's *Pageant of Susan B. Anthony* raised important questions in 1915. Was it necessary to restrict definitions of pageantry to include only "the dramatic portrait of the community" or could biographical pageants also be part of the definition? Was it appropriate to restrict the development of pageantry at this point in time through any arbitrary definitions? Could the same pageant be repeated in another community and have validity? Were conditions in society changing in any way that could mean a change in the nature and form of pageantry? Did the need for artistic quality in the pageant mandate further exploration before arriving at a set formula or standard?

The APA had a membership that consisted of practicing artists with professional backgrounds in theatre, music, dance, and art. Among these were Percy and Hazel MacKaye, Thomas Wood Stevens, George Pierce Baker, and Frederick Koch in theatre, Arthur Farwell in music, Florence Fleming Noyes and Mary Porter Beegle in dance, and Daniel Brewster in art. The APA also had members whose prime initial focus had been as educators or social workers and these included William Chauncy Langdon and Lotta Clark.

The artists saw the organization and the pageant movement as a vehicle for exploration of new artistic ideas and the development of art as a social force. For the educators and social workers artistic quality was not as important as the cooperative process involved and the impact on society.

The MacKaye-Brown controversy in 1915 came at a time when artists within the APA had some concern about the artistic merit of numerous local pageants and limitations imposed by insistence on making community the theme. The artists' concerns coincided with efforts all over the country to organize celebrations in honor of Shakespeare's tercentenary. The idea of the APA becoming involved in a national effort to celebrate Shakespeare's birthday could mean an invigorating new influx of ideas and possibly greater control over local efforts. Even if there were still anniversaries to celebrate, those with professional backgrounds in the arts had some hesitations about a pageant format that had become repetitious in response to these birthdays—Indians, followed by Civil War soldiers, followed by Spirits of Liberty and Industry. The idea of the whole country focusing on one theme could mean repeating the same pageant in different communities. This was certainly not on the original agenda of the APA, but had great appeal for many of the artists in the association.

By 1916 a large number of pageants listed in the APA bulletins were in some way connected with the Shakespeare tercentenary celebrations. The APA found new strength in a broader definition of its mission, and it assumed a stronger guiding role for communal festivals all over the United States.

In 1917 America entered World War I. The APA joined a national effort of even greater significance than the Shakespeare celebrations and became part of the move to mold a unified national identity. During the war effort, the APA moved from guiding pageants in each community to dispersing specific material and instructions and creating nationwide pageants.

On September 6 and 7, 1918, the APA held a conference in Boston on "Pageants for War Service." Bulletin No. 58 (September 15, 1918) was devoted to a report.

> Many aspects and phases of the vital service to the community in such times as these . . . became the subject of general discussion. . . . This discussion forcibly brought out the universal demand for dramatic means of symbolizing or typifying the present need for community self-expression of a national as well as an individual problem. Societies all over the country are eager to give dramatic performances of a patriotic appeal, if only the material and the inspiration be given them. The speakers formulated clearly that the knowledge of sources of such material and the inspiration was almost wholly lacking. The subject of the meeting therefore eventually resolved itself into the questions—what can the American Pageant Association do for our country today? What can it offer of Community Service? The policy of the American Pageant Association has been heretofore mainly restricted to the collection, editing and distribution of all kinds of information about Pageants, besides serving as a clearing house for the discussion or publication of suggestions as to production, organization, dancing, etc., rather as the theories and beliefs of the various authors, than officially representing the Association as a whole. Today it appears it must depart from this established policy if it is to be able to help the existing situation. It must boldly offer specific dramatic texts and books of the play, and be prepared to give definite instruction and information.

The APA held the conference jointly with the War Camp Community Service Control Bureau of Entertainment, which had been established by the Playground and Recreation Association of America. This War Service Bureau had a staff of 3,000 workers in 755 towns near military training camps, and the APA worked with them in setting up a Department of Community Drama.

A resident director was appointed, Constance D'Arcy MacKay, whose "purpose and duty would be to stimulate, through all local secretaries of the War Camp Community Service Organization, the fostering and development of local drama and local dramatic organizations, in all parts of the country." The APA was to provide information about preparing performances, make texts available, and provide lists of pageant directors. They also wanted to commission a new text "to visualize more adequately the situation of America in the world war as it exists at the present."

Perhaps the most important statement in the 1918 conference report had to do with the APA's feeling that it must reach a wide audience, meet the needs of national unity in facing the war, and tailor its own standards to the current situation. The APA stated a new mission in the September 1918 Bulletin, and envisioned the organization doing the following:

> It must, for the time being, give less regard to consideration of technique and perfection of form, and help in the preparation of material calculated to meet a more elemental, wider and more popular demand; entertainments capable of being given more simply, with less preparation and finish, and planned especially to meet the new set of conditions found in camp town and communities. In other words, it must at least temporarily resign from its passive part as Historian of the growing and forming Art of Pageantry, to become a definite Actor in this its new phase. It behooves us then, as a society, to take account of stock. . . . The members present realized not only the demand of this opportunity, but also its future possibilities in greatly furthering and raising the standard of dramatic community presentations, as well as stimulating the future of American local drama throughout the country.

By turning the tables and "meeting popular demand" the APA was allowing pageantry to become reduced in meaning and substance. Pageants written by a pageant master for performance in any community negated the elements that had made the form exciting in its early days. By calling for standardized texts and nationwide distribution of prescribed pageants, the organization was furthering the commercialization they had decried in their original efforts. Pageants produced "more simply, with less preparation and finish" would ultimately make the pageant an uninteresting, formulaic tool for didactic purposes, lacking creative exploration and excitement.

In 1919 the APA held a conference on the upcoming pilgrim tercentenary celebrations, but the organization was floundering. In 1920 the president of the association, Thomas Wood Stevens, wrote to Frank Chouteau Brown, "I am so completely in the woods that I don't know whether there is an association or not."[12] Bulletin No. 66 of the APA is dated December 1, 1919, and is titled "The Pilgrim Spirit." Bulletin No. 67 is dated May 15, 1921, two years later. The last bulletin issued was No. 68 on June 21, 1921. Some of the leaders of the APA continued to produce pageants sporadically during the 1920s but they were functioning without an organizational base.

In 1930 a small booklet appeared, *Who's Who in American Pageantry,* issued by the American Pageant Association "in the endeavor to establish a uniform standard for pageants and pageantry in America." The association never published anything again. The APA probably made one last attempt to reorganize with the idea that they could have some role in the celebration of the Massachusetts Tercentenary in 1930 and the George Washington Bicentennial in 1932.

No attempt to revive the APA could have been successful, for after World War I pageantry was no longer an exciting idea for social and artistic reform. Thomas Wood Stevens made these comments in 1939, in his personal notes on pageants.

> After the war the pageant game began to be attacked on one side by commercial racket-
> eers and from below by cheesecloth shows in the high schools. . . . We prepared careful
> bulletins to guide people; but the rackets could make more money by not following our
> advice, and the high schools didn't have the skill.[12]

Stevens was referring to companies such as the John B. Rogers Producing Company of Fostoria, Ohio, when he talked about "commercial racket-
eers."[13] Founded in 1903, the company sold and rented costumes and
scripts for winter amateur indoor shows, in addition to sending out directors. In 1919 they produced their first historical pageant and soon their
business was booming. They were out to make money and used commercial
theatre directors in the production of formula spectacles devoid of social or
artistic value. Other large firms in the commercial-pageant business were
the Wayne P. Sewell Producing Company of Atlanta, the Empire Producing
Company of Kansas City, Missouri, and the Universal Producing Company
of Fairfield, Iowa.

By the 1920s the word "pageant" was used to identify hundreds of
productions that were far removed from those created by Langdon, Baker,
the MacKayes, and the other APA leaders. Teachers created pageants in
elementary and high schools which lacked imagination and were often based
on texts issued for mass consumption. Symbolic dance interludes which had
been innovative in the first two decades of the twentieth century looked
dated and silly by 1930. Dialogue which had derived from a fresh investigation of local history had a secondhand sound when repeated by ten- and
twelve-year-olds under the guidance of teachers intent only on getting
through a history lesson. "Water pageants" and "beauty pageants" and
"tableaux vivants" were spectacles presented to pass the time in mindless
entertainment and had none of the components of the utopian idealism
encompassed in the earlier pageants.

Thomas Dickinson, in *The Case of American Drama*, wrote propheti-
cally about the demise of the pageant:

> The best thing the pageant can do is to create its own place in the heart of America and
> then give way to other forms. The best mark of its success will be that it compels the
> demand for the service of other higher forms and so renders itself unnecessary.[14]

During the years 1913 through 1920 the APA conferences and bulletins
provided opportunities for exchanging ideas and raising questions. The one-
page APA bulletin articles had titles such as "The Dances of American
Pageantry," "Problems of Color and Costume in Pageantry," "The Spoken
Word in Pageantry," "Necessity of Originality in Pageant Work," "The
Pageant as a Form of Dramatic Literature," "Pageantry as a Means of Improving American Standards of Dramatic Art," "Possibilities of the Pageant

as Local Historian," "Possibilities of the Lyric and Ode in Modern Pageantry," "Resources of the Pageant Stage," "Pageant Music," "Pageantry in Americanization Work," and "Determining the Stage and the Episodes."

The annual APA conferences from 1914 through 1919 usually lasted two or three days and consisted of presentations by members and nonmembers. Nonmembers who spoke at these conferences were civic leaders, college presidents, artists, critics, and teachers, including the following: John Collier, People's Institute and School for Community Centre Workers, New York; Kenyon L. Butterfield, President, Massachusetts Agricultural College; George F. Kunz, Chairman, City Hall Fourth of July Committees, New York; Durr Friedly, curator, Metropolitan Museum of Art, New York; John J. Walsh, City Planning Board, Boston; John A. O'Shea, Director of Music, Boston Public Schools; and Clara Barton of the Red Cross.

The APA of the old days was a microcosm of the larger community that the pageant movement was mobilizing, bringing together a diverse group of individuals from different walks of life. Percy MacKaye in the 1950 issue of *Theatre Arts* recalled the excitement generated by pageantry that came through in all the APA literature and activities.

> The most important contribution my masques had to make is the one I find it most difficult to write about. . . . How can I make the present generation understand what it meant when an entire community put its heart and soul into such a production, when in "Caliban" a bootblack played Pericles and a banker carried his train; when the medical student who acted the role of St. Louis asked me to excuse his coming late to rehearsal, explaining that he had just rushed there from his marriage ceremony; when every day 1,000 to 21,000 people came merely to attend rehearsals and watch the thing grow.[15]

A Pageant of the North-West, Grand Forks, North Dakota, 1914
Sakakawea (Sacagawea), the Bird woman. The first spelling of this important
historical figure was the one used by Frederick Koch in this pageant.
(Courtesy Brown University Library)

6

Pageantry and Theatre

Imagine a pageant in a small town in Iowa, or on New York's lower East Side, in the year 1911, or maybe 1912 or 1913. For young John or Giovanni, for Mr. and Mrs. Smith or Cohen, it could have been their first time participating in live theatre. They may have danced, or sang, or said a few words. Their assignment may have been to dance about the harvest on the farm, to join the circle in a traditional Russian Hopak, to recite a poem about settling the West, or to participate in a dialogue about crossing the ocean to the New World. The pageant was an event to remember and cherish for many—young and old, migrant and immigrant, landed gentry, wealthy businessmen. For others, it was probably a passing fancy or even a terrible bore.

The fact that pageantry was a major influence in shaping American theatre was due largely to its power as a catalyst for change in which two individuals figured prominently: George Pierce Baker and Frederick Henry Koch. In their work at Harvard, Yale, the University of North Dakota, and the University of North Carolina, they passed on to future generations lessons they learned in creating their own pageants through their explorations with music, poetry, dance, and new staging and lighting techniques.

As pageant directors and writers Baker and Koch tested their ideas about regional playhouses, American playwrights and American thematic material. As teachers they transmitted to their students a passion about theatre as a creative and moral force in society, a belief encouraged by their pageant work. Eugene O'Neill, Sidney Howard, Agnes Morgan, Paul Green, Munroe Pevear, Theresa Helbrun, Robert Edmond Jones, John Reed, Heywood Broun, Thomas Wolfe, Hallie Flanagan—these are only a few of the illustrious figures for whom Baker and Koch were mentors.

George Pierce Baker

George Pierce Baker (1866–1935) was initially hired by Harvard to teach rhetoric in 1888, almost immediately after he had graduated from the col-

George Pierce Baker
(Courtesy Harvard Theatre Collection, Harvard College Library)

lege. By 1897 he was lecturing on modern drama to the women of Radcliffe, and in 1899 he began teaching this subject at Harvard. From the 1890s to the turn of the century, he spoke whenever possible to clubs and community groups, and his focus was the treatment of drama not just as a literary form but as a force in modern life.

In his teaching and lectures Baker analyzed the American theatre and deplored the lack of American drama; he considered this condition the fault of both public and playwright. Hope for an American drama lay in the effort to create a demand for art as well as entertainment; the best theatre is art which is relevant to the life and spirit of the people.[1]

A European sabbatical, 1901–2, brought Baker in touch with the new small art theatres in France, England, Germany, Ireland, and Russia. Independently run, they showcased new playwriting talent and staging techniques, introduced foreign dramatists, developed subscription audiences, and provided alternatives to conservative state-run and commercial playhouses.

The first of these, the Théâtre Libre, was created in 1887 by André Antoine in Paris. It became a model for others dissatisfied with traditional modes of presentation and lack of innovation in existing theatres. The Moscow Art Theatre, the Viennese Volks-Theater, Ireland's Abbey Theatre—all encouraged Baker's belief that a way must be found to create endowed civic playhouses and new plays drawn from our heritage and relevant to the twentieth century.[2] It was to be a few more years before he began to see pageantry as a way of channeling these goals.

Baker returned to his teaching with new enthusiasm and in 1903 he had his Radcliffe students write plays as their final projects. In 1904 he instituted English 46 at Radcliffe, and the assignments were to write a one-act adaptation of a novel or short story, an original one-act, and a three-act play. The success of the first playwrighting course offered at Radcliffe led to a similar course at Harvard, listed in the 1905–6 catalogue as English 47, "The Techniques of the Drama, Lecture and Practice." In a radical departure from Harvard tradition, academic credit was granted for original creative work in drama as well as for the history and theory of drama.

Baker lectured in France during his 1907–8 sabbatical. He had opportunities to observe the new English pageants and renew his acquaintance with theatrical innovations in Europe. Not too long after Baker returned to the United States he began to focus on pageants as a solution to the problems he had been wrestling with for several years—development of American talent, audiences and community civic theatres—endowed to avoid reliance on mass popular appeal.

In 1910 Baker created the *Peterborough Memorial Pageant* presented on August 16, 18, and 20 at the MacDowell Colony in Peterborough, New

Hampshire. Baker's introduction to the published text of his Peterborough pageant provides an understanding of the importance he placed on his first pageant venture:

> In two ways the Peterborough Memorial Pageant is experimental. Believing that pageantry stimulates local pride in past achievement, strengthens community spirit, and reveals unexpected artistic resources, those responsible for this pageant wish it to help in demonstrating that for artistic and pleasurable results pageantry need not be confined to great centres, need not necessitate vast expense, but is perfectly possible for small communities. The Peterborough Pageant aims to prove, also, that movement, color, pantomime, and music should count more in pageantry than the spoken word. Scenic effects have been omitted in the belief that the natural setting of this pageant would make these seem offensively artificial. Because of this setting and because of the use of the MacDowell Music, suggestion rather than realism is the basis of the pageant.[3]

Working with Baker for their New Hampshire venture were two former students. Chalmers Clifton arranged Edward MacDowell's music for chorus and orchestra and Hermann Hagedorn wrote the lyrics. The script carried the notation, "Born from the dreams of men, interpreted in them, history begins and is represented." The pageant was subtitled "The House of Dreams" and Baker further elaborated on his main theme in an article in *New Boston:* "I wanted the pageant to convey clearly the message of Peterborough history, that labor is born of man's dreams and in labor the dreams come true."[4]

Opening with an invocation to the muses, and interspersed periodically with their exaltations, the story of Peterborough's settlement unfolded. Over 200 participated—rich and poor, young and old, single people and entire families. Audiences of 1,500 saw an Indian wedding before the white man came, the landing of the Irish in the Portland, Maine, harbor, the farmers mustering at the Revolutionary War call to arms. They watched soldiers return to Peterborough after the Civil War and saw the village in the twentieth century welcoming people of all nations. The pageant concluded with a "Song of Triumphant Labor."

SETTLERS	Oh, high beat the sea, Our hearts sang free, From famine came we Oh, afar, afar!
INDIANS	Wild lands we found Wild men and stony ground, Pain and woe and bitter wound, Famine, fading hopes and war!
COLONIALS	Up, wake the soil! Through war's turmoil,

'Neath strong arms that toil
Fields they bloom, bloom!

REVOLUTIONARY FIGURES

Brave men and wise,
Fair towns and cities rise,
Tyrants fall and kingship dies
Labor, labor, spade and loom!

MILLING GROUP

Wild wood and stone
To empire grown!
For Labor, a throne
And for man, space!

CIVIL WAR AND LATER

Proud roofs and spires!
Loud mills and roaring fires!
Mighty sons of fearless sires!—
   Teeming land and titan race!

THE FOREIGN RACES

Wake, aliens, wake!
Old ties must break.
Here new loves shall wake!
   Come, be free, free!
Whip, thong and scourge,
Forget, and anger purge!
Joy and labor yet shall merge.
   Enter, brothers! Be ye free.

THE ENTIRE GROUP

Right, toil and Light!
Be they our might!
Strong-winged be our flight
   Where the dream leads!
Right! Mark our way!
Rouse, TOIL, the sleeping clay!
Light! Sweep on, through dark to day,
Kindling man to dreams and deeds!

The *Peterborough Memorial Pageant* brought local and national history to life, educated the audience, and sought to give them faith in dreams and democracy. Baker sought to portray the energies of a new country born of struggle and built with labor nurtured in freedom. He showed the harshness of life in Ireland for Peterborough's original settlers and the hope of a better life in the United States; the striving for freedom of the new immigrants in the town and the difficulties of life in an unknown environment.

Conventional staging and realistic effects were replaced with suggestion and symbolism. The pageant was performed at 3:30 in the afternoon to take advantage of natural light, and the outdoor site was chosen to heighten the visual impact and meaning of the various scenes. Solo dances and group movement were interwoven with music and poetry.

The wedding scene avoided a literal presentation of the ceremony and festivities. Using the spinning wheel as a symbol of the colonial era, the audience was presented with a spinning song and dance which captured the hopes and joys of the young couple. A dance about "Old Black Baker and the Devil" brought to life New England mythology. The importance of cotton mills in the life of Peterborough (the first was established in 1809–10) was sung by the weavers: "Weave hope and toil! Fly, shuttle through! Weave me my doom of dreams-come-true!"

Baker was encouraged by the way the community rallied around the pageant. In his *New Boston* article, he went into great detail about the way in which the whole community participated. He pointed out that employers adjusted working hours around rehearsals, that townspeople closed stores on the three days of the pageant, and that many walked miles to attend rehearsals. He was impressed by the change in values he observed:

> Like any community, the town had its accustomed leaders and at the outset rather looked to them to lead in the pageant, but pageantry set its own values or readjusted. It created, I am sure, a new respect in a conservative New England community for the things of art, for at bottom all of us New Englanders think of the fine arts as matters for women . . . not wholly virile. No community which has had a properly managed pageant will ever think just that again.

The *Peterborough Memorial Pageant* was very successful and Baker became interested in pageantry as a force in American theatre and civic life. He presented pageant ideas to the Oregon Conservation Commission and the New York Child Welfare Exhibit[5] and served on two committees for Boston-1915: as executive director for the Fine and Industrial Arts Committee and as a member of the General Advisory Committee.

While formulating ideas for a pageant about the pilgrims, George Pierce Baker planned a trip for the summer and fall of 1912 to study theatrical innovations in England, Ireland, Germany, and France.[6] He wanted to understand experiments in lighting, set design, staging, and theatre construction that were being grouped under the heading "the new stagecraft."

Baker's previous sojourns abroad had acquainted him with this movement, which had already influenced his symbolic staging and integration of the arts in the Peterborough pageant. During his 1912 trip Baker had personal interviews with Gordon Craig, Ernst Stern, Max Reinhardt, Adolph Linnebach, and Max Littman. He renewed acquaintance with William Butler Yeats and Lady Gregory, whom he had met in 1911 when their group, the Abbey Theatre, toured America. Yeats and Gregory fostered Irish nationalist playwrights, and their work had been an important cornerstone in Baker's thinking for several years.

While abroad, Baker spent a good deal of time reviewing the new

Peterborough Memorial Pageant, Peterborough, New Hampshire, 1910
(Courtesy Brown University Library)

devices in use on the German stage—the *Drebühne* or revolving stage and the *Schiebebühne* or sliding stage—the various kinds of horizons or cycloramas, and the new Fortuny lighting. He watched an Abbey Theatre production using Gordon Craig's new devices—mobile screens which moved with the lighting and the actors, thereby creating a dynamic illusion. Most impressive to Baker was the work of Max Reinhardt (1873–1943) and he spent time at his Deutsches Theater.

Reinhardt, as a director, sought to free the theatre from the dominance of literary drama and stressed vast scenic effects, integration of poetry, music, and elaborate crowd movement which exploded the confines of the proscenium-arch stage. Reinhardt's 1912 American production of the musical pantomime *Sumurun* was often mentioned by those involved in pageantry. His emphasis on each production requiring its own particular conceptual development guided the thinking of many pageant masters. Baker commented on his reaction to seeing Reinhardt's production of *Henry IV*:

> No other producer whose work I have watched has caught so closely as Reinhardt the Elizabethan sense that the mere use of a few characteristic details or changes in them will kindle the imagination to supply the rest of the required scene. . . . There has been much talk lately, and some of it has reached America, that Reinhardt is not really a great manager, but is, rather, the trainer of supernumeraries and crowds—the somewhat spec-

tacular producer seen at his best in "The Miracle" and "Sumurun." After "Henry IV" I
do not believe this. He is a great producer in the best sense of the word. Here, as in
"Sumurun," I had the delight of feeling the unity of artistic effect, the perfect composing
of details, which is present only when a master mind is managing.[7]

Three other meetings in Germany had an impact on Baker—those with
Ernst Stern, Adolph Linnebach, and Max Littman. Stern (1876–1954)
worked closely with Reinhardt as a designer for most of his experiments.
He was able to capture the feeling of any particular theatrical work by
avoiding elaborate realistic detail and emphasizing shape, mass, and color.
Adolph Linnebach (1876–1963) was one of the innovative German figures
Baker had wanted to meet, but after watching Linnebach's production of
Everyman in Dresden he concluded that the most interesting aspect of the
production was the striking lighting effects.

A visit with Max Littman (1862–1931) proved rewarding. Littman was
a theatre architect who had designed several important theatres: the
Prinzregenten in Munich (1901), the Schiller in Berlin (1906), and the Munich Art Theatre (1908). Discussions with Littman centered around Baker's
interest in plans for building municipal theatres in New England. In Baker's
notes about the meeting he commented that Littman "is the first architect
I have seen who is as much interested in, as fully equipped about, what is
behind the curtain as in front of it. When we get that in the U.S. we shall
have the right kind of work."[8]

One of the figures who looms large in "the new stagecraft" movement
is Adolphe Appia, and his name appeared in Baker's notes about his trip.
Appia (1862–1928) was involved with experiments in total theatre that provided an overall symbolic illusion and a three-dimensional experience emphasizing space, volume, mass, and light as opposed to any naturalistic
statement. There is no record of Baker meeting Appia, but Baker brought
back to the States lantern slides of the scene designs of Adolphe Appia,
Gordon Craig, and Ernst Stern.[9]

George Pierce Baker returned from Europe in January 1913 and sought
to integrate what he had learned into both his teaching at Harvard and his
pageant work. The 47 Workshop was established that winter as a laboratory
theatre for Harvard playwrights, directors, and designers, and Baker encouraged his students to explore new ideas such as those of Craig, Appia,
and Reinhardt. When Baker produced *A Pageant of Hollis Hall*, June 4,
1913, in Cambridge, Massachusetts, he wrote a revealing introduction to
the published text. "All pageant writing is dramatic experimentation, for
each pageant differs from all others in site, numbers, amount of available
historical material or special conditions set the writer by those in charge."[10]

Over the next few years Baker continued to encourage his students' creative explorations in the 47 Workshop while he used pageantry as a way of experimenting with his own ideas about American theatre. After producing *The Allegheny Centennial Pageant* in 1915 at Allegheny College in Pennsylvania, Baker began intensive work on *The Pilgrim Spirit* which was the crowning achievement of his pageant career. He submitted a formal plan to the Pilgrim Tercentenary Commission in 1916 and a year later wrote that he saw the pageant "as the composite work of American dramatists, poets, composers."[11]

The Pilgrim Spirit was presented from July through August 1921 in Massachusetts for audiences numbering around 5,000 at each of the performances. Utilizing 1,300 actors and a chorus of 300, the pageant was a celebration of the three hundredth anniversary of the pilgrim's landing and their sacrifice of friends, country, safety, family, even life for intellectual and spiritual freedom.

In the summer of 1920 Baker went to England and Holland to do historical research, visiting places connected with the pilgrims. Voluminous correspondence during 1921 shows his concern with securing the best American talent he could find for writing verses and music to be integrated with his text.[12] On February 11, 1921, Baker wrote to Robert Frost. "I am delighted you are interested, and I want to do anything I can to make the collaborating easier for you." On March 25 Frost sent Baker a telegram, "Leave last one to me." On April 1, Baker wrote to Frost: "I am delighted to know that you are writing the verses for the end of the Pageant. Feel free so long as the verses will not take more than five minutes in the singing."

Each of the poets Baker invited to write for the pageant was to receive one-hundred dollars upon completion of his work. Either the fee was too low or Baker's demands too specific, and much of the correspondence indicates he had to push hard to get what he wanted. Edwin Arlington Robinson was another poet invited to contribute, and a letter of March 16 records Baker's frustration. "I . . . have a poem from E. A. Robinson, but as this is not entirely satisfactory I expect to see him in a few days before any payment is made." The same letter includes a terse comment on Frost: "Mr. Frost is at work on a poem."

The final version of the pageant was in five episodes with twenty scenes. The music was written by George W. Chadwick, Frederick S. Converse, Arthur Foote, Chalmers Clifton, Henry F. Gilbert, Edgar Stillman-Kelley, E. B. Hill, John Powell, and Leo Sowerby and was played by a wind orchestra of seventy pieces with Clifton as conductor. The 300-voice chorus was trained by George S. Dunham. Special verses were written by Josephine Preston, Peabody Marks, Robert Frost, Hermann Hagedorn, and Edwin Arlington Robinson. Costumes were designed and made under the direction of Rollo Peters, lighting was by Munroe R. Pevear, and dances were by Virginia Tanner. Baker had originally requested Robert Edmond Jones to work as a collaborator, but Jones was too busy and turned him down. Baker also drew on the expertise of Elizabeth and Ruth Burchenal of the American Folk Dance Society in recreating authentic Dutch dances from 1600 to 1620.

The pageant presented not only the familiar stories about pilgrim life at Plymouth, but illustrated the growth, meaning, and influence of the ideas which inspired the pilgrim fathers. Baker's development of the thematic material, his utilization of native talent, and his staging represented the ultimate in his ideas about pageantry.

The set for *The Pilgrim Spirit* was Plymouth Harbor, with the famous Plymouth Rock to the right of center stage. The waterfront area was cleared to create a park and theatre. A Mayflower replica was recreated by designer Rollo Peters, as was a Norse vessel. Twenty-six rows of grandstands with a seating capacity of ten thousand were built surrounding the stage area. Two massive forty-five-foot-high towers housed Pevear's huge lighting installations: fifteen miles of wire, fifty fifteen-hundred-watt floodlights, and fifty thousand-watt projectors utilizing three-hundred kilowatts of power. Pevear was able to flood the entire four-hundred-foot by four-hundred-fifty-foot stage area with light. Using specially designed spotlights called "pilgrims" he could pinspot a lone figure within a seven-degree beam. With all of this massive equipment, Pevear could provide light for the stage one hundred and fifty feet away or highlight the Mayflower far out in the harbor.

Baker's staging was bold and daring, and it was achieved by his unified conception of space, lighting, and mass. Pevear's lighting contributed greatly to the rhythmic and architectural flow and gave Baker's pageant a powerful sweep and energy. One of the characteristics of the work of Appia, Craig, and Reinhardt was the insistence on moving away from naturalistic acting, staging, sets, and lights in order to achieve the symbolic essence of any given script. In his utilization of the natural environment combined with lighting, mass groupings and integration of music, poetry, and text, Baker achieved a symbolic statement about the search for freedom.

The first episode of the pageant portrayed the pre-pilgrim explorers and traders in seven scenes, and through lights and images Baker provided a collage of early settlers. First the audience saw the arrival of the Norsemen. In the next five scenes lights pinpointed various groupings in the vast playing arena—English, French, Dutch, each holding a national flag and a banner giving the name of the leader, the contemporary name for the area settled, and a date. As Pevear noted in a *Boston Globe* article headlined "Plymouth Pageant Ready to Be Shown" (July 10, 1921):

Practically the entire cast can appear on the stage at one time with all except one group in complete darkness. By means of the projectors, tableau after tableau can be shown without having the actors proceed across the stage or needlessly delay the action of the pageant.

In the last of the five scenes depicting early immigrants, the Englishman Captain Thomas Hunt was shown kidnapping several Indians. As they were bound and thrown into boats, one of the Indians was shown grieving, the lighting pinpointing his single sorrowing figure in the midst of the vast stage. This was followed by a blackout, after which a greenish light came up slowly for forty-five seconds on a stage completely empty except for smoke and haze. This represented the pestilence of 1618, which killed many Indians. Baker, in his notes, wrote that he would let "the Indian airs recur till they dominate; then suggestions of the pestilence that strikes down the Indians; then the quiet waiting of the field for newcomers." Baker had hoped to have a group of Maine Indians (Pawnees) participate. Budget restrictions finally eliminated this possibility.[13]

The second episode, set in 1593, began in a prison where two Puritans awaited death and used one of their wives to smuggle illicit writings out of the cell. The scene ended poignantly with sounds of barely audible sobs and a single bell tolling 10:00 P.M. In the next scene, set in 1603, Baker established a contrasting mood with a full stage: about fifty horses, one-hundred-and-ten courtiers, over a dozen dignitaries, two dozen sheriff's men, and about one-hundred onlookers. Augmented by marching bagpipers, the crowd was shown accompanying King James on his way to London. The scene ended with the King's pronouncement: "A Puritan is a Protestant scared out of his wits. I shall make them conform or I will harry them out of this land." Hermann Hagedorn wrote the words and Edgar Stillman-Kelley the music for the final chorale sung by the King's men:

> Harry them with snare and sling
> Harry them with fire
> Harry them with jeers
> Harry them with spite
> Harry them with fears
> Harry them with might
> Strike down their hands and bind them
> Crash prison doors behind them
> Harry them by night and day
> Till they bow down and obey!

The music critic Olin Downes in a *Boston Post* review, "Dramatic in the Extreme" (July 21, 1921) wrote that this scene was "profoundly felt." As the singing ended, the audience heard the Puritans cry out, "We will keep pure, though we die." This was followed by three almost simultaneous images, related to a secret meeting of the Puritans. First was a post station, a small area of the stage where riders exchanged horses and drank ale. Then a cross-fade of lights showed children serving as lookouts. Another cross-fade showed over one-hundred-fifty Puritans in a secret conference.

Music by Frank Converse provided the opening mood for the third episode. As noted in the text, "lanterns and lights of a duplicate of Rembrandt's *Night Watch* approached center from various parts of the field." Baker utilized several groupings of about seventy people in each to represent various Dutch towns. Each group carried a banner with the name of the community and its prominent Puritans. About one-hundred torches carried by various individuals provided the actual lighting, which to Baker symbolized the intellectual and spiritual light illuminating the Puritans' search for freedom. After the 1609 truce between France and Spain was announced, the entire ensemble of about three-hundred people danced. The stage lights dimmed and the torches remained lit for a few moments, giving the scene its final impact. The third episode ended as the audience saw the pilgrims leaving Delftshaven on August 1, 1620, and the chorus sang a hymn with words by Edwin Arlington Robinson and music by Leo Sowerby.

In the fourth and final episode Baker opened by juxtaposing a group signing the Mayflower Pact in a lighted area stage center against a simultaneous spotlight on the Mayflower replica in the distance. In this way Baker crossed barriers of time and space and eliminated a literal telling of the story. As the single beam of light showed the Mayflower, the orchestra played an original score by Chalmers Clifton, "Voyage to the New World." The finale began in darkness as the chorus sang a hymn based on William Bradford's *History of Plymouth Plantation* set to music by Arthur Foote. As noted in the text "the lights, going up slowly, reveal BRADFORD sitting at a table writing history, his only illumination a tallow dip. As the music ends, BRADFORD stops his writing to think. The lights, penetrating the darkness beyond him a little, show the figures of his fellow workers CLIFTON, BREWSTER, ROBINSON, CARVER, STANDISH, FULLER, WINSLOW, like statues, near at hand."

Robert Frost's poem at the end of the pageant stated the message of hope and freedom emerging from sacrifice and risk, as exemplified in the first two stanzas:

When landing weary from the narrow deck,
You stumbled up the rugged beach and fell,
Here still afraid of God, though safe from wreck,
You spoke a vow that was a prayer as well,
And first it was like fire in the grass and trees,
Across the open, up a wooded slope;
And then like sunlight, over both of these—
A vow that was a prayer, that was a hope.

Your hope of landing was your gift to men,
As freely of it as was yours to give
You gave it to us to be ours to hope again,
And hope forever to be free and live.

After Frost's poem was sung to John Powell's music, the script instructions read:

Enter the Pilgrims convoying forty-eight young women bearing the State flags. Down the center toward the ship go the State flags. So group that all eyes are on the MAY-FLOWER. On the last two stanzas of the chorous the lights are full on the MAY-FLOWER, the Pageant Ground and the harbor are ablaze with light, and great search-lights are sweeping the sky. As the last line is sung the Field darkens quickly till there is light only on the MAYFLOWER.

With the light on the Mayflower, a solemn voice summarized the message of the pageant. "With malice toward none and charity for all it is for us to resolve that this nation under God shall have a new birth of Freedom." The lights then faded and the pageant ended.

As Baker lectured, taught, and created pageants during the years 1910 to 1921, he helped lay the foundation for what was soon to become a burgeoning Little Theatre Movement—an umbrella for a variety of efforts to foster new plays and audiences. A 1910 lecture to the people of Manchester, New Hampshire, was called "The Civic Theatre."[14] It outlined existing negative conditions: cheap vaudeville and picture shows, the rising cost of good theatre tickets, and the lack of community support. And then he noted:

Why not a civic pageant to draw the people together? Find an occasion. Put Manchester and its manufacturers and past life into the pageant. Bring all walks of life together. Then in common desire for dramatic expression find your scheme. A simple building—anything at first. . . . Then in time, see if the city will not build and lease a fine building.

There were many different aspects to the Little Theatre Movement. Thomas Dickinson in *The Insurgent Theatre*, published in 1917, commented: "In this book I am trying to give some form to events of a half dozen years in the American Theatre. These events are of great variety and present at first a view of no great consistency. At the outset the only point of agreement is the implied conviction on the part of the workers that the things of the old theatre must be destroyed and a new theatre be built up in its stead."[15]

Some of the insurgents wanted to create art theatres—small playhouses where the focus was more experimental and less geared to popular approval. For others the phrases little theatre and civic theatre were more appropriate descriptions of a broader goal—the development of subsidized playhouses supported by local communities where native talent and new plays could be showcased alongside standard repertory. There were diverse methods for funding proposed: subscriptions, private endowments, or federal, state, and local monies.

According to Thomas Dickinson, "the first group of little theatres came about in 1911 and 1912. The second and larger crop came three years later in 1915."[16] Many in the American Pageantry Movement were active in various aspects of the Little Theatre Movement and individuals from both groups were usually involved with the Drama League, founded in 1910 to further national awareness and support of theatre. George Pierce Baker never supported a narrow perspective on the future of noncommercial theater in America, but in his lectures and teaching advocated a variety of solutions for the future vitality of American drama. Pageants were for him at the core of any changes that could be implemented, as they created a cohesive focus in a community along with a spirit of enterprise and appreciation.

Kenneth MacGowan, in his book *Footlights across America*, included a map prepared in 1925 showing "how far the pupils of George Pierce Baker have spread his influence."[17] The map shows his students all over the United States working as actors, directors, critics, playwrights, and administrators.

Among Baker's students when he first started teaching playwriting in English 46 and 47 were many who went on to work on Broadway, to create pageants, and develop little theatres Off-Broadway. Agnes Morgan was instrumental in helping Alice and Irene Lewisohn transform the early pageant work at the Henry Street Settlement House into a professional repertory company and school—the Neighborhood Playhouse. Allan Davies and Leonard Hatch became playwrights and directors; Edward Brewster Sheldon became a successful dramatist; John Reed and Robert Edmond Jones produced *The Paterson Strike Pageant*; Jones was involved with MacKaye's *Caliban* and had an illustrious career as a designer in professional theatre aside from his pageant work.

A short list of some of Baker's students during the period 1913 to

1925—his active period with pageantry and the 47 Workshop—would include Eugene O'Neill, Sidney Coe Howard (playwrights), Hallie Flanagan (Federal Theatre Project head), Munroe Pevear and Donald Oenslager (lighting designers), Theresa Helbrun (producer) and Samuel Hume (director). Some of these assisted Baker in his own pageants, some created their own. John Reed participated in the formation of the Provincetown Players in 1915, the first group to produce O'Neill's plays not long after his 1914 student days with Baker at Harvard. In 1918 Theresa Helbrun, Lee Simonson, and Maurice Wertheim put their efforts into transforming the Washington Square Players into the Theatre Guild.

Samuel Hume, a former student of Gordon Craig's, came to Harvard to work with Baker in the 47 Workshop.[18] He became active in the APA and, after directing the *Cranbrook Masque* in Detroit in 1915, developed a little theatre there. Following that he became a major artistic force as director of the Greek Theatre, University of California, Berkeley.

After *The Pilgrim Spirit* much of George Pierce Baker's energy was devoted to building a professional theatre department and a physical structure to house experimental work and student and professional productions on the Harvard campus. His efforts were not successful and in 1925, when offered the opportunity of heading a new well-funded theatre program at Yale, he left Harvard for his new venture. Baker developed an internationally known School of Drama, renowned for its professional training on the graduate level.[19] He did create one more pageant in 1930, *Control, A Pageant of Engineering Progress*, for the fiftieth anniversary of the American Society of Mechanical Engineers.

Pageantry had been an important focus in Baker's attempts to create a vital new theatre in America; it is closely intertwined with the legacy he left his students and his own achievements.

Frederick H. Koch

A young student who came to study with George Pierce Baker from 1908 to 1909, at the beginning of Baker's involvement with pageantry, was Frederick H. Koch (1877–1944). He had been teaching English at the University of North Dakota since 1905, where he had organized groups of students in dramatic productions. Realizing he wanted to do more with theatre at his university, he enrolled in a master of arts program at Harvard with a concentration in dramatic literature. Koch went on to become a leader in the APA and his own pageants were crucial in his work.

When Koch returned to the University of North Dakota in 1910 he founded an amateur group "to cultivate dramatic appreciation and self-expression through the production of good plays." It was called the Sock

Frederick H. Koch
(Courtesy Brown University Library)

and Buskin Society and counted Maxwell Anderson among its original members. Four years after founding this group Koch, in combined authorship with eighteen of his students, wrote and produced *A Pageant of the North-West*. A new outdoor theatre was created for the pageant, The Bankside Theatre. It was situated near a gently curving stream, the English Coulee which flowed across the university campus.

> The Bankside Theatre was the first to utilize the natural curve of a stream as the foreground of the scene, between the stage and the amphitheatre. It is unique in that entrances and exits can be made by water as well as by land, a feature often useful and exceedingly picturesque. . . . The reflections in the quiet stream of the moving tapestry of the play and the setting of nature, either by day or by night, are lovely indeed. Yet on this very spot, by this same stream, not so long ago that living residents cannot remember it, the buffalo herds ranged at will and the Indians met the white man in friendly trade. This may well be taken as a symbol of the marvelous transformation of the primitive soil into an institution of fine arts of the people. Here in this open theatre, then, an original type of community drama has already flourished. . . . The first of these communal plays, *A Pageant of the North-West* . . . represents the dramatic story of the making of the great North-West. It marked a distinct contribution because it demonstrated that the community, under proper direction, cannot only enact its own traditions and outlook, but, more than this, actually create the pageant-form, thus cultivating communal literary as well as histrionic art.[20]

The success of *A Pageant of the North-West* led Koch to encourage his students in the writing of individual original plays, and the first series of these were produced in December 1916.

That same year in June twenty students worked with Koch and wrote a pageant/masque, *Shakespeare, the Playmaker*. This was "designed to commemorate the tercentenary of the death of William Shakespeare, to represent him as a man of his own times, a craftsman of the folk, and to suggest his vision of the new world of America."[21]

The *North-West* and *Shakespeare* pageants reinforced Koch's views that people could work together and create drama that had individual and group meaning.

> These communal dramas were designed and written entirely by . . . students at the University, representing the various races—English, Scandinavian, Russian, Polish, Bohemian, Irish, Scotch, German, Italian—that have gone into the making of our big state. All sections of the state were represented. And the entire composition was enriched by reason of the widely varying points of view of the different writers. As one of the amateur playwrights whimsically phrased it:
>
> > If you can see the world with me
> > And I can see the world with you,
> > I'm sure that both of us will see
> > Things that neither of us do!
>
> Is not such a conception heartening in these days of our strivings towards universal democracy?[22]

A Pageant of the North-West, 1914
Paugauck, Indian omen of evil. The speaking parts were all played by
full-blooded Indians.
(Courtesy Brown University Library)

Concurrent with his pageant activity Koch had enlarged the activities
of the Sock and Buskin Society and renamed it the Dakota Players. Koch
encouraged the group to produce original plays, which he called "native
prairie plays" as distinct from pageants. Soon he evolved a broader concept—"folk-plays" which better identified what he was trying to do. In the
Carolina Play-Book Koch recalled the development of these folk-plays.

> In succeeding years came a wide range of simple folk-plays, portraying scenes of ranch
> and farm life, adventures of the frontier settlers, and incidents of the cowboy trails. . . .
> They were simple folk-plays of the Dakota prairie, sometimes crude but always near to
> the good, strong, wind-swept soil, telling of the long and bitter winters in the little sod
> shanty, singing too of the springtime of unflected sunshine, of the wilderness gay with
> wild roses, of the fenceless fields welling over with lark song, of the travail and the
> achievement of a pioneer people. From the first our particular interest was in the local-
> ity—in the native materials—and in the making of fresh dramatic forms. For we felt that
> if the young writer observed the locality and interpreted it faithfully it would show the
> way to the universal.[23]

A Pageant of the North-West, 1914
The Spirit of Prophecy.
(Courtesy Brown University Library)

The Dakota Players toured all over the state, creating new audiences wherever they went. A writer for the *Dakota News-Bulletin* (April 17, 1917) commented on the reaction to the young thespians:

> The splendid enthusiasm which greeted the amateur actors wherever they went meant more than mere admiration for the work shown. . . . It was like the spirit which pervades a big family reunion . . . a feeling of kinship, for the people of the soil were welcoming the sons and daughters of their commonwealth in plays that promise not a little . . . towards a new Dakota Drama.

Rural community pageants were another outgrowth of Koch's work with his students, as once they had graduated he encouraged their leadership in playmaking all over North Dakota. In 1917 and 1918 three women alumnae of the Dakota Players were responsible for the creation of rural community pageants: *The Dickey County Historical Pageant,* written in collaboration by twenty citizens representing all parts of that county; *A Patriotic Pageant of Dickey County,* written and performed in the same manner; and *The New Day,* produced in an outdoor theatre at Saint Thomas, on the northern border.

Koch was understandably proud of the accomplishments of the people he had trained. The women were encouraged along with the men to be creative leaders. When he wrote in 1918 about the rural community pageant he saw it as a new omen for art and democracy.

> This new type of the rural community drama has been created under the quickening leadership of Dakota girls. . . . They have taken back to the home-town and countryside a fresh vision, a new folk-consciousness, expressing itself in rural pageantry, in a play-form uniting all the people—not simply of a village, or a city, but now of an entire county-community—in a larger expression of life. So these County Pageants cherish for the country people a new folk-ideal—an expression more democratic, a new song of the countryside.[24]

Koch's own pageants had attracted national attention, as had the rural community pageants and folk plays he encouraged his students to write and produce. In 1918 the head of the University of North Carolina's English Department, Dr. Edwin Greenlaw, invited Koch to join his faculty, anxious to see if the rich history and legends of the South could also be developed into pageants and folk plays.

One of the first things Koch did upon assuming his new post was to establish a Bureau of Community Drama to assist groups all over the state in promoting community expression by means of plays, pageants, and festivals. Almost simultaneously he embarked on writing a pageant celebrating the tercentenary of Sir Walter Raleigh's death, as North Carolina owed its settlement to Raleigh's arrival in the New World. He saw the pageant as the most powerful way of bringing creative expression to his new home state and felt it was the best way of exploring the rich native material of North Carolina.

Since there was no formal drama course at the University of North Carolina, Koch created English 31-32-33:

> A practical course in the writing of original plays. Emphasis is placed on the materials of tradition and folk-lore, and of present-day life. The essentials of stagecraft are illustrated in the production, by The Carolina Playmakers, of selected plays written in the Course. The Course is limited in number.

English 31 became a cornerstone in the great surge of regional drama Koch helped generate. It was not a course for complacent students who wanted someone to tell them what to think or what they should know. There were no textbooks and class was conducted in seminar fashion. Students were given selections from dramatic masterpieces to read and told that they too could, and would, write their own plays. Koch talked extensively about folk plays and communal drama but never lectured on dramatic technique or became involved with critical analysis of existing texts.

Koch wrote about his teaching techniques, and it is clear that the communal emphasis in pageant making remained a successful guideline for him.

> The approach is frankly experimental, and constructive toward sound dramatic expression. The instructor directs the attention of the student to the dramatic happenings in the life with which he is most familiar . . . to the restless lives of the workers in a mill village; to the balladry of sea-faring men on the shifting banks. . . . The spirit of the group is communal. The students come to the meetings of the course with vague ideas for plays-in-the-making. Perhaps the boy from the Piedmont section will begin: I know about a country boy's courtship which ought to make a play. The old man used to stamp on the floor of his bedroom as a signal for the boy to go home. One night the boy—we'll call him "Lem"—conceived the idea of pretending to leave. He called out to the girl a loud "good-bye" and banged the outside door. Then after a little he slipped in through the window in his stocking feet to finish saying "Goodnight." But the father came and discovered the trick, "That's a good one," someone laughs. "But how did the father happen to come in?" . . . A lively discussion ensues . . . and . . . with much re-shaping of the plot, revising the characters, recasting of the dialogue, the comedy of *In Dixon's Kitchen* finally emerges.[25]

As Koch's students began to gain confidence in their ability to write original material he established "The Carolina Playmakers," a producing vehicle for their work. Three plays were chosen for presentation from those written in English 31 during their first season in 1919, and rehearsed over a period of three weeks. When the plays were presented the authors answered questions from the audience and responded to criticism. The young authors could then better assess their own efforts and revise if they so desired. This process of presentation and review was followed for many years as the Carolina Playmakers produced the work created in English 31.

Thomas Wolfe and Paul Green, who both became well-known writers, were among the English 31 students in the early years. Wolfe went on to further training with George Pierce Baker, but became a novelist instead of a playwright. Green's first full-length play, *In Abraham's Bosom*, produced by the Provincetown Players in 1926, won a Pulitzer Prize. Green took Koch's class while he was a graduate student in philosophy, and maintained that before English 31 he had always been more interested in writing short stories and poetry.

> Then in 1918 Prof Koch came riding from the Dakota prairies, his arms full of plays and his head full of dreams. In no time a stage was set up and everybody near and far, little and big, black and white realized for the first time that he, said body, was an artist of some sort—mainly a dramatic artist—I chose the last. And after a few productions, I was caught fast in my choice and had struck acquaintance with all the bat-like terrors that inhabit the shadows of the stage.[26]

It was Green who perhaps understood most deeply Koch's belief in pageantry and folk art. In 1937 Green's *The Lost Colony* was first produced in Manteo, North Carolina, in a specially constructed outdoor theatre. Green's work was closely related to *Raleigh, The Shepherd of the Ocean* which Koch had planned for the Raleigh Tercentenary in 1918 but did not have produced until 1920.

The Lost Colony spawned a new wave of twentieth-century outdoor communal dramas. After the success of *The Lost Colony* Green wrote other outdoor pageants, among them *The Highland Call*, *The Common Glory*, *Faith of Our Fathers*, and *The Stephen Foster Story*. Kermit Hunter, who did graduate work at the University of North Carolina, wrote more than twenty outdoor dramas, among them *Unto These Hills*, and other North Carolina graduates have extended the genre as far as Alaska.

Green called *The Lost Colony* and his other outdoor spectacles "symphonic drama." In his book *Dramatic Heritage* he wrote, "In the original sense it means 'sounding together.' That is, all the elements of the theatre working together—words, music, song, dance, pantomime, masks, mental speech, and so on."[27] The form was based on the same content as the pageants that Koch and others wrote, but for Green the difference lay in the development of character and the continuity of the action. In Green's symphonic dramas he wanted to make his characters individual types, not usu-

Waterside Theatre, Roanoke Island, North Carolina
This theatre was built in 1937 expressly for Paul Green's symphonic
outdoor drama, *The Lost Colony*, which is still being performed today.
(Photo by Foster Scott; courtesy Lost Colony *office)*

ally the case in the pageants. He wrote, "There is a conflict of wills, a goal—a story-line continuity."[28] But for Green many elements of the older pageants were still important:

> By the symphonic use of the various elements of the theatre, especially music, there came a freedom and fullness of possible story statement not otherwise to be had in dealing with large groups of people in action. Short cuts and intensification could be quickly indulged in which the audience would accept without question. Conventions could be quickly established . . . time could be telescoped through a symbol—even could become that symbol. Space might be compressed or expanded. . . . Tomorrow is already here.[29]

The success of *The Lost Colony* was not only directly related to Koch's interest in pageantry through historic content and structure but also through his establishment of a strong regional base for theatre. In 1935 Hallie Flanagan, director of the Federal Theatre Project, appointed Koch regional director for Virginia, North Carolina, and South Carolina. When the citizens of North Carolina were unable to raise sufficient money to produce *The Lost Colony* Flanagan made the funds available, aware they would be well used because of Koch's many years of work in establishing community support and regional audiences for contemporary American theatre.

Koch was involved with two more pageants: *A Pageant of the Lower*

Cape Fear Valley (1921) and *A Century of Culture* (1937), which brought together playwrights from fifty different communities and 5,000 actors. Pageantry remained a reinforcing outlet for his own creative energies and ideas about folk plays and American drama, but most of Koch's time after 1921 was devoted to other activities: touring the Carolina Playmakers, teaching budding young writers, and organizing statewide activities through the Bureau of Community Drama.

By the 1920s a string of southern plays, influenced by Koch's work, had hit the New York stage: Paul Green's *In Abraham's Bosom* (1926–27); Lulu Vollmer's *Sun-Up* (1923–24); Hatcher Hughes' *Hell-Bent* (1923–24); Dorothy and DuBose Heyward's *Porgy* (1928); Jack Kirkland's adaption of Erskine Caldwell's *Tobacco Road*; and Lynn Riggs' *Green Grow the Lilacs* (1931), later to be translated into the musical *Oklahoma*.

Although Frederick H. Koch helped bring the people and legends of the South to life on the professional stage, his commitment to integrating theatre with daily life in small and large communities remains one of the supreme achievements of his career. He reached out to every corner of North Dakota and North Carolina—whether it was through the creation of pageants, folk plays, and festivals, or through touring standard repertory and original drama.

In 1923 Koch was the prime mover in organizing the statewide Carolina Dramatic Association, which began to hold a Dramatic Festival and State Tournament each year. By 1935 this association embraced sixty-five dramatic groups—city and county high-school groups, little theatre and community organizations, and college and junior-college clubs. Koch also guided the Bureau of Community Drama that he had established in North Carolina into a powerful force for local drama; in 1923 the bureau assisted 292 towns with homegrown productions by providing directors, scenery, and costumes.[30]

By the late 1920s pageantry was no longer a strong influence in the work of either Frederick H. Koch or George Pierce Baker, and it was no longer a shaping force in American theatre. The work of the movement's leaders had been accomplished, as American writers presented their work all over the country, utilizing native themes and new ideas of production and staging.

According to Joseph Wesley Zeigler, the Little Theatre Movement of the 1920s faded out, and was not the precursor of the growth of regional theatres in the 1950s and 1960s. "By the end of the 1930s, their high-flying quest had failed."[31] Zeigler himself points out that the Cleveland Playhouse[32] "begun in 1916 by 'serious amateurs'" is "still going strong today."[33] So are others—such as the Pasadena Playhouse begun in 1917. The continuity of these small playhouses through the decades is important, as is the impetus they derived from the American Pageantry Movement. Even when little theatres did not fulfill their idealistic mission and fell by the wayside, they proved that it was possible to generate community support and participation, that there could be plays in the provinces.

The outdoor theatres that dot our landscape today are also an important legacy of American pageantry. It would be interesting to give the millions who sit under the stars during the summer listening to concerts and watching plays some background on the early pageant masters whose vision helped build the facilities they enjoy. They were responsible for developing the idea in our country of relating performing arts to the natural environment, using the Greeks as their model. The great playwrights of ancient Athens united people in plays that spoke of their history; performances were not simply passing entertainments but important rituals of community life staged in spaces built for vast numbers. The pageant masters built their outdoor theatres with the idea that this kind of environment was more egalitarian than formal indoor playhouses with elaborate settings and class-oriented seating. It would be interesting to trace the history of today's outdoor theatres and to see how many structures built for the early pageants still exist.

Whether pageants were performed indoors or outdoors, there was considerable experimentation with the visual aspects of theatre lights, sets, and staging. The use of non-proscenium environments challenged the conventional entrances, exits, and presentation of individuals and groups in the playing space, and opened up new possibilities for flexible staging. The vast indoor and outdoor spaces, the thematic content, and the episodic structure of the pageant forced the lighting designer to be bold and less realistic. With such large spaces used for stage area and with so many different episodes passing through changes of country and century, specific realistic sets were out of the question. Instead, symbolic suggestion was explored. The philosophical thrust of pageantry, in addition to the existential problems confronted by form, structure, and environment, fostered both an inventive minimal realism and a symbolic visualization that encouraged others to go further in these directions.

And finally, the theatrical legacy of American pageantry is evident every day as students in university drama departments take classes and stage their plays. Frederick Koch and George Pierce Baker always linked their work in pageantry with a belief in education. For them theatre belonged to everyone and should take its rightful place in the university along with science, religion, and history. They helped make drama part of the curriculum in higher education, for the amateur and professional alike.

Ruth St. Denis, *Light of Asia Pageant*, UCLA KROToñah, CALif., 1918
(*Courtesy Hollywood Bowl Museum*)

Pageantry and Dance

Woodland nymphs and skipping water sprites—these are the images often conjured up when the words *pageant* and *dance* are brought together. Picture instead men and women dancing of war, hate, and greed; boys and girls dancing of work and freedom; audiences watching daringly exposed male torsos and female arms and legs. Picture large groups moving together expressing fear, love, and hope. Add to this Native Americans performing their traditional sun and rain dances and European immigrants moving in lines and circles in centuries-old patterns celebrating rites of passage and everyday concerns. And finally, picture young people from North Dakota dancing about the prairies or young people from Massachusetts dancing about the devil and the New England conscience.

The American Pageantry Movement gave dance a role in society for men, women, and children who were not dancers, just citizens. It helped change the negative image of body inherited from the puritans and the notion of theater dance as an exotic European development and import. Dance in pageants went beyond frivolous movement for chorus girls or spiritual exercise for soulful ladies. Pageants provided legitimacy and new horizons for dance and became part of the search for grass-roots indigenous material to create an American art form as opposed to imported commercial spectacles such as *The Black Crook*.[1]

Twentieth-century American pageantry was not the only factor creating new directions in dance but it gave moral and artistic purpose to many who saw dance as a vital contemporary art form. The Pageantry Movement and artists such as Ruth St. Denis and Isadora Duncan were responding to similar concerns, creating art that would address the expressive and spiritual needs of a changing society. It is not surprising that American pageantry had its initial and major growth period during the years 1905 through 1915—the same years that marked the emergence of Ruth St. Denis and Isadora Duncan as international artists with revolutionary ideas about the expressive potential of dance.[2]

University courses in pageantry influenced the development of American dance from 1911 through 1925. The first such courses took place in New York, at Columbia University's Teachers College, a graduate institution which attracted people from all over the world. Internationally known faculty such as John Dewey, Edward Lee Thorndike, and Jesse Feiring Williams were involved in educational reform at the college. Ideas developed at Teachers College spread to other institutions of higher learning as many individuals in the field of education who came for advanced degrees or special summer institutes went back to their own teaching institutions.

Although the courses dealing with pageants, school festivals, and dramatic expression were part of teacher training at Teachers College, the emphasis of the degree process was on self-development and personal exploration rather than on sterile rigid teaching formulas. In the eyes of these revolutionary educators schools were seen as integral to the development of a democratic society, not just places to impart a defined body of knowledge hallowed by tradition. The entire curriculum of Teachers College had been constructed so that educators would have the knowledge and skills enabling them to make contemporary educational institutions responsive to the needs of society in twentieth-century America.

Several dance-education pioneers attended Teachers College during the period 1911–25, when pageantry courses exerted an influence. All acknowledged the experience at Teachers College as having a significant impact on their teaching and writing. Margaret H'Doubler's study there in 1915 was important in her development of dance at the University of Wisconsin. Martha Deane, a key figure in shaping the dance program at UCLA from 1924 through the 1940s, was influenced by her earlier work at Teachers College. Gertrude Colby received a diploma from Teachers College in 1911, first taught there in the summer of 1912, and became a full-time faculty member in 1914. She was influenced by her studies at that institution, bringing her ideas to UCLA as director of Women's Physical Education, 1921–23. Bird Larson, another acknowledged dance pioneer, received her degree from Teachers College in 1913 and joined the faculty full time in 1916. Mary Wood Hinman, an early teacher of Doris Humphrey, was a guest faculty member at Teachers College during the summers of 1916 and 1917—a situation that gave her a chance to exchange and develop ideas with colleagues.

Three courses offered at Teachers College during 1911–13,[3] used the words *pageant* and *festival* in their titles: Physical Education 123-124 ("Conference—Constructive work in the dramatic game, the school festival and pageant," 2 to 4 credits); Physical Education 80 ("Conference on the School Festival and Pageant," 2 credits); and Speech 7, cross-listed in Physical Education ("School Plays and Festivals," 2 credits). These courses were team taught by individuals from three departments: Anna Cecilia Thornton, Physical Education (whose main interest seems to have been dance); Charles Hubert Farnsworth, Music; and Azubah Julia Latham, Speech.

Physical Education 9-10 and 59-60 were first offered in 1911 and repeated for several years. Titled "Practice" and "Advanced Practice" they were related through content and goals to pageantry. Physical Education 9-10 (8 credits) included practice and lecture which, the bulletin noted, "treats dance as a form of art, and presents the evolution of dance drama and the relation of the dance to the other arts. The meaning of dance is studied in relation to its origin and place among primitive people. The practice work in dancing follows the evolution of the dance through national dancing and includes a knowledge of the rhythms of dance."

Physical Education 59-60 (8 credits), "Advanced Practice," had the following description: "The historical study of dancing is a continuation of the course 9-10, and will include some of the dance-dramas of the 17 and 18 centuries. The constructive work aims to give practice in the interpretation and in the composition of dances." Physical-education faculty for these two courses from 1911 to 1913, listed here with their backgrounds, were Maud March (Anderson School, 1893), George T. Holm (no degrees listed), Ann Cecilia Thornton (Diploma, Teachers College, 1911), Jesse Feiring Williams (Oberlin, 1909), Mary Porter Beegle (B.S., Columbia, 1910; Diploma, Chalif School, 1910), Eva Allen Alberti (A. M., Alfred; Dean, Department of Action and Pantomime, American Academy of the Dramatic Arts, the latter as listed in her biographical sketch).

In 1913–14 two new courses relating to pageantry were introduced. Education 91-92 (4 credits), "Plays and Festivals" (cross-listed in Physical Education), was team taught by Professors Farnsworth (Music), Wood (Physical Education), Dow (Fine Arts), Latham (Speech), Abbot (English), and Thornton (Physical Education). Education 193-194 (4 credits), "Dramatic Expression in Physical Education" (also cross-listed in Physical Education), was team taught by Alberti, Williams, and Thornton. The course description shows a direct relationship to pageantry and provides information about the dance content:

This course aims to give Physical Education students and others an understanding of and appreciation for the art side in Physical Education and the relation it bears to the sister arts—music and literature. The course will consider the correlation of motor activities with the subject matter of the grades and will show how such material as folk and interpretive dances, pantomime, mimetic exercises of sports and games, marches and drills can be used in developing the dramatic instinct of the child and also the place such activities have in the dramatization of poems, fairy stories, short pantomimic plays, and in the organization of festivals. The subject matter will be studied from the viewpoint of construction and the principles involved in the technic of production.

All the courses in pageantry at Teachers College through 1914 show similar concerns for dance: emphasis on dance as an art form with a history; relationship of dance to the other arts; production and presentation as a final goal; interpretation and composition of dances; folk dance, dramatic dance, and expressive dance. In 1914–15 the previous pageantry courses were repeated and a new one was listed, "Physical Education 81-82" (3 credits), "The Pageant and the Dance." Taught by "Miss Beegle and assistants," it consisted of lectures and demonstrations described as follows:

> Lectures upon the educational, social and civic significance of festival activity will be followed by a historical sketch of the various forms of pageantry. Methods of planning and preparation will receive thorough exposition. Attention will be given to the fundamental types of dancing and their place in the pageant and festival. The subject of dramatic structure, selection and adoption of music, costumes and the pictorial aspect of pageantry will be treated in a practical way so that teachers and social workers may have a definite working plan as well as thorough insight into the pedagogic and social significance of pageants and festivals.

The 1916 summer-session bulletin listed two new courses taught by Mary Wood Hinman: Physical Education 63—"Dances for Boys" (1 credit) and "The Dramatic Game" (1 credit). Hinman taught the dance course for boys again in 1917 in addition to "Folk and National Dances—Elementary" (1 credit).

The pageant courses were defined by 1915 and continued in similar fashion through 1921. Gertrude Colby, who was to become an important force in educational dance, taught all the pageant courses at various times from 1915 through 1921, team teaching with Alberti, Williams, Holm, and Beegle. Colby, Alberti, Beegle, and Thornton not only taught but were involved in pageant production. In 1912 Colby staged the dances for *The Pageant of Schenectady*;[4] Alberti and Thornton, along with Williams, presented *The Conflict* (subtitled *A Health Masque in Pantomime*) at Teachers College, May 1913;[5] Mary Wood Hinman was master of the pageant for *Father Penn* (1915, Pennsylvania State College).[6] In 1914 Mary Porter Beegle coauthored *The Pageant of Elizabeth* (in New Jersey), and was author/director of *The Romance of Work* (New York), in addition to pageants she created during summer courses at Dartmouth.[7]

The 1912 Dartmouth College summer course is mentioned in all the early literature on pageants as being the first course of its kind, although it actually followed the 1911 courses at Teachers College. The Dartmouth course attracted individuals from a variety of places who wanted to learn more about the new form of expression which promised to be useful in schools and communities. The 1912 course was short and according to the summer bulletin was one in which "problems involved in organizing festi-

Mary Porter Beegle and Chorus, *The Romance of Work,* 1914
(Courtesy Brown University Library)

vals and pageants were discussed by prominent festival workers in a manner at once absorbing and practically helpful." Among the lecturers for the course were Mary Porter Beegle (on the faculty of Teachers College); William E. Bohn (head of English at the Ethical Culture School);[8] Charles H. Farnsworth (head of music at Teachers College); and William Chauncy Langdon (by then self-employed as a pageant master).

The 1913 Dartmouth summer course met daily for six weeks and consisted of three separate sections. "School Festivals" was taught by William Bohn and Mary Porter Beegle (by that time also on the faculty of Barnard College). The Dartmouth course was open to men and women for two credits and the description was as follows:

> A course in the materials and management of festival work in schools. Miss Beegle will lecture on the history of various forms. . . . Special attention will be given to the history of the dance and early dance drama, and to the fundamental types of dancing and their place in the festival activity and the literary materials available for use.

The other components of the 1913 Dartmouth summer venture were "Elementary Festival and Pantomime Dancing" and "Advanced Festival Dancing," each offered for one credit. In both courses we see, possibly for the first time, the use of the words *natural dancing,* later used by Gertrude Colby in 1919 for a new course with that title offered at Teachers College.[9] The "Elementary Festival and Pantomime Course" had a full description in the Dartmouth College summer bulletin:

> This course will deal with the simple dance forms, suitable for use in festivals and plays, and also for the purposes of instruction in the school gymnasium and on play-grounds. Practice in a selected group of national and folk-dances will be supplemented by a study of the fundamental principles of natural or interpretive dancing.

It is interesting to note the range of dance materials the students were exposed to, and the variety of skill development and creative activity they experienced. "Advanced Festival Dancing" emphasized folk dancing less and was "intended primarily for students who wish to gain skill and facility in natural dancing and in adapting dance forms for use in festivals. A variety of symbolical and interpretive dances will be studied." It is not clear what the "dance forms" were but it is likely that they could have been a mixture of folk, national, and historic material. Symbolic and interpretive material explored for pageant use covered a wide range, as the pageants utilized dances about many abstract ideas, such as war, independence, work, and the forces of nature.

Part of the summer bulletin information for 1913 shows that prospective students were encouraged to inquire about the Dartmouth summer classes from representative alumni in Maine, New Hampshire, Vermont, Massachusetts, Rhode Island, Connecticut, New York, New Jersey, Pennsylvania, and the District of Columbia.[10]

Beegle seems to have had quite an impact on her students, making them think very seriously about dance. The Dartmouth summer-school documents include a clipping dated 1913 about a woman named Mrs. Robert M. Seymour from St. Paul, Minnesota. One of the St. Paul newspapers included an article about Mrs. Seymour, "who will give a study course on 'English and American Dance' this winter as a part of her work as assistant director of the St. Paul Institute" and who was "spending the summer at Dartmouth College gathering material." The article consisted mainly of a letter from Mrs. Seymour and one item was about "dancing becoming an art."

> Undoubtedly dancing is in process of development into a great and noble art, and nothing is more significant than the widespread interest among physicians, scientists and educators in the present movement to organize the dance. . . . Everywhere in the East public attention and interest is directed toward amusement as a social force . . . the theatre, drama, the festival and the dance—an effort to put order into a much neglected side of civic life.

The Dartmouth summer-school work in pageantry and festivals was expanded in 1914. Closely allied in working with Beegle that summer was a man named Jack Randall Crawford, an instructor in dramatic composition at Yale. Crawford, having acquired a bachelor and master of arts degrees from Princeton in 1901 and 1903, had also studied drama in Berlin in 1902 and in London and Paris in 1903–7. Crawford's studies in London coincided with the development of pageants in that country, and he was listed in 1914 in the Dartmouth bulletin as "a successful playwright who has also had experience as a producer, both in London and in this country."[11] As a result of Beegle and Crawford's collaboration at Dartmouth they coauthored *Community Drama and Pageantry* (Yale University Press, 1916), a book that was to have a significant influence on the development of dance in the university, and was also one of the most important books on pageantry at the height of the movement.

There were five courses in the Dartmouth summer session of 1914 that related to dance and pageantry. "Elementary Festival Dancing" (1 credit) included an "introduction to the elementary principles of natural or interpretive dancing"; "Folk Dancing and Pantomime," was "a more advanced course, introducing the student to the technique of the Russian school, and aiming to develop increased facility in a selected group of national dances." The description for "Festival Dancing, Advanced Course" noted that it was intended "primarily for advanced students who wish to gain skill and facility in natural dancing and in adapting forms for use in festivals. The interlude as an art form will be studied, together with a variety of symbolic and interpretive dances." The last of the dance courses was called "Theory and Practice of Teaching" (1 credit):

> Lectures on the theory and practice of teaching dancing as a means of physical education. The place and scope of physical education in general education, and the relation of the dance to this problem; the value of creative self-expression for children; the history of dance and the dance-drama; the dance as an art form and its relation to the other arts; problems in the actual technic of teaching.

The two-credit course "Festivals for School and Community" covered all aspects of pageantry and included within its scope the production of a pageant, *The Magic of the Hills*. This pageant, presented August 11 and 12, 1914, was directed by Mary Porter Beegle. The book was by Jack Randall Crawford and the music by Henry Dike Sleeper of Smith College, who was also in residence teaching in the summer session. The summer before, the pageant course had staged *Sylvia Decides*, but the 1914 pageant seems to have been more ambitious. A newspaper clipping from Boston's *Evening*

Transcript, included with Dartmouth summer-school documents, particularly singled out the impressive dancing:

> The success of the midsummer pageant last year, given by the Dartmouth Summer Session, has brought a plentiful harvest of enthusiasm for this year's performance. The number of actors and dancers has been greatly increased so that it will be a pageant of much larger scope than the last. . . . The addition of a number of undergraduates will be of great assistance to the producers of this pageant and the increased number of dancing classes . . . will give a great variety of new and beautiful dancing this year. . . . The dance of the Talisman, the dance of the Storm Winds, the dances of the Fog Wraiths, and many others, will have the wonderful and effective natural background in the glade.

The Dartmouth activities calendar for 1914 listed many lectures which took place on the summer evenings for the students and the neighboring community. Among these were several lectures on dance by Mary Porter Beegle, including such topics as natural dancing, festival dancing, types of folk dance, and interpretive and dramatic dancing.

Pageant courses in the university were not simply a phenomena of the Eastern schools. There were summer courses in Illinois and Wisconsin, and in Los Angeles there were several examples of regular pageant courses during the academic year. In 1917 when UCLA was a State Normal School, "Pageantry and Folk Dancing" appeared in the bulletin, with no description or faculty listing.[12] The next mention of pageant-related courses appeared in the summer bulletins of 1921 and 1922 for what had by 1919 become the University of California, Southern Branch. In 1921 "Dramatic Games and Folk Dancing for Playground and Elementary Schools" was offered. In 1922, Theodore A. Viehman, instructor in the Drama Department of Carnegie Institute of Technology, Pittsburgh, was a guest teacher in the Physical Education Department. He offered "Pageant Organization and Production" which was "arranged to aid high school teachers in planning school pageants, festivals and dance pantomimes. A festival of dance pantomime will be chosen for production by the class."

Other pageant-related courses at UCLA through 1925 were "Pageant and Festival Organization and Production" (summer 1923, taught by Mary Patricia O'Donnell, Teachers College); "Dramatic and Folk Dancing for Playgrounds and Elementary Schools" and "Mexican and Spanish Pageant Production" (summer 1924). The latter had a particularly interesting description, with the bulletin noting as follows:

> It will be based upon the early history of California dealing with the life, customs, pastimes and dress of the early Spanish and Mexican settlers. Historical facts will be adhered to. . . . A festival will be chosen for production.

In 1925 Martha Deane offered "Dancing and Pageantry," "a study of the sources of pageantry material with theory and practice in the organization and production of pageants and pantomimes."

The University of California, Berkeley, had pageant-related courses starting in 1920: "Dramatic Games and Dancing for Playgrounds and Elementary Schools" and "Dramatic Expression for School and Playground." In the summer of 1923, Theodore Viehman taught "Pageant Organization and Production" for men and women. Beginning with 1918–19 the Berkeley Physical Education Department listed "Partheneia Practice" as a non-credit class. The *Partheneia* was the word used for the annual pageant masque presented by the students on the campus from 1912 through 1931.[13]

By the time Margaret H'Doubler created the first dance major at the University of Wisconsin in 1926–27, pageantry courses were becoming relics of the past. Wisconsin was one of the states most active in the Pageantry Movement and summer pageantry courses were taught at the university as early as 1914.[14] H'Doubler, combining her own explorations of dance with those she had gleaned from pageant courses and productions, took dance one step further toward acceptance as an art form and a discipline when she made dance a major field of endeavor in academics.

During the same period of time that university courses in pageantry were created, books explaining and defining pageantry were being written and they all contained different degrees of material on dance. *Pageantry and Pageants* by Esther Willard Bates (1912), *The Dramatic Festival* by Anne A. T. Craig (1912), and *A Handbook of American Pageantry* by Ralph Davol (1914) include dance material as it related to specific pageants. *Festivals and Plays in Schools and Elsewhere*, edited by Percival Chubb (1912), contains a chapter written by Mary C. Allerton, "Dancing in the Festival." Although not a long chapter, it shows the importance of expressive dance to those involved in the pageant movement.

> Man first expressed his thought by movement. Sign or movement language, preceded spoken language. Even after the development of the spoken word the language of movement remained more vivid in meaning to ancient and primitive peoples. From this speech by sign, this motor expression of thought and feeling, developed the ceremonies connected with the observance of the vital periods and events of their lives. Great joy or sorrow, phases of nature, seedtime and harvest, the occupations of their lives, and their religious worship were instinctively expressed in motor form. . . . Dancing has existed among all peoples down through the history of mankind; industry, religion, love, war, being the factors in its development. . . . Because of this . . . should boys and girls, young people and grown-ups, come into their own by practice and appreciation of this mother of the arts.[15]

Scenes from *The Masque of Maidenhood,* University of California, Berkeley, 1912
This type of Greek pageant was known as a *Partheneia.*
(Courtesy University Archives, Bancroft Library. University of California, Berkeley)

Allerton went on to say that there are four kinds of dances that can be used in pageants and festivals: descriptive or pantomimic; symbolic; the folk dance; and the formal or set dance. She gave examples of each form and a brief description of how each developed and what it meant. The book was mostly written for work with children, and her illustrations showed boys and girls performing a variety of colorfully named dances: greeting the sun; dance of the hours; dance of work; age preventing folly from entering the palace of Columbia; the virtues dance before Columbia; boys performing a Morris dance.

Community Drama and Pageantry (1916) by Mary Porter Beegle and Jack Randall Crawford has very extensive material on dance, particularly significant as it was developed through their work at Teachers College, Yale, Barnard, and Dartmouth. Written as a scholarly treatise on pageantry, the book consists of extensive bibliographic material and eleven chapters: The Principles of Pageantry and Community Drama, Types of Community Drama and Pageantry, Writing the Pageant Book, Production, Acting, Grouping, Color, Costume and Setting, The Dance, Music, and Organization.

The chapter called "The Dance" begins with a discussion of four approaches to dance in America: ballet as a system with rigid rules; dance as a form of physical training; dance as a means of recreation; and innovative dance as practiced by "Isadora Duncan and the revolutionists of the Imperial Russian Ballet."[16] The authors concluded that ballet has validity but not for their purposes, while dance as recreation is not suitable for use as it is "almost entirely taken up with reviving old forms instead of new." Dance as physical training was also rejected, on the grounds that it finds its best expression as rhythmic gymnastics and its worst as a substitute for bodily exercises. Innovative dance, however, "not only preserves the forms and traditions of an art that was once flourishing" but also shows "that the dance itself is today a vital creative art which can be made to grow and develop new forms and even new techniques."

For Beegle and Crawford the purpose of dance as an art was "to achieve creative self-expression through interpretation of ideas by means of rhythmic movement. To distinguish this theory of the dance from any other application of this art, the term 'natural dancing' is used." Natural dance has technique, but one that changes with what is being expressed. It requires physical training and a well-formed body "but this body is used as a medium of expression for the mind." They concluded that "natural dance when taught with feeling and judgment, is preeminently the art of the dance best suited for community drama and pageantry."

Dance is then defined as "that portion of the spectacle in which for a particular reason the emphasis is shifted to pure movement," and three general classifications are listed: the plot dance, the illustrative dance, and the dance interlude. An example given for the plot dance is from the second scene of the authors' *The Magic of the Hills* produced at Dartmouth. During an attempt to capture an Indian princess, a group of Fog Wraiths came from the hilltops to save the princess and carry her off. Their movements were "symbolic of the slow and billowy coming of the mist," and this dance was an integral part of the plot bringing the action to the next episode. A parallel is drawn with the plot dances in the Russian ballets, such as *Le Dieu bleu*:

> *Le Dieu bleu* has a striking plot dance. The scene is by a lotus pool in India. A maiden whose lover has been carried by the priests is lying forlorn by the pool. Horrible monsters appear from a cave and threaten her. Then the lotus flower opens and the Blue God steps forth. In a long solo dance he subdues and drives away the monsters one by one.

The illustrative dance is one which "may be used either to depict the manners and customs of a particular period or nationality, or as a symbolic dance to enhance the poetic value of a scene." An example is a dance by a Spirit of Fire in a scene where "primitive people are shown kindling fire. This dance would be illustrative of primitive people's fear and awe of the nature forces and of the tendency to personify their conceptions." Beegle and Crawford feel this kind of illustrative dance is equally applicable to contemporary episodes where "The Spirit of Steam or of Electricity could be represented as dominating and directing the modern works of man." Beegle and Crawford conclude the discussion of symbolic dancing by comparing it to lyric poetry. "It is a way of expressing ideas through an ordered pattern of beauty, and hence may have the same emotional qualities that lyrics possess." This kind of dance does not have to carry the plot forward, and may be used to reflect or create a mood.

The third category they discuss is the dance interlude, "employed in those portions of the dramatic action which may be given an allegorical meaning or other independent treatment." It could consist of anything from "a single personified figure to a complete dance drama." One of the examples given is from the authors' *Pageant of Elizabeth*, where they wanted an allegory reappearing at intervals throughout the performance.

> The purpose of the interludes was to illustrate the growth of the city. A figure, veiled at first, was shown, inchoate and formless, since the city had not yet come into being. About this figure there was a dance of Indians and nature spirits, who were unconscious of the figure's presence. After each episode, which covered a lapse of years, the figure stood forth more and more clearly, until in the final interlude it became the personification of the city of the present day, no longer veiled. The figure was now surrounded by allegorical personages representing art, science, education, commerce and civic unity.

Other examples of dance interludes are given. Beegle and Crawford state that an episode about the coming of French settlers could be followed by a dance interlude picturing French peasants at the close of the vintage season; included would be actual festival customs. Other interludes could form a complete dance drama consisting of a plot from local legend or folklore.

The remainder of the chapter on dance is devoted to an extensive discussion of basic principles relating to dance composition relevant in a general way to a higher quality of dance in the pageants. Beegle and Crawford discuss and give examples of ways to develop mood, action, rhythmic progression, and climax. They are concerned with the principles of repetition, contrast, pause, and rise and fall of movement. Regarding the actual selection and organization of movement patterns they are concerned that the readers understand that movement is composed of basic elements that are combined and recombined, and not steps that are strung together. Other aspects of dance composition covered in the chapter are entrances and exits, groupings, and projection.

It would be a fairly safe assumption that the material in *Community Drama and Pageantry* formed the basis for course content when Beegle was involved at Teachers College, and possibly also when she was not directly involved.[17] Norma Gould, a pioneer dancer/teacher in Los Angeles, listed the book as a text for her 1924 course at the University of Southern California. Since her unpublished class notes, assignments, and lectures have been found, they are a more specific example of content and procedure available.[18]

The objectives of Gould's course were "to prepare students to become directors and composers of pageants and to give aesthetic pleasure to the student of pageantry as well as to the audience who will view their pageants later. The study of pageantry to be approached as one branch of dramatic art." Course requirements were "to have a working knowledge of dance, pantomime, music, costuming, setting, lighting and make-up. To have an appreciative knowledge of all good literature, history, myths, legends and fairy tales, geography, and customs of all peoples (ancient and modern)."

Gould included regular research assignments as well as composition of a pageant, with the promise that the best would be presented in connection with the May Festival. There were seven units organized around lectures and assignments: Origin of Pageantry, History of Pageantry, Principles of Pageantry, Pageants for School, Colleges, and Universities, Pageant Composition, Pageant Production, and Pageant Organization. The students had to keep a notebook and devote one section to "Dance Composition."

Many of Gould's lectures relate to various aspects of dance. Giving her orientation in an essay, "Pageantry," that was found as part of the course notes and could have been separate lecture introductory material, or an article, she wrote:

> My first desire to combine the study of pageantry with my original work in the Art of Dancing, grew out of a love for the nature worship and ritual of the ancient peoples of all countries, and the contribution of these to art.

Gould's first lecture, the "Origin of Pageantry" has rich material on various forms of religion and the celebration of religion in drama and dance; in Lecture II, "Ritual Dancing," she notes, "Dance was one of the most complete forms of expression. Dance to early man was not a gymnastic exhibition or an amusement—but it was a serious and intimate part of life, an expression of religion and the relation of man to non-human powers." Lectures III, VI, VII, and VIII are about the "Contributions of Ritual to Art," "Solar Myths," "Dramas of the Savage People," and "Ancient Mysteries" and there is discussion about gesture, movement and feeling, mythology, magic, and a knowledge of all of this as pageantry source material.

Lecture XVII has material on how to compose a dance in terms of structure, movement, music, mood, action, and basic elements and is very close to the Beegle and Crawford chapter. Gould's basic premise about dance as it is to be explored in the context of pageants is stated in this lecture: "Dancing is an expression through the medium of bodily movement; a revealing of mental and emotional states."

Norma Gould had started her dance teaching career in 1908 in Los Angeles and from 1912 through 1914 she and Ted Shawn, the American dance pioneer, performed together and shared a studio. By the time Gould and Shawn were partners, pageantry was alive and well on the West Coast. As early as 1910 Mrs. Edward MacDowell, widow of the composer and a strong believer in pageantry, had been in California on a speaking tour. Spurred on by the success of *The Peterborough Memorial Pageant* which she had sponsored in the summer of 1910 she wanted to spread the word about this new form that combined music, poetry, and movement. In a letter dated December 18, 1910, she wrote to George Pierce Baker, the creator of *The Peterborough Memorial Pageant*, "In every place I have spoken, several have asked me about you, and there is a large movement on foot, all through the West in regard to the subject of Pageantry."[19]

Gould and Shawn were hired in 1913 as entertainers by the Santa Fe Railroad, and they performed in employee recreation centers on the route from Los Angeles to New York. In 1914 Gould and Shawn studied at the Unitrinian School of Personal Harmonizing in New Canaan, Connecticut. The school was run by the Canadian poet Bliss Carman and Mary Perry King, both of whom were involved in pageantry. After Gould and Shawn left the school in February, they went to New York. There Shawn met the internationally known dance innovator Ruth St. Denis, and by the summer of 1914 he and St. Denis were marital and artistic partners.

Ruth St. Denis joined Percy MacKaye, Mary Porter Beegle, Frank Damrosch, Alfred Hertz, and Florence Fleming Noyes on April 4, 1914, as one of the judges for the pageant staged for Barnard College's Greek Games.[20] Originally started in 1905 as an athletic contest between the freshman and sophomore classes, it was not until Beegle took over supervision of the Greek Games in 1913 that music and dance became a substantial component of the event.

Beegle's involvement with the Greek Games coincided with her burgeoning interest in pageantry. When she joined the Barnard faculty in 1913 Beegle was certainly influential in bringing her ideas on natural dancing to the young women she taught. Her work as supervisor of the Greek Games provided an opportunity for showcasing her efforts along these lines, and allowed her to help create a pageant by bringing together poetry, dance, and music in a thematically based production.

Ruth St. Denis, along with the other judges at the 1914 Barnard Greek Games, were to decide whether it was the freshman or sophomore class which created the best original work in dance, chorus, and costume. The presentation of the freshman class had original music by Aline Politzer and Lucille Taylor, words by Babette Deutsch, dance by Dorothy Leet, Helen Leet, and Gertrude Livingston, and costumes by Gertrude Livingston.

There were eighteen young women in the dance and the synopsis read as follows:

> The maidens enter intertwining their freshly plucked garlands and singing in praise of Pan. While they dance, a shy call betrays the fauns in hiding. They leap out eager to dance, but the maidens retreat in terror. But gradually they overcome their fright and join with the fauns. Suddenly the Great Pan blows upon his pipes. The fauns vanish at the summons and the maidens, gathering their neglected garlands, carry them penitently to the altar.

The dance the sophomore class created, for thirteen women, was a bit more elaborate. It started with the pipes of Pan, and a band of dryads. Soon there appeared water nymphs, Diana (guardian of all maidens), and Syrinx, fairest of all the nymphs, who is eventually transformed into a slender reed.

Ruth St. Denis, as she watched the women dance at Barnard, and as she may have watched pageants in New York during the years 1913–14, certainly absorbed the way others were developing expressive ideas in movement. She may have been particularly interested in the way large groups moved in these pageants, as she was doing work only as a solo

Peterborough Memorial Pageant, Peterborough, New Hampshire, 1910
The muses invoking the spirit of dreams.
(From Ralph Davol, A Handbook of American Pageantry *[Taunton, Mass.: Davol Publishing Company, 1915])*

performer in those early years. It was not until she and Ted Shawn joined forces in a tour which began on April 13 in Paducah, Kentucky, that she performed as a concert artist with others. After Shawn and St. Denis married on August 13, 1914, their tours included one or two pieces for "St. Denis, Shawn and Co." but the company usually consisted of only two-to-five other people.[21]

The first major extended group dance that St. Denis and Shawn created was a pageant at the Berkeley Greek Theatre on July 29, 1916. Titled *The Dance-Pageant of Egypt, Greece, and India* it utilized forty dancers from the Denishawn School and Company, in addition to about sixty students from the summer-session classes at the University of California.[22] Also involved in that pageant was a new student at the Denishawn School—Martha Graham. Prior to the Denishawn production there had been a *California Pageant* on the Greek Theatre stage in 1912, and a dance and music demonstration in 1915. The student/faculty pageant-masques, *Partheneia,* were presented at the nearby outdoor space, the Faculty Glade.[23]

The production staged by St. Denis and Shawn, when seen in the context of American pageantry, assumes familiar dimensions. The Berkeley pageant was in three parts (or episodes, in pageant terminology) and each of these had two sections. The overall theme was the life and spiritual beliefs of ancient civilizations. In the Egypt section the entire cast came on stage—

Ted Shawn and Ruth St. Denis, "Tillers of the Soil"
From *The Dance-Pageant of Egypt, Greece, and India,* University of California, Berkeley, 1916.
(Courtesy University Archives, Bancroft Library. University of California, Berkeley)

as if the Nile itself were there—all wearing individual trailing veils of green and white. After the image of the river had been successfully embedded in the imagination of the audience, St. Denis and Shawn did a duet, "Tillers of the Soil," about plowing, sowing, reaping, hunting, and fishing. The Greek section was next and included a Bacchic feast and a dance version of the myth of Orpheus and Eurydice. There was also a Pyrrhic dance for sixteen young men—probably similar to those used in other pageants of the time.

The third section, on India, featured a couple traveling through successive lives and finally coming to a state of self-realization. According to Suzanne Shelton, in her book *Divine Dancer: A Biography of Ruth St. Denis,* in each segment "the broad walk before the Greek Theatre stage was transformed into a river—the Nile, the Styx, the Ganges."[24] This too would be in keeping with the use of real or imagined bodies of water in many of the outdoor pageants. The music for the Berkeley production was played by the San Francisco Orchestra, conducted by Louis Horst, and compositions were by Walter Myrowitz, Arthur Nevin, and Ada de Lachau.

Ruth St. Denis and some of the students from the Denishawn School participated in the 1918 pageant *Light of Asia* in an outdoor theatre called

Krotonah in Los Angeles. That same year Gould, Shawn, and St. Denis were involved in the *Red Cross Pageant* in Pasadena. St. Denis played the leading role in the June 1925 *Pageant of Lexington* written by Sidney Howard for the two-hundredth anniversary of the Massachusetts city. St. Denis, wearing a wig of long loosely flowing tresses, played the role of Freedom. A reviewer in the *Lexington Minute Man* (June 19, 1925, "Splendor of Pageant Grips Thousands") noted that St. Denis "moves her audience into profound reverence." He felt that her performance had a quality of floating "over the greensward with that poetry of motion so characteristic of her." E. Bigelow Thompson, in *The Boston Evening Transcript* (June 13, 1925), wrote: "Poised, intense body in rhythm with the mood, she sets the pace for those who would follow, clear in diction, intelligent in the business of the outdoor theatre, alert to its descriptive distances."

Ted Shawn summarized his ideas about pageantry in *Dance We Must,* published in 1946:

> A pageant is something in a class by itself, being neither strictly dancing nor strictly legitimate drama, but it leans more towards pure movement than towards drama. There is usually a considerable space between the performers and the audience, and it is generally played in the open, with stage conditions thrown together for the occasion. . . . The movements should be broad and simple in outline, with well marked movements of masses of people so that the idea conveyed is that of people doing something very simple but very effective. In this field we have the most logical fusion of dance and drama problems, and the pageant director should work in the greatest harmony with the one who is responsible for the dancing.[25]

Three other dance pioneers had close associations with American pageantry: Isadora Duncan, Doris Humphrey, and Lester Horton. Duncan danced in Percy MacKaye's *Caliban* in New York's Lewisohn Stadium in May 1916 to great acclaim. "One of the most effective individual incidents . . . was the appearance of Isadora Duncan who preceded the Grecian pageant on the sands by a solo dance in which she crossed the entire stretch of sands followed by a soft yellow spotlight. She seemed to be wearing only a long flowing veil which revealed every charm of her graceful figure."[26]

Duncan's association with the ideas and practice of pageantry predate *Caliban.* Probably her earliest associations relating to pageantry were the ideas she absorbed and shared with Gordon Craig, from the beginning of their affair in 1904. Duncan's brother, Augustin, was a close friend of the MacKaye family, and he performed with Hazel MacKaye as a member of the touring Coburn Players. Gordon Craig, in a letter to Percy MacKaye dated February 3, 1915, called Isadora "distinguished, remarkable and exasperating."[27] He chided her for lack of discipline and selfishness in giving "no help whatever to the Theatre—only to herself." Craig's assessment may

Caliban, 1916
Morris Dancers.
(*Courtesy Dartmouth College Libraray*)

have related to Isadora's lack of total commitment to his ideas. She drew from him what she wanted and needed, and probably did the same in selecting ideas from dance in pageantry.

Isadora Duncan had allies in America among those who were seeking to change society politically and artistically. She was a friend of Max Eastman, editor of the radical *New Masses*, and of Robert Edmond Jones, the theatrical designer—both of whom were involved in the 1913 *Paterson Strike Pageant*. Walter Damrosch, who conducted the symphony orchestra for Duncan's New York concerts in 1908 and 1911, wrote music for pageants. Although Duncan may have liked the image of herself as a powerful solitary revolutionary figure battling the conventions of dance and the world, she must certainly have found encouragement and added impetus for her work from those involved in American pageantry.

Doris Humphrey was to become one of the leading dance innovators and choreographers from the 1930s through the early 1950s. She came to study with Ruth St. Denis and Ted Shawn at the Denishawn School in 1917 and went on to found her own company in 1928 with Charles Weidman. Her first major dance teacher, Mary Wood Hinman, was closely involved

Dances from *Caliban*, 1916
(Courtesy Dartmouth College Library)

with the American Pageantry Movement. Humphrey was a student of Hinman's at the private progressive Francis Parker School in Chicago. By the time she graduated in 1913, she had participated in pageants Hinman created for the students at the Parker School. During the years 1915, 1916, and 1917 Hinman was a pageant master and a member of the summer faculty of Teachers College. She directed her own studio and was on the staff of Hull House in Chicago—the settlement house founded by Jane Addams. In addition to teaching her own classes, Humphrey also assisted Hinman during this period.

During the summer of 1914, Humphrey was involved in teaching dance at the Outdoor Players Camp in Peterborough, New Hampshire. In Marcia Siegel's *Days on Earth* there is a picture of a pageant that took place at the camp during that summer.[28] The picture shows groups of young people in a variety of dance poses outdoors in a wooded setting. The camp was adjacent to the MacDowell colony, which in 1913 had presented the *Peterborough Memorial Pageant*. Humphrey writes in her autobiography that while she was teaching at the camp "an invitation came from the nearby MacDowell Colony. Mrs. MacDowell had engaged a young man, who was going to produce a play with dancing on her outdoor stage. Were there volunteers from our camp who would like to be in it? I was the first to offer, and there were two boys who wanted to go, too."[29] Given the strong interest of Mrs. MacDowell in pageantry, it is likely that the outdoor play with dancing was in fact a pageant.

American pageantry was a direct and formative influence on the work of west-coast choreographer Lester Horton. As a young man growing up in Indianapolis he arranged the dances, helped with the staging and costumes, and was a performer in the pageant *Song of Hiawatha*, produced in that city in 1926 and 1927. Clara Bates, the director of the pageant, took the production on tour throughout Indiana and Ohio in 1927 and 1928, and in 1929 accepted an invitation from a friend to bring *Hiawatha* to Los Angeles. When the pageant was repeated in 1929 in the outskirts of Los Angeles, Horton was listed as the director, with music by Charles Wakefield Cadman, Homer Grunn, and Sol Cohen. That same year Horton composed the dances for *Fire* by Mary Austin, another outdoor pageant production. In 1932, the year Horton launched his career as a concert choreographer, he created another pageant, *Takwish, the Star Maker*, produced in an outdoor theatre outside of Los Angeles.[30]

American pageantry and American modern dance shared many ideas and values. Both the early modern dance and pageantry movements rejected existing forms as being too commercial and lacking spiritual values and aesthetic coherence. Early American modern dance grew out of a search for native American forms, democratic expression, interest in the movement of other cultures, and a search for spiritual truth in dance. The Pageantry Movement grew out of a search for native forms, democratic expression, an interest in multi-cultural American heritage, and a search for spiritual truth in theatre.

Both the modern dance and the Pageantry Movement placed strong emphasis on education, development of the individual, and the individual creative process. Both the modern dance and the Pageantry Movement placed emphasis on forms of expression that contained historic and symbolic material. Early modern dance de-emphasized technique in favor of expression, as did pageantry. For both, the concept of art was a lofty one, but not an elitist concept. Early modern dance drew to itself people dissatisfied with traditional forms of art that emphasized an appeal to the elite and to a limited audience. The aristocratic traditions of the past were rejected by both pageantry and early American modern dance, which emphasized an art for the people, expressing their inner lives, their social and political concerns.

Isadora Duncan's words probably best express the joint feelings and goals that motivated the modern-dance pioneers and those involved in pageantry, bringing them together in search of new ideas that would express our heritage.

> In one of his moments of prophetic love for America Walt Whitman said, "I hear America singing," and I can imagine the mighty song that Walt heard, from the surge of the Pacific, over the plains, the Voices rising of the vast Choral of children, youths, men and women singing Democracy. When I read this poem of Whitman's I, too, had a Vision: the Vision of America dancing a dance that would be the worthy expression of the song Walt heard when he heard America singing. This music would have a rhythm as great as the undulation in, the swing or curves, of the Rocky Mountains. . . . It would be the vibration of the American soul striving upward through labour to Harmonious life. . . . Let them come forth with great strides, leaps and bounds, with lifted forehead and far-spread arms, dancing the language of our pioneers, the fortitude of our heroes, the justice, kindness, purity of our women. . . . When the American children dance in this way, it will make of them Beautiful Beings worthy of the name of Democracy. That will be America dancing.[31]

8

Pageantry and Music

The subject of pageant music is still a very chaotic one. It is very easy to have ideals in the matter, but impossible, as well as wrong, to attempt to force them upon an enormous national community, with pageant activities going on in so many widely separated places and with such different interests at stake. A few principles of fundamental nature, however, seem to have asserted themselves. The foremost is that pageant music should be created for the pageant and not adapted. If the pageant movement is not creative, it is nothing, and everything in its artistic constitution should be created. This is the only way to move forward with power and dignity.

—Arthur Farwell

One of the foremost composers of music for pageants, Farwell expressed these concerns in the APA Bulletin No. 43, December 1, 1916. Although some pageant writers commissioned music for their work, many used whatever hymns, folk, or classical music was available to them. Farwell's creed that "pageant music should be created for the pageant and not adapted" was followed by some pageant masters and on occasion complete original scores were composed for individual pageants.

Farwell was responsible for the music in Langdon's *The Pageant of Darien* and MacKaye's *Caliban*. Walter Damrosch was the composer for MacKaye's *The Gloucester Pageant*. Chalmers Clifton was the composer for J. Willard Hayden's *The Pageant of Lexington* and was the music arranger for Baker's *The Peterborough Memorial Pageant*.

Other distinguished composers of the era were asked to write sections of music for pageants. Ernest R. Kroeger and Frederick S. Converse shared in the musical composition for *The Pageant and Masque of St. Louis*. Converse did the same with Farwell for MacKaye's *A Bird Masque*, performed in Meriden, New Hampshire. Baker divided the compositional tasks for *The Pilgrim Spirit* among nine individuals: George W. Chadwick, Frederick S. Converse, Arthur Foote, John Powell, Leo Sowerby, Chalmers Clifton, Edgar Stillman-Kelley, E. B. Hill, and Henry F. Gilbert. Langdon, in *The Pageant of Thetford*, commissioned James T. Sleeper, but also used some Bach, Dvořák, and Tchaikovsky, as well as some contemporary Farwell.

George Pierce Baker's correspondence with various composers for his pilgrim pageant sheds light on difficulties involved in commissioning pageant music and shows clearly why the published books of script did not include scores. A letter to Baker from Henry Gilbert, a prospective composer, dated August 5, 1920, raised all the relevant issues.

> Although some of my compositions have been arranged for *band*, I, myself, have never written one and scored it especially for band. This arranging for *band* is a special branch in itself. Not many composers are able to do it. Therefore all expenses incidental to the arranging of my music for band will have to be borne by the management, independently of my fee for the composition. . . . Now in regard to *composition*. Considering my circumstances, I should require to be paid a sum of money for this composition. . . . While I am keenly appreciative of the honor, I cannot afford to donate my services. But I hesitate to name a definite sum as your specifications are so indefinite. For instance, you say "a short overture." Can you not give me a more definite idea of this by telling me how many minutes you wish it to occupy? You have not told me when the Pageant is to be produced, nor how many performances there will be, or whether you will pay me a royalty on performances or whether you wish to settle for a lump sum. Nor for how long you wish the *use* of the music. All these things have a very important bearing on what I should charge. One point must be understood and made clear, however; that is that the copyright and ownership of the music must revert *to me* when you are through with it. My first thought on reading your letter was that $1,000 would be a right price for the amount of work which you wished me to undertake. I figure that it will take my entire time for three months, and . . . this sum seemed to me to be but modest. This is $1,000, in addition to the $500 for *band* arrangement. . . . If, however, the Pageant is to be frequently given and I am to get a royalty on performances, another arrangement, not calling for such a large outlay at the start, might be feasible.[1]

Baker must have felt confronted with an impossible task, given a total budget of $2,000 for all composer fees, and knowing there was no more money forthcoming from the Pilgrim Tercentenary Commission. He had probably given no thought to royalties or who would own the music, and he could see his dream of original American music going down the drain. Negotiations would require diplomacy and skill, and Baker must have had these in large quantities, as a letter from Gilbert dated January 17, 1921, shows the composer a bit more ready to compromise.

> Referring to our telephonic conversation yesterday, let me say that I was somewhat pained that you should have so misunderstood my attitude. Far from wishing to bring

about a "hold up" on the part of American composers, my efforts were entirely directed toward simplifying matters and protecting my own interests. . . . You must not misunderstand me and think that I regard this matter purely in the light of a "job" for so much money. I certainly feel that you have paid me honor in selecting me . . . but now, when I considered the thing as a whole, I immediately saw the great commercial possibilities of it. I, therefore, feel that I should have some kind of contract. . . . This contract should cover the following points. That full credit for the composition of his music shall be given to Henry F. Gilbert. . . . That the "Commission" shall pay all expenses arising in connection with arranging this music. . . . That the "Commission" shall have the free use of the music in connection with all performances of the Pageant . . . but that apart from this, the following rights are to be the absolute property of Henry F. Gilbert: copyright, performing rights, publication rights, phonograph—or any music reproduction machine—rights, motion picture rights.

Baker's problems with Gilbert were not finished. Gilbert's concern about copyright required more clarification, as a letter to Baker on January 26 indicates:

As I understand it the copyright of the music vests in me—therefore if the Commission published it in any way, or form, either as part of the Pageant book or otherwise, and derived money from the sale of such copies either in the Pageant book or separately—a *part* of this money . . . should be paid to me in the form of royalties upon such sales.

Gilbert was not the only composer to question final ownership of the music. Composers expected to sell their music and wanted opportunities to have their work played and used as separate entities. Baker had correspondence with each of his composers about these issues. A letter from Baker to Stillman-Kelley dated May 26 shows why original pageant music was not commissioned more often and why, when it was commissioned, it was not published with the text.

I understand that a music publisher is—as I should think would be the case—eager to publish your music. . . . The following is a quotation from a recent letter to me from a member of the Commission speaking for it as a whole: "At a recent meeting of the commission the question of the rights of authors . . . came up . . . and it is the feeling that no arrangement should be made that will prevent the Commission or the Commonwealth from having the right to make and sell the composite pageant book." My understanding of this is that so long as your music is not published until the Pageant is over, you are quite free to do so if the publisher understands that the publication must in no way interfere with the sale or use of the Pageant Book. . . . Though I should much like to have the music printed in the Pageant Book I suspect that this will prove impossible because of the involved expense and the necessity of selling the book at a low price.

The Pilgrim Tercentenary Commission returned original scores to the composers and they utilized opportunities to have their music played either by symphony orchestras or for other pageants. Gilbert's suite was played by the Boston Symphony in April 1922, and later that summer Powell's *Pilgrim* music was used by the Virginia Historical Society for a pageant they were producing.

The very nature of pageantry was collaborative and many composers found it difficult to write on demand and match their music to poetry, text, and dramatic action. Not many pageant masters had the patience Baker exhibited in writing to his composers. For many composers, the demands of integrating their work with that of other creative artists was a new and difficult experience. One of the things Baker did to facilitate matters to was send out the organizational structure for the wind orchestra. He also suggested that "a convenient arrangement of score consists in putting Clarinets (violins and violas), Baritone Horns, (Cello) and Tubas (contra Basses) in the place occupied by the string quintette in orchestra scores." He also tried to establish a time frame for receipt of material. He stipulated that "a Piano or Vocal Score should be made and a copy thereof forwarded to the Master of the Pageant not later than March for use in rehearsal."

Baker did not receive many of his scores on time and letters went back and forth concerning interpretation, sequence, staging, and all sorts of other details. George Chadwick, on February 21 wrote to Baker:

> I quite agree with you that Mrs. Marks' verses are very beautiful. . . . I think I shall have no difficulty in setting them so that the spirit of the words will be reflected. Perhaps you had better let me know as soon as possible what you decide about transposing the first and last choruses. The first chorus might be repeated before or after the last one. The contrast of the women and young girls is quite delightful for music. I fear it might be difficult to get this inside of five minutes, but I will do my best. I return the words of Bradford's speech, which I should have done some time ago.

A month later, well after the deadline that had originally been presented, Baker and Chadwick were still negotiating aspects of his assignment. On March 14 Baker wrote as follows to Chadwick:

> I have talked with Mrs. Marks again, and she entirely agrees, if you and I wish to close the poem on "Unsleeping, unsleeping" of the third stanza before the end. This would bring the two stanzas of the Young Girls—"Thistledown" and "Run, boys, run"—together, to be followed by the stanza of the Older Woman ending on "Unreturning." That in turn would be followed by their stanza, the second on the last page, I think, which ends, "Unsleeping, unsleeping." I quite appreciate your desire to treat the scene on the sands at Provincetown more elaborately, but my most difficult problem is to represent all that must be treated in the time that I can use. The inevitable result is that I must treat whatever is represented very briefly, and I am forced to ask poets, composers, and all my other aids, to help to that end.

The letters of the two gentlemen must have crisscrossed in the mail, as Baker had questions about "unreturning" and "unsleeping" and about some other matters. On March 15 he mailed a letter to Chadwick referring to an earlier piece of correspondence:

> Rereading your letter, I am considerably puzzled by the first paragraph when you say that "not one syllable of her lines will be understood by the audience." We expect to have the chorus directly in front of their seats. Do you mean that it is not possible to train a chorus so that the words will be distinguishable, or that the words chosen by Mrs. Marks are not well fitted for musical expression? I dislike to approach her on the matter until I am sure on this question. Nor do I like to ask her for more lines, for she has kept well within the conditions I laid down for her as to time,—at a considerable cost of labor to herself, I suspect. As my last letter must have warned you, I do not want to emphasize "Unreturning," because that idea is better fitted for the scene of the return of the Mayflower; but the prayer-like intensity of the lines under "Unsleeping," I am glad to have emphasized. Why not directly communicate with Mrs. Lionel Marks at 192 Brattle Street,—telephone Cambridge 3674 M? If you must have more lines, of course we will give them to you, but I really do not dare to let these musical numbers swell for the Pageant is likely to get out of hand in all directions as to length.

In one final communication to Baker, Chadwick wrote:

> The important thing is—do I get one more line after "All of our treasury, we offer here to Thee"; otherwise I shall be obliged to repeat either one or the other of these lines, which I dislike to do. As soon as this point is settled, I can finish this piece.

Each piece from each composer presented different problems. Converse was writing a march and a dance, and Baker wanted to pause between the two for three lines of speaking. He wrote Converse, "Will that be all right for you provided you know within this week?" Sowerby, who was writing his music to the verses of Edwin Arlington Robinson, requested permission to write a recitative between the verses and the dialogue. That was to be a problem as it would make the section too long. Baker asked Sowerby in an April 12 letter, "How long do you feel you really should have for the recitative, and how long for the verses? I suggested to Mr. Robinson to cut his poetry to one stanza, and jam into that all he wants to say. Tenderness, wistfulness growing into trust in Divine providence, is what I feel the recitative should carry. The whole scene should be filled with uncertainty and a sense of great adventure."

One composer who did not have any problems with either the collaborative or financial aspects of pageantry was Arthur Farwell (1872–1952), who made the decision to become a composer in his freshman year as an electrical engineering student at MIT.

Arthur Farwell, ca. 1921
(Courtesy Brice Farwell)

After graduation in 1893 he studied with Homer Norris, George Chadwick, and Edward MacDowell. In 1897 he went to Europe, where he studied with Englebert Humperdinck, Hans Pfitzner, and Alexandre Guilmant. While in Europe he was deeply impressed with Richard Wagner's operas and their use of legend and folk material, and he returned to the United States with the idea of basing his compositions on native American material. During the summer of 1899 he began researching the life and music of the American Indians, and as he composed he looked for publishers who would accept his work.

Faced with difficulty in publishing his own work, in 1901 he founded the Wa-Wan Press in Newton Centre, Massachusetts.[2] The press was active with Farwell as publisher until 1912 and its mission was to publish the music of American composers without concern for the commercial value of their work. Farwell was joined in his venture by Henry F. Gilbert (1868–1928). From 1901 to 1912 the Wa-Wan Press published the works of thirty-seven American composers, nine of them women.[2] An essay by Farwell in the 1903 edition of the Wa-Wan Press puts forward the ideas that were soon to be integrated with his work in American music and community singing.

> The present edition, containing works by three composers whose names have not heretofore appeared in our publications, brings to an end the second year of The Wa-Wan Press. This effort of two years, aiming to sound the newest, the most characteristic and progressive note in our national musical art, has necessarily involved an exhaustive study of the present conditions of that art. It is impossible that this study should not lead to certain broad conclusions in regard to the present status of American composition, conclusions impossible to arrive at without this shifting from the enormous mass of imitative and characterless works constantly being produced, those which give evidence of fresh impulses, of new imaginings—in short, of a genuinely creative spirit tallying other phases of modern progressive thought.[3]

Farwell went on to stress the importance of utilizing American sources for music and he listed these as "ragtime, Negro songs, Indian songs, Cowboy songs, and, of the utmost importance, new and daring expressions of our own composers, sound speech previously unheard." In the same issue of the Wa-Wan Press, Farwell published "A Letter to American Composers" and stated in the first paragraph a manifesto that guided his compositional work.

> Speaking for the little group of composers and appreciators that has worked faithfully with us for the past year and a half, to bring about more purposeful and advantageous conditions in our musical life, especially as regards compositions, I take this opportunity of addressing all composers who feel the pulse of new life that marks the beginning of a new era in American music, and who will see in this new movement a definite hope for their own artistic future and a reason for their entire devotion to the highest ideals. This

group of workers, already mentioned, has striven to draw out of the dawning, though widely distributed realities and possibilities of American musical life, the elements and forces necessary to form a definite movement which shall make for the untrammelled growth of a genuine Art of Music. Such an art will not be a mere echo of other lands and times, but shall have a vital meaning for us, in our circumstances, here and now. While it will take the worthier traditions of the past for its point of departure, it will derive its convincing qualities of color, form, and spirit from our nature world and humanity.[4]

During the years of the press Farwell made four continental tours, lecturing about American music and playing his own compositions developed from Indian themes. In 1904 the Southwest Society of the Archeological Institute of America, based in Los Angeles, invited Farwell to collect and record southwest Indian music. He worked with Charles Lummis, and together they visited numerous tribes and recorded their songs, which Farwell later transcribed. In 1905 he spent a summer studying the Indians in Arizona and did some more field work in California.

Upon returning to the East he founded the American Music Society in Boston, and in 1907 the National Wa-Wan Society of America, whose board included George Chadwick, Charles Martin Loeffler, Frank Damrosch, and Lawrence Gilman. Twenty centers were established across the country for the study of American music and the *Wa-Wan Press Monthly* was published as an informational newsletter about the policies of the society. In 1908 Farwell combined the National Wa-Wan Society with the American Music Society to form the National American Music Society. The *Wa-Wan Press Monthly* was replaced by the *Bulletin of the American Music Society*, which printed four issues from 1908 through 1909.

Farwell joined the editorial staff of *Musical America* in 1909 when he moved to New York and the next year was appointed supervisor of municipal concerts. Farwell held this post through 1913, and in this capacity supervised band and orchestra concerts in the city's public parks and on the recreation piers. He fought for more free music in the parks, and was particularly proud of the Central Park orchestral concerts which attracted audiences of thousands. In conjunction with his role as supervisor he developed opera nights, regular performances of new American orchestral works, and afternoon folk dancing for children.

By 1913 Farwell had become active in the APA and was asked to make a presentation during the Conference of Cities organized to coincide with *The Pageant and Masque of St. Louis*. On May 31, 1914, the conference met on the general topic "Municipal Music and Folk Dancing": Frank Damrosch gave a talk on the "People's Choral and Musical Societies"; F. X. Arens spoke on the "People's Orchestra." David Mannes spoke about "Music Settlements," Louis Elson and J. C. Freund on "The Development of American Music," and Luther Gulick on "The Development of Folk Dancing in America." Arthur Farwell's topic was "Municipal Concerts: Music and the Pageant."

The St. Louis Pageant and Masque proved to be an inspiring experience for Farwell. He wrote an article for *Review of Reviews*, calling the production "from the civic standpoint a celebration for the one hundred fiftieth anniversary of the founding of St. Louis, from the sociological an ideal cooperative enterprise of the most stupendous nature, and from the artistic a world-event in the history of drama."[5] He went on to herald the pageant as a great new art form and spoke about its importance for music.

> Pageant has become a familiar word to Americans of late years, but the pageant, as the potential form of a new people's drama rivaling in significance for American life that of Greek life and that of the Greek drama for ancient Greece, it is a less familiar conception. Neither the public at large nor casual observers in general are given to long-range comparisons . . . and it is not surprising that only those most intimately concerned are at present aware of the actual present status and the vast future possibility of our new American community drama as an unprecedented art-phenomenon of modern democratic evolution. We are prone to consider as legitimate art only that which falls within the scope of accepted forms, forgetting that there was a time when opera did not exist, or symphony, or painting and drama as commonly understood today. The birth of a new and great art-form is too infrequent an occurrence to keep the public mind in the condition readily to accept such a thing when it occurs. The great public issue depending upon the production of community dramas of this nature rests in the fact that they provide for the mass of the people an access to the arts of music and dance and of drama, realistic and imaginative, which has been denied them in the narrower, traditional, and financially forbidding art-world. In fact, such community drama presents a form which may well be considered as the most complete flowering of the present wide-spread movement to bring to the whole people the refreshment and inspiration of the arts. It is with this aspect of the pageant that the writer has been particularly concerned, and through which both experience and observation have shown him the possibility not merely of community drama, but of a veritable community music-drama, capable of realizing for our American democracy a public art-life the possibility of which has been unsuspected, or doubted, and even denied. For considerable groups of the public the pageant, in any form, provides also the possibility of preparing and participating in the dramatic and musical activities, which serves to knit into the common life an experience and familiarity with artistic matters never to be attained by merely casual attendance at the theatre and concert hall. Richard Wagner conceived his music-drama as a national and democratic function. But it has been shut away in opera houses.[6]

Shortly after his trip to St. Louis Farwell accepted the director's job at the Third Street Music School Settlement in New York in 1915. This gave him the opportunity of working with a large range of people as he supervised a staff of 100 and a student body of 1,000. He probably enjoyed the multicultural environment of the settlement school, and took great satisfaction in educating the eager immigrants who flocked to its doors. The school offered instruction at prices ranging from ten to sixty-five cents a lesson.

Farwell conducted two of the school's four orchestras and helped guide the chorus. On one occasion he presented his students in a Carnegie Hall concert—800 chorus members accompanied by an orchestra of 200.

An invitation to compose the music for MacKaye's 1916 production of *Caliban* provided Farwell with the opportunity of creating a major score for a mass public. It was a challenge that would give him great critical visibility as a composer. It would also allow him to create a unique American score and to see democracy in action through music, drama, and dance. There are no records that Farwell shared the concerns that plagued the composers working for Baker on the Pilgrim pageant—copyrights, the complications of the collaborative process, or the music's fate after the performances.

Farwell was devoted to the possibility of using the pageant form as a way of making an original statement about American music and educating the public. A review in the *Boston Sunday Herald* on June 24, 1916, gave the flavor of his music and some specific detail.

> An orchestra of more than 100 pieces will play the "Caliban" which the composer Arthur Farwell intends shall appeal to the modern dramatic sense. The music is scored for a large orchestra, particularly in the brass section, which will consist of eight horns, eight trumpets, six trombones and four tubas. The strings are relatively few in number and are employed only to lend orchestral color. The more powerful portions of the music is scored so that it is complete with brass, woodwind and percussion. One of the most impressive effects will be 20 trumpets sounding the introduction. Two trumpets will sound first and others will fall in until all 20 are ringing. Mr. Farwell has composed new and special music for the pantomimes of the Roman, Germanic and Italian interludes. A special orchestra will play for them on the "Yellow Sands." A few archaic effects in the score will add variety and contrast. The most impressive is the choral dirge "Gray, Gray," in which the composer and author comment on the death-like and uncreative aspects of Puritanism, which, they say, has put a check on artistic expression, from which this country is only beginning to free itself. Mr. Farwell has resorted to an American Indian theme to gain the desired archaic effect in the Egyptian interlude in the chant of the priest. The other archaic number is the early English song "Sumer is icumen in." The Prospero motive consists of a high trumpet call, which descends an octave and returns again by brilliant consonances, and in the lower register by hidden dissonances.

The opportunity to write an original pageant score for a work on the scale of *Caliban* proved to be an enormously satisfying task for Farwell. He felt his attempts to write music that would be artistic without being elitist had been successful and was pleased that the pageant form allowed him to experiment with a variety of musical ideas. Several months after the *Caliban* production, in the December 1916 issue of the *APA Bulletin*, Farwell wrote with glowing comments and enthusiasm about pageant music.

> The country is full of composers, and many of them have already proven themselves thoroughly in this respect. The ordinary musical markets are too Europeanized to want

or to invite their work. The pageant movement in America should make a special point of doing this. Aside from the principle of creative progress involved, it is distracting to hear familiar music, laden with other associations, used with a pageant which should direct attention wholly upon itself. . . . It has been constantly proven that pageant music for any audience whatsoever should be absolutely of the best—a thoroughly and highly artistic product. The composer can safely go beyond his audience. . . . We are to look at pageant music not as an off-shoot from the world of music in general, but as something more vital and creative than most of that which arises otherwise. For it marks a departure from the artificialities and descendent importations which constitute much the greater part of the affairs of our musical world, and fills a distinct need of the people for something which is appropriate and belongs to them. From the inspiration of pageants should come songs, choruses, processionals, dances, and many other forms of music of a vigorous nature, scarcely to be expected from the work of a closeted composer, who is not working in touch with the active life of the people.

Concurrent with Farwell's work on *Caliban* was his role as first president of the newly initiated Community Chorus of New York City. With Harry Barnhart as director of the chorus, rehearsals were held on Sunday afternoons preceding the regular orchestral concerts in Central Park. During the summer regular concerts were presented on Sunday afternoon, and part of the time was devoted to audience participation.

A grand finale for the successful first season of the Community Chorus was an evening called Song and Light and 800 participated in the performance. With the orchestra located on a platform over the water in Central Park and the chorus placed on the north shore of the lake at the head of the mall, 60,000 people attended two free evenings. Lights and screens hung in the largest trees to illuminate the event.

Kenneth S. Clark wrote about these final concerts of the Community Chorus in a *Musical America* article dated September 23, 1916.

Most unyielding of the citadels stormed by the campaigners for community music is that of New York City, which has been captured outright by the "Song and Light" Festival of the New York Community Chorus along the shores of Central Park's lake on the evenings of September 13 and 14. . . . Some 30,000 "hit the trail" on the first evening, while on the second night an even larger throng capitulated. This, too, was accomplished in the midst of a street car strike that made traveling to the Central Park lake a matter of much inconvenience. However, as one of the far-seeing journalistic observers remarked of this birth of a real "neighbor spirit" in the most unneighborly of cities, "the world is not all wars and strikes and lockouts and murders and suicides and political campaigns. Beauty is not dead. Melody still exists, and so does wholesome human fellow feeling. That the "Song and Light" Festival has been able to crystallize this community feeling in spite of the inherent resistance of a great cosmopolis is perhaps the greatest triumph in America's community music movement.[7]

Farwell also composed two new works for the Song and Light evenings and acted as assistant conductor. At Christmas the Community Chorus presented a concert in Madison Square Garden, and 1,000 voices were accompanied by an orchestra of ninety. The major offering on the Madison Square Garden program was a performance of Handel's *Messiah*. Writing on "Community Music and the Music Teacher" in the 1916 *Proceedings* of the Music Teachers National Association, Farwell noted that when rehearsals began eighty percent of the singers had not previously heard the music.

An invitation to lecture on music at the University of California, Los Angeles, brought Farwell to the West Coast in 1917, where the next phase of his career took place. Concrete evidence of his influence still stands there in the form of a huge outdoor amphitheatre—the Hollywood Bowl.

Farwell was not a stranger to Los Angeles due to his earlier work with Lummis. Through his work in pageantry he became acquainted with the impresario L. E. Behymer who had been a founding member of the APA and a staunch believer in its philosophy. Behymer was a well-known and omnipresent figure in the affairs of Los Angeles, and along with Farwell was to have an influence in creating the Hollywood Bowl.[8]

Farwell's role in the creation of the Hollywood Bowl was primarily through his work in establishing a Community Chorus in Hollywood modeled on the one he and Barnhart had in New York.

A brief article in the July 2, 1918, edition of the *Los Angeles Times* reported on a concert of a new Community Chorus. The unsigned report mentions with some awe that there were 500 singers led by Arthur Farwell, who was quoted as saying "music is for all the world instead of a select few . . . regardless of race, education, status in the community."

Farwell's Community Chorus concerts of 1918 were popular in Hollywood and by 1919 a permanent Hollywood Community Chorus had been formed. One of the young women who had been inspired by Farwell's belief that "music is for all the world" was Artie Mason Carter, and she became the first president of the new Community Chorus. She at that time had recently arrived in Los Angeles accompanying her husband, who was establishing his practice as a doctor. Carter had studied music all her life and was trained as a pianist. Her background also included serious professional study in Vienna with the world-renowned piano pedagogue Theodore Leschetizky.

Artie Mason Carter wanted to see her Chorus perform as often as possible for a variety of occasions. In 1919 she initiated an Easter sunrise service for the Hollywood Community Chorus in the Whitley Heights Section of Hollywood. Farwell had written in 1916 that eighty percent of the singers in the New York Community Chorus had never heard the music for one of their concerts before they began rehearsals. Carter found this to be true of the people in the Hollywood Chorus, and felt a mission to expose and educate them.

The 1919 Easter sunrise service had been a great success which Artie Mason Carter wanted to repeat in 1920, but in an even more dramatic fashion, using not only a live chorus but a live orchestra. William Andrews Clark, a wealthy Los Angeles resident, had founded the Los Angeles Philharmonic in 1919 and in 1920 Carter asked him to donate the orchestra's services and join the chorus in song to celebrate Easter. He agreed and that year the sunrise service was held in Barnsdall Park, a dramatic hilltop site overlooking the city.

When faced with the decision as to where to hold the Easter sunrise service for the third time, Carter decided that because of its increasing popularity she wanted a large environment. She recalled her experience singing with the Hollywood Community Chorus under Arthur Farwell in a newly purchased site, what was soon to be called the Hollywood Bowl, but at that time was still called Bolton Canyon by the community.

The Hollywood Bowl site, a large natural amphitheatre nestled in the Santa Monica Mountains, had been envisioned as the location for a religious pageant as early as 1914 by a real-estate developer, Charles Toberman. At that time, he could not convince the community to engage in such a venture. In 1916, in accordance with the nationwide pageantry celebration of the Shakespeare Tercentenary, Hollywood believers in the power of pageants to educate and entertain decided to stage *Julius Caesar*. Both the impresario Behymer and the real-estate developer Toberman supported this pageant enterprise, and wanted to hold it in the undeveloped Bolton Canyon—the future Hollywood Bowl site. The people of Hollywood supported an outdoor production of *Julius Caesar* as they felt this would be the first step in the direction of a community theatre. Bolton Canyon was rejected and a neighboring site, Beachwood Canyon, was chosen as being better and more accessible.

Julius Caesar was an enormous success and one Hollywood reporter claimed that as a celebration of Shakespeare and as a pageant it was far superior to New York's *Caliban*. The idea of producing more pageants and establishing a permanent site for outdoor theatre became increasingly attractive to the artistic and civic leaders of Hollywood. In 1918, Christine Wetherill Stevenson, a wealthy patroness of Philadelphia's Little Theatre Movement, arrived in Los Angeles and immediately produced a religious pageant about the life of Buddha, *The Light of Asia*. For her production, which ran for thirty-five performances to popular acclaim, she chose an outdoor canyon site at the upper end of Vine Street, called Krotonah.

WORLD'S GREATEST
DRAMATIC OFFERING

HOLLYWOOD-SHAKESPEARE-TERCENTENARY

PRESENTATION OF

JULIUS
CAESAR

DIRECTON OF RAYMOND WELLS

FOR THE BENEFIT OF THE
ACTOR'S FUND OF AMERICA

BEACHWOOD NATURAL AMPHITHEATRE
HOLLYWOOD MAY 19

ONE EVENING ONLY---8 P.M.

5000 IN BEAUTIFUL
SPECTACULAR PAGEANT

GLADIATORS, DANCERS, CENTURIANS, SOLDIERS—ALL ROMANS

LEGIONS OF BRUTUS AND
ANTHONY IN BATTLE

MONSTROUS SPECTACLE AND WONDERFUL DRAMATIC OFFERING

REPRODUCTION OF ANCIENT ROME

WITH GREATEST OF SHAKESPEARIAN CAST

TYRONE POWER	DeWOLF HOPPER	SARAH TRUAX
WILLIAM FARNUM	DOUGLAS FAIRBANKS	CONSTANCE CRAWLEY
THEODORE ROBERTS	TULLY MARSHALL	MAE MURRAY
FRANK KEENAN	CHARLES GUNN	GRACE LORD

SEATS ON SALE AT

MASON OPERA HOUSE
127 SO. BROADWAY

HOLLYWOOD BOARD OF TRADE
6553 HOLLYWOOD BOULEVARD

MAKE YOUR SEAT RESERVATIONS EARLY

AMPLE CAR SERVICE FROM HILL ST. STATION
LOS ANGELES AND FROM ALL POINTS ON

PACIFIC ELECTRIC RAILWAY

Hollywood Bowl, 1922
(*Courtesy Hollywood Bowl Museum*)

By 1919 there was a strong community impetus to acquire a site for "a community park and art center and kindred projects of a civic nature, and not for personal, individual or corporate gain or profit." These words were part of the mandate of the newly formed Theatre Arts Alliance, among whom were L. E. Behymer, Charles Farwell,[9] Ruth St. Denis, and Ted Shawn. Their mandate continues, echoing statements in the writings of MacKaye, Baker, Farwell, and others involved in pageantry and the thrust toward civic theatres.

> To encourage and develop, through a community spirit and civic patriotism, the finest forms of arts and crafts and individual talents, and to promote appreciation of and inculcate love for beautiful creations and productions of every sort, kind and nature . . . and to present and produce and exhibit dramatic operatic and musical attractions, cantatas, pageants, community singing, oratory, sculpture, lectures, debates, discussions, and intellectual and recreative performances of every kind and nature for the edification, entertainment and benefit of the public . . . to afford opportunities for the study, presentation and exhibition of all the arts, and opportunities for all classes of people to find congenial channels for the expression of their highest and best of qualities.

This mandate, issued by the Theatre Arts Alliance, produced results and in 1919 the Hollywood Bowl site of 58.57 acres was purchased because of its perfect acoustics and the beauty of its natural environment. One of the first events to take place on that site was a free concert presented by Farwell's Community Chorus—with people sitting on blankets and spread informally on the relatively flat spaces that were surrounded by hills.

One of the next major events at the now community-owned Hollywood Bowl site was *The Pilgrim Pageant*. Once again, Hollywood was joining another nationwide pageant effort—the celebration of the Pilgrim Tercentenary, and Hollywood's production preceded George Pierce Baker's monumental Pilgrim pageant by one year.

On November 27, 1920, *The Pilgrim Spirit* was presented at the Hollywood Bowl in the afternoon. *Holly Leaves* (now a defunct publication) reported in its December 4 issue that the pageant brought together "the largest crowd ever assembled in Hollywood and estimated at from 10,000 to 15,000 people, who gave their approval of the production in spontaneous and repeated applause which filled every nook and cranny of the great 'bowl.'" *Holly Leaves* called the production an "unqualified success" and praised not only the performance but the site as well.

A veritable human picture reel of compelling force . . . was the Historical Pageant given last Saturday afternoon in the natural amphitheatre in the foothills just west of Highland Avenue. . . . Success, 100 percent, attended the pageant interpreted by speech, music, dramatic action and dancing, the ensemble composing a symphony attuned to the grandeur of the wonderful natural scenic setting with the eternal hills as a background and the blue dome of the high heavens for the canopy. The mood and spirit of the vast company was in harmony with the whole, and as each episode merged into the next with pleasing smoothness and precision, the kaleidoscopic effect was most attractive. The stage was a large space cleared and leveled in the pit of the bowl, tepees hung with furs and skins, and Indian campfires contributing to the primitive motif. The weather was a "perfect day," with Nature in her happiest mood and the sun's radiance flooded the canyon and added luster to the scene. The crowd began to assemble shortly past the noon hour, and people attended picnic style, and making themselves comfortable. The sight from the pit of the thousands closely seated together on the ground away up the hillside and around the natural amphitheatre was one never to be forgotten.

Artie Mason Carter had sung at the Hollywood Bowl in 1919 with the Community Chorus and as part of the audience at the 1920 pageant had been able to evaluate the site even better for its acoustics and atmosphere. Arthur Farwell's ideas about the importance of reaching out to all people through music had made a profound impact on Carter. The Community Chorus concept was a democratic one, and the emphasis was on group participation in an egalitarian setting.

Carter decided that the Easter sunrise service, utilizing both chorus and symphony orchestra, should be at the Hollywood Bowl—a place where hundreds of people could be accommodated and where the music would be heard to great advantage wherever they sat.

Her decision to have the sunrise service on the new site was also based on her growing desire to create a more permanent facility for her vision of music as encompassed by the Community Chorus. Hollywood in the first two decades of the twentieth century was a relatively new and rapidly growing community with no large public arena for any of the arts. Hollywood's first census report, filed in 1907, listed 3,415 residents. By 1920 there were 20,000—many of them recent immigrants from all over the country. They came for a variety of reasons—for opportunities in the movies and the new industries that were springing up and for the available cheap land and housing. Many of the civic leaders were concerned about educating the new arrivals and with providing positive and fruitful recreational experiences.

Carter's experience in the Community Chorus, her success with the orchestra and chorus working together for the Easter sunrise service, and her passion for music came together in the fall of 1921. She mobilized the community to support a new and radical idea—symphonic concerts during the summer evenings at low prices, presented in the somewhat informal environment of the Hollywood Bowl. She knew from her work with the Hollywood Community Chorus that many of Hollywood's residents were unfamiliar with the great symphonic literature. She also saw that people enjoyed the music in the Community Chorus once they became familiar with it. She knew from Farwell that music in America had to develop an audience and that music had to be heard and experienced outside the formal confines of the concert hall.

With a target date of starting the concert series in the summer of 1922, Artie Mason Carter sought volunteers from the community to raise money, construct a stage and seats, and work at whatever else needed to be done. The members of the Hollywood Community Chorus were at the heart of the fund-raising efforts. The nearly 1,000 members each sold ten books of season tickets at ten dollars per book for forty concerts, raising more than $90,000.

The money being raised was needed primarily to pay the orchestra for the ten weeks of concerts; running the physical plant and printing and selling the programs were to be done by volunteers. When sufficient money had still not been raised just before the scheduled opening, Carter went on the radio to make a final appeal. Her words sound familiar in the context of Farwell's ideas about music for the people, pageantry, and community singing.

How I wish, dear people, that this wonderful unseen audience might be picked up bodily and transported to our Bowl, a picturesque cauldron of Nature that is to overflow with music and song. My message to you is that the tremendous undertaking of giving sixty concerts during a period of ten weeks, beginning July 11, was not born of self-greed or commercialism, but is an outgrowth of Community Faith.

Behind all the enthusiasm of Carter was the guiding hand of Arthur Farwell. Not only was he influential in introducing her to music as a form of "community faith" and democracy, he had been the first to utilize the Hollywood Bowl as a populist musical performance space; and after Carter developed the summer concert series Farwell helped shape the programs. For several years he served on the volunteer committee that worked with Carter in selecting the music for what was then called "Symphonies Under the Stars." He also appeared as a guest conductor.[10]

Thousands today attend summer concerts at the Hollywood Bowl, as well as at Central Park, Ravinia Park, Wolf Trap, and Saratoga Performing Arts Center. Dressed in jeans, sandals, or perhaps something more elegant, people come to sit on lawns, or in reserved seats.

The notes sound through the stillness of summer skies in Chicago, Los Angeles, and New York. People of all races and occupations—secretaries, businessmen, lawyers, teachers, students—are joined together by the emotion of the music. On these evenings, the pageant leaders' dream becomes a reality—if only for a while—as art provides a common basis for spiritual sharing and understanding.

Conclusion

The legacy of the American pageantry movement can be felt in cultural and community values today. The writings about pageants of the early twentieth century suggest a pervasive and enduring positive influence on many of the people involved—both audience and participants. Pageants brought together individuals and groups of diverse backgrounds: social, political, economic, and ethnic. The weeks of shared planning and preparation, rehearsals and performances inevitably broke down social barriers and provided a unifying experience.

The strengths of pageantry of the early twentieth century—the first and in some cases perhaps the only opportunities for individuals to participate in dance, music, and theatre events; the educational value of studying the history and literature of the subjects celebrated; the concept of community involvement; the spirit of volunteerism; the art of story-telling on a grand scale kept alive—are what survive in the latter part of our century. The continuation today of some pageants founded early in the century as well as contemporary variations on the pageant form attest to the universality of the original vision.

In Thetford and St. Louis, social, political, and economic reforms were credited to the pageants of 1911 and 1914. The suffrage pageants clearly mirrored an important social issue of the time. All of the pageants which raised issues of change played a role in creating awareness and a spirit of activism.

But activism among special interest or minority groups was not the express mission of pageantry, and its waning as a movement can be explained in part by those "limits" of the original vision. However well-intentioned the pageant masters, the socioeconomic gulf between pageant leadership and pageant participants was enormous. Unification of purpose by means of obfuscation or assimilation of the very differences that served as the hallmark of the "melting pot" could not survive indefinitely. A leadership that could not or would not acknowledge the contemporary realities of strife and deprivation suffered by immigrants and other ethnic groups among audience and participants could not hold the unending support of a pluralistic society.

Modern-day manifestations of the spirit of pageantry can be seen nationally and locally in nearly every community. The American bicentennial celebrations of 1976 echoed the historic awareness and educational benefits of pageantry as did the centennial observances for the Statue of Liberty in 1986. Olympic celebrations from Los Angeles were telecast—and thus shared—by the world. But an examination of events closer to home resound with the same enduring qualities—school or church pageants are often a child's first introduction to the world of participatory story-telling—and the ramifications on individuals are perhaps more profound and long-lasting—if more intangible—on this more personal level.

If any lesson is to be learned from studying this important cultural movement it is that the desire to "make art" at the grassroots level has a rich history in twentieth century America. The excitement and opportunity for personal expression within a community context had a positive impact on large numbers of people and gave meaning to the idea of a partnership between art and democracy.

Appendixes

Pageant of Patriotism, Taunton, Massachusetts, 1911
Poster.
(Courtesy Brown University Library)

Appendix A

Chronology of American Pageants, 1908–1917

The APA bulletins, found in the Library of Congress, listed pageants by year but only through 1917, and they are listed here exactly as they appeared in the bulletins. At one point, the APA decided to clarify their listing notations: D (director), A (author), C (composer). When provided in the APA bulletin, the information is included in this listing also.

The Pageants of 1908

June 6 & 8. *A Pageant of Education*. Boston, Massachusetts. Lotta A. Clark.

July 4. *A Parade of Nations*. Springfield, Massachusetts. William Orr.

July 20–31. *The Quebec Tercentenary Pageant*. Quebec, Canada. Frank Lascelles.

October 7. *The Bridge Celebration*. Hartford, Connecticut. Frank Lea Short.

October 9. *The Founders' Week Pageant-Parade*. Philadelphia, Pennsylvania. Ellis P. Oberholtzer.

The Pageants of 1909

January 26 & 27. *The Pageant of the Italian Renaissance*. Chicago, Illinois. Thomas Wood Stevens.

February 21 & 22. *A Colonial Pageant*. Springfield, Massachusetts. Esther W. Bates.

May 29 & 31. *The Pageant of Westchester Country*. Bronxville, New York. Violet Oakley & Eugene Sanger.

July 5–9. *The Lake Champlain Tercentenary Indian Pageant*. L. O. Armstrong.

July 31. *Duxbury Days, An Historical Pageant*. Duxbury, Massachusetts. Margaret MacLaren Eager.

October 7, 8, 9. *Pageant of Illinois*. Evanston, Illinois. Thomas Wood Stevens.

The Pageants of 1910

April 28, 29, 30. *Old Worcester Ways, an Historical Pageant.* Worcester, Massachusetts. Margaret MacLaren Eager.

May 3 & 5. *Historical Pageant.* Charlestown, Massachusetts. Lotta A. Clark.

June 14. *The Ripon Historical Pageant.* Ripon, Wisconsin. J.F. Taintor.

July 14, 15, 16. *Pageant of Old Deerfield.* Deerfield, Massachusetts. Margaret MacLaren Eager.

July 25. *Missionary Pageant.* Northfield, Massachusetts (Repeated September 27, at Montpelier, Vermont). Mrs. Henry W. Peabody.

August 16, 18, 20. *MacDowell Memorial Pageant.* Peterborough, New Hampshire. George P. Baker.

August 21. *Camp Lanier Pageant.* Eliot, Maine. Peter W. Dykema.

August 25, 26, 27. *Pageant of Ipswich.* Ipswich, Massachusetts. Margaret MacLaren Eager.

November 10, 11, 12. *Pageant of the Perfect City.* (Boston, 1915 Civic Pageant), Boston, Massachusetts. Lotta A. Clark.

November 14, 15, 16. *A Church Pageant.* St. James Episcopal Church, Milwaukee, Wisconsin. Rev. Frederick Edwards.

The Pageants of 1911

April 22–May 20. *Pageant of Darkness and Light.* Boston. George Pickett, Francis Annesley & Hazel MacKaye.

May 4 & 5. *Pageant of the History of Minnesota.* St. Paul, Minnesota. Lee Woodward Ziegler & Lilly A. Long.

May 27 & 30. *Pageant of Patriots.* Brooklyn, New York. Constance D'Arcy MacKay & Margaret Wilson Shipman.

May 31, June 1, 2, 3. *Historical Pageant at Northampton.* Northampton, Massachusetts. Margaret MacLaren Eager.

June 1, 3, 10. *Pageant of Progress.* Lawrence, Massachusetts. Alice B. MacDonald & Mrs. Cyrus E. Dallin.

June 10. *Pageant of New London.* Connecticut. Clara W. Newcomb.

June 12 & 15. *Pageant of the Old Northwest.* Milwaukee, Wisconsin. Thomas Wood Stevens.

June 17. *Normal School Pageant.* Salem, Massachusetts. Frances Dean & Genorie Solomon.

June 26. *In the Days of the Medici, Florence.* State Normal School, Clarion, Pennsylvania. Anna B. Lilly.

July 1, 3, 4. *Pageant of Hartford.* Hartford, Vermont. Margaret MacLaren Eager.

July 1–3, 4. *Pageant of Patriotism.* Taunton, Massachusetts. Ralph Davol.

July 4. *A Pageant for Independence Day.* Chicago, Illinois. Thomas Wood
Stevens & Kenneth Sawyer Goodman.

August 12. *Pageant of Martha's Vineyard.* West Tisbury, Massachusetts.
Barbara S. Look.

August 12, 14, 15. *The Pageant of Thetford.* Thetford, Vermont. William
Chauncy Langdon.

August 12, 14, 15, 16. *Pageant of Bennington.* Bennington, Vermont. Margaret MacLaren Eager.

The Pageants of 1912

April 19 & 20. *Pageant of Charlestown.* Charlestown, Massachusetts. Lotta
A. Clark.

May 25. *Greenwich Village Children's Historical Pageant of New York.*
New York City. Margaret L. Conger

May 30, 31, June 1. *Historical Pageant.* Schenectady, New York. Constance
D'Arcy MacKay.

June 5, 6, 7, 8. *Pageant at Brattleboro.* Vermont. Margaret MacLaren
Eager.

June 17. *The Pageant of Wheeling, West Virginia.*

June 24. *A Festival of Nations.* State Normal School, Clarion, Pennsylvania.
Mary Boyce & L. Guy Carson.

July 4. City Hall, New York.

July 4. *Pageant of Healdsburg, California.*

July 4. *Pageant at Lancaster.* Massachusetts. Joseph Lindon Smith.

July 4. *Pageant of Oxford, Massachusetts.* Miss Strang.

July 5. *The Trail Breakers Pageant.* Baker, Oregon. Rev. J. Neilson Barry.

August 10 & 13. *Pageant of Martha's Vineyard.* West Tisbury, Massachusetts. Barbara S. Look.

August 14 & 15. *Pageant at Warwick, Massachusetts.* Anne B.C. Fisher.

August 15, 16, 17 & 24. *Pageant at St. Johnsbury.* Vermont. William
Chauncy Langdon.

August 19–24. *Pageant of Saratoga.* Saratoga Springs, New York. Margaret
MacLaren Eager.

August 26, 27, 28. *The Lake George Pageant.* Lake George Village, New
York. Margaret L. Conger.

September 17, 18, 19. *Pageant at Edwardsville.* Illinois. Thomas Wood
Stevens.

October 7–15. *Historical Pageant.* Philadelphia, Pennsylvania. Ellis P.
Oberholtzer.

Historical Pageant, Philadelphia, 1912
Poster.
(Courtesy Brown University Library)

October 10–12. *Erasmus Hall High School.* Brooklyn, New York. Eugene W. Harter.

Week of November 10–17. *Y.W.C.A. Foreign Pageant.* Harriet L. Boutelle et al.

The Pageants of 1913

March 31, April 1. *Pageant of the Old South Church.* Boston, Massachusetts. Joseph Lindon Smith & Henry Copley Greene.

April 12. *The National Young Women's Christian Association Pageant.* Richmond, Virginia. Lotta A. Clark.

May 8. *The Irish Pageant.* New York. Anna Throop Craig.

May 13. *Old English Pageant.* Rock Hill, South Carolina.

May 17. *Mt. Holyoke Pageant.* South Hadley, Massachusetts. M.G. Cushing.

May 24. *The Wisconsin Pageant.* University of Wisconsin, Madison, Wisconsin. Thomas Wood Stevens.

May 30. *Young Women's Christian Association Pageant*, Baltimore, Maryland.

May 31, June 14. *A Pageant of the Odyssey.* Millbury, Massachusetts. Virginia Tanner.

June 5, 6, 14. *The Arlington Pageant.* Arlington, Massachusetts. Mrs. Cyrus E. Dallin.

June 7. *New York City Pageant of the Paterson Strike (Paterson Strike Pageant).* John Reed.

June 13–17. *The Pageant of Salem.* "Kerwood," Salem, Massachusetts. Margaret MacLaren Eager.

June 14. *Hollis Hall Pageant.* Harvard University, Cambridge, Massachusetts. George P. Baker.

June 16. *The Weston Pageant.* Weston, Massachusetts. Joseph Lindon Smith.

June 17. *The Pageant of Wheeling, West Virginia.*

June 17. *Pomona College Pageant.* Claremont, California. M.G. Frampton.

June 24, 25. *Pageant of Meriden.* Meriden, New Hampshire. William Chauncy Langdon.

June 25. *National Y.W.C.A. Pageant.* Silver Bay, New York. Katherine H. Scott.

July 3–5. *Pageant of Oxford.* Oxford, Massachusetts. Emily Tudor Strang.

July 4. City Hall, New York.

July 4. *The Pageant of the Nations.* Newburyport, Massachusetts. Anne Withington & Dr. Frank W. Snow.

July 4. *Pageant of American Childhood.* Worcester, Massachusetts. Lotta
A. Clark.
July 4. *The Pageant of Portland.* Portland, Maine. Constance D'Arcy
MacKay.
July 4. *The Historical Pageant at Carmel.* California. Perry Newberry.
July 4. *Pageant of Healdsburg.* Healdsburg, California.
July 4. *Pageant at Peoria.* Illinois. Women's Club.
July 4 & 5. *The Medway Pageant.* Medway, Massachusetts. Esther Bates.
July 24–26, 28–30. *The Pageant of Saratoga.* Saratoga Springs, New York.
Margaret MacLaren Eager.
August 5–7. *The Pageant of Machias Valley.* Machias, Maine. Virginia Tan-
ner.
August 7. *National Y.W.C.A. Pageant.* Asilomar, California. Amelia
Johnson & Louise Brooks.
August 12, 16, 19. *Pageant of Lake Tashmoo.* Martha's Vineyard. Barbara
S. Look.
August 15, 16, 18, 19. *Pageant of Old Deerfield.* Deerfield, Massachusetts.
Margaret MacLaren Eager.
August 30, September 1, 6. *Pageant of Darien.* Darien, Connecticut. Wil-
liam Chauncy Langdon.
October 19, 21. *Portola Pageant.* California.
October 21. *National Y.W.C.A. Pageant.* Syracuse, New York. Martha P.
Tracy.
November 7. *National Y.W.C.A. Pageant.* New York City. Laura Hickox.
November 18. *National Y.W.C.A. Pageant.* Patterson, New Jersey. Carolyn
March.

Festivals, Masques, etc.

February 21, 22. *Washington's Birthday Pageant.* Montpelier Seminary,
Montpelier, Vermont.
March 3. *Suffrage Allegory and Pageant Parade.* Washington, D.C. Hazel
MacKaye & Elmira L. Tinnen.
May 7–9. *Greek Festival at Nashville.* Tennessee. Sydney Hirsch.
May 13. *Old English Pageant.* Winthrop College, Rock Hill, South Caro-
lina. D.B. Johnson.
July 4. *Uncle Sam's Birthday.* Washington, D.C. Hazel MacKaye & Elmira
L. Tinnen.
May 27. *Miss Wheeler's School Festival at Providence.* Rhode Island. Sarah
Hincks & William Chauncy Langdon.
July 16. *Festival at Rockport.* Massachusetts. Virginia Tanner.

August 21, 25. *MacDowell Musical Festival.* Peterborough, New Hampshire. Mrs. Edward MacDowell.

August 24. *Festival at Hanover.* New Hampshire. Mary Porter Beegle & William C. Bohn.

September 11. *"Sanctuary" Bird Masque.* Meriden, New Hampshire. Percy MacKaye.

September 23. *Peabody Dramatic Historical Festival.* Elizabeth C. Osborn.

December 24, 31. *Grace Chapel Christmas Festival.* New York City. William Chauncy Langdon.

The Pageants of 1914

January 21. *"The Pageant of the Trees."* Maugus Hall, Wellesley, Massachusetts. Isabelle Fiske Conant and Anna Eastman Frost.

February 7. *Pageant of the History of the First Church of Christ.* Pittsfield, Massachusetts. Margaret MacLaren Eager.

February 7. *National Young Women's Christian Association Pageant.* Baltimore, Maryland. Anna Pyott.

March 24, 25. *A Pageant, Being Episodes in the History of Chester County.* West Chester, Pennsylvania. Cora E. Everett.

March 26, 27. *A Pageant of Trees.* Wallaston, Massachusetts. Anna Eastman Frost.

March 28. *National Y.W.C.A. Pageant.* Oakland, California.

April 7. *National Y.W.C.A. Pageant.* Dayton, Ohio. Mable E. Stone.

April 19. *"The Progress of Women"* by Men's League for Woman Suffrage, 69th Street Armory, New York City. Hazel MacKaye.

April 25. *National Y.W.C.A. Pageant.* Philadelphia, Pennsylvania. Florence Fetherston.

April 28. *National Y.W.C.A. Pageant.* Quincy, Illinois. Grace Channon.

May 5. *National Y.W.C.A. Pageant.* Indianapolis, Indiana. Pearl Forsythe.

May 6. *Nashville Spring Festival.* Nashville, Tennessee.

May 11. *An Elizabethan Pageant (Masque) Tennessee College.* Murfreesboro, Tennessee. Elizabeth Prentiss Whitmarsh.

May 12. *May Day Festival.* Byrn Mawr College, New York. Mrs. Daly.

May 13. *Masque of the Moon Princess.* South Hadley, Massachusetts. Constance D'Arcy MacKay.

May 15. *Pageant of the Association of Working Women.* "The Romance of Work." New York City. Mary Porter Beegle.

May 16, 23. *"The Fire Regained."* Baltimore, Maryland. Edward T. Emery.

May 22, 23. *A Pageant of May.* Walla Walla, Washington. Porter Garnett.

May 23. *A Dream of Freedom.* (A Woman's Suffrage Pageant) Cleveland, Ohio. Hazel MacKaye.

May 25. *Pageant of the History of Education In Georgia.* Celebration of the 25th anniversary of the Agnes Scott College, Decatur, Georgia. Miss McKinney, Miss Markley.

May 25. *Pageant of American Costume.* Denton, Texas. S. Justine Hunt.

May 26–28. *A Pageant of the North-West.* Grand Forks, North Dakota. Frederick H. Koch.

May 27. *A Symbolic Pageant of the Normal School of Warrensbury.* Missouri.

May 28. *The Mansion Garden.* Quincy Mansion School, Wollaston. Anna Eastman Frost.

May 29. *Tree Day Festival.* Wellesley College, Massachusetts.

May 29–31. *The Pageant of St. Louis.* St. Louis, Missouri. Thomas Wood Stevens.

May 29–31. *The Masque of St. Louis.* St. Louis, Missouri. Percy MacKaye & Joseph Lindon Smith.

June 1. *"Universal Peace."* A Pageant, State Normal School, Bellingham, Washington. Frances S. Hayes.

June 6. *A Pageant of Nations.* New York City. Festival Committee, New York Center, Drama League of America.

June 9. *The Pageant of Concord.* Concord, New Hampshire. Constance D'Arcy MacKay.

June 12. *The Pageant of Patriots.* Piqua, Ohio. Constance D'Arcy MacKay and Nella McCabe.

June 13. *Pageant of New Harmony.* New Harmony, Indiana. Charity Dye & Mrs. Mary H. Planner.

June 13. *The Heart of the World.* Nasson Institute, Springvale, Maine. Esther Willard Bates.

June 17–20. *The Pageant of the Mohawk Trail.* North Adams, Massachusetts. Margaret MacLaren Eager.

June 22. Tenth Campus Pageant: "William Penn, Exemplar of Brotherhood and Peace," State Normal School, Clarion, Pennsylvania. L. Guy Carson.

June 22, 26. *The Padres.* (Pageant Drama) Santa Cruz, California. Perry Newberry.

June 23, 27. "The Pathfinder" (Pageant Drama) Santa Cruz, California. Perry Newberry.

June 25, 26. *Historical Pageant of Georgia.* Atlanta, Georgia. Given by the D.A.R. Mrs. Wm. Lawson Peel.

July 2. *The Pageant of Nevada History.* Reno, Nevada (repeated on October 19). Jeanne Elizabeth Wier.

July 14. *Pageant at Healdsburg.* California.

July 29. *A Masque of Rockport (1614–1914).* Rockport, Massachusetts. Virginia Tanner.

July 29. *Pageant of the University of Wisconsin.* Madison, Wisconsin. Lotta A. Clark.

August 1. *The Pageant of Littleton.* Littleton, Massachusetts. Alice Endora Chapman.

August 5–8. *Historical Pageant of Utica in the Mohawk Valley.* Utica, New York. Margaret MacLaren Eager.

August 10. *Historical Pageant-Parade,* Battle Anniversary of Stonington, Connecticut. Virginia Tanner.

August 10, 11. *Pageant of Rutland.* (200th Anniversary) Rutland, Massachusetts. Charles E. Carroll & Oscar F. Adler.

August 11, 12. *A Midsummer Festival.* Dartmouth College, Hanover, New Hampshire. Mary Porter Beegle.

August 12. Academy Festival, "Every Student," Thetford, Vermont. Helen Slade.

August 15, 17–19. *The Pageant of Cape Cod.* Sandwich, Massachusetts. William Chauncy Langdon.

August 23. *A Graphic and Allegorical Pageant: Five Epochs in United States History.* Silver Bay, New York. George W. Braden.

September 1, 2. *The Chatham Pageant.* Chatham, New York. Albert S. Callan.

September 9–11. *Pageant of Plattsburgh and the Champlain Valley.* Plattsburgh, New York. Margaret MacLaren Eager.

September 12, 13. *A Pageant of Chicago.* Ravinia Park, Illinois. Ruth Coffin Collins.

September 14–16. *Pageant of St. Clair County.* Belleville, Illinois. Thomas Wood Stevens & Joseph Solari.

September 19. *The Pageant of the Charles River.* Newton Lower Falls, Massachusetts. Isabelle Fiske Conant & Anna Eastman Frost.

October 5. *Social Centre Pageant.* Sauk City, Wisconsin. Ethel Theodora Rockwell.

October 6, 7. *Pageant of the Emma Willard School.* Troy, New York. Elsa M. Eager.

October 8–12. *The Pageant of Warren.* Rhode Island. Margaret MacLaren Eager.

October 10, 12. *Pageant of Ridgewood.* New Jersey. Mrs. Frances G. Wood.

October 15–17. *The Brooklyn Historical Pageant.* Brooklyn, New York. Postponed until next spring. Ellis P. Oberholtzer.

October 28. *The Pageant of Elizabeth.* New Jersey. Mary Porter Beegle & Jack Randall Crawford.

The Pageant of Cape Cod, Sandwich, Massachusetts, 1914
Poster.
(Courtesy Brown University Library)

November 1–4. *The Roger Bacon Pageant.* Columbia University, New York City.

Festivals, Masques, etc.

February 24. "Rainald & The Red Wolf," A Medieval Masque, Art Institute, Chicago, Illinois. Thomas Wood Stevens & Kenneth Sawyer Goodman.

April 4. *Greek Games.* Barnard College, Columbia University, New York.

May 1, 2. *A Pageant of Spring.* Unity House, Minneapolis, Minnesota. Grace Hodsdon Boutelle.

May 6. *Nashville Spring Festival.* Nashville, Tennessee.

May 11. *An Elizabethan Pageant* (Masque), Tennessee College, Murfreesboro, Tennessee. Elizabeth Prentis Whitmarch.

May 12. *May Day Festival.* Bryn Mawr College, New York. Mrs. Daly.

May 13. *Masque of the Moon Princess.* South Hadley, Massachusetts. Constance D'Arcy MacKay.

May 16. *Elizabethan Fete.* Kansas City, Missouri. Marcus Ford.

May 22, 23. *A Pageant of May.* Walla Walla, Washington. Porter Garnett.

May 29. *Three Day Festival,* Wellesley College, Massachusetts.

May 29–31. *The Masque of St. Louis.* St. Louis, Missouri. Percy MacKaye & Joseph Lindon Smith.

June 6. *Festival & Pageant of Nations* (Auspices of People's Institute & Social Center, P. S. 63), New York City. L. W. Barclay.

June 12, 15, 17. "Sanctuary," A Bird Masque, Buffalo, New York. Hazel and Percy MacKaye.

June 26. "The Pageant of Peace," A Masque, Santa Cruz, California. Mrs. Dennison Wilt Thomas.

July 14, 15. "The Pipes of Pan," A Masque, Peterborough, New Hampshire. Hazel MacKaye & Florence Fleming Noyes.

July 29. *A Masque of Rockport (1614–1914).* Rockport, Massachusetts. Virginia Tanner.

August 11. "Orfeo," A Masque, by Pooliziano (J. B. Symonds, Translator). Marie Ware Laughton & Livingston Platt.

August 11, 12. *A Midsummer Festival.* "The Magic of the Hills." Dartmouth College, Hanover, New Hampshire. Mary Porter Beegle and Jack Randall Crawford.

August 12. Academy Festival, "Every Student," Thetford, Vermont. Helen Slade.

October 14. *Fall Festival,* Star Spangled Banner Pageant, Madison, Wisconsin. Ethel Theodora Rockwell.

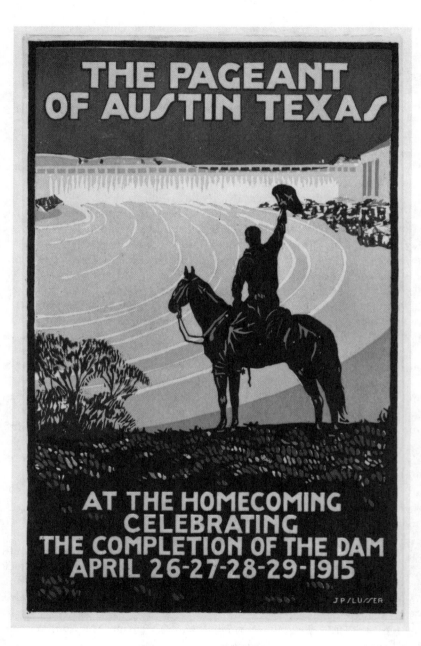

The Pageant of Austin, Texas, 1915
Poster.
(Courtesy Brown University Library)

The Pageants of 1915

February 17, 18. Pageant, "Triumph of Life," Passaic, New Jersey. Charles Keeler.

February 19 and March 2. "The Progress of Civilization," Historical Pageant. Coburn Classical Institute, Waterville, Maine. (D) Adele Gilpatrick.

April 8. "Every Child," A Masque of Youth. Greenfield, Massachusetts. Margaret MacLaren Eager.

April 9. *Partheneia.* Berkeley, California. Porter Garnett.

April 26–29. *Long Beach Historical Pageant.* Long Beach, California. Glenn Hughes & Wilfred Lucas.

April 26–29. *Pageant of Austin.* Austin, Texas. William Chauncy Langdon.

April 29, 30, May 1. Historical Pageant of Fresno: "Dionysius and the Raisins," Fresno, California. George E. Hunting.

May 8. *The Romance of Work,* A Pageant, Philadelphia, Pennsylvania. (D) Mary Porter Beegle.

May 11. *Pageant of Saluda.* North Carolina. (D) Mrs. Robert C. Chapin.

May 15. *Symbolic Festival, A Story of Springtime.* Landsdowns, Pennsylvania. George N. Braden.

May 15. *Musical Pageant of Hiawatha.* Trenton, New Jersey. Marvin A. Riley.

May 20, 21. *A Pageant of Trade.* The High School of Commerce, Cleveland, Ohio. L. Gertrude Hadlow.

May 20, 21, 22, 24. *Pageant of Long Beach.* California. (D) Perry Newberry.

May 21, 22. *Brooklyn Historical Pageant.* Brooklyn, New York. (D) Virginia Tanner.

May 22. *May Festival, A Woodland Myth.* (repeated June 15) Wheaton College, Norton, Massachusetts. Irene U. Telford & Lillian Keith.

May 24. *The History of Texas.* College of Industrial Arts, Denton, Texas. S. Justina Smith.

May 24. "Peace and War," State Normal School, Valley City, North Dakota. (D) Helen Rand.

May 24–29. Pageant and Masque, "The Golden Legend of California," Exposition Park, Los Angeles, California. Alfred Allen.

May 25. *William Woods College Pageant.* Fulton, Missouri. (D) Ethel P. Rockwell.

May 27. *Pageant of Columbus.* Mississippi Industry Institute and College, Columbus, Mississippi. (D) Emma O. Pobl & Frances I.J. Gaitber.

June. *A Mission Pageant.* Balboa Park, San Diego, California.

June. *The Abnaki Pageant.* State Camp at Vermont.

June. *Historical Pageant.* Roanoke, Virginia.

Pageant of Lincoln, Lincoln, Nebraska, 1915
Poster.
(Courtesy Brown University Library)

June 3–5. *The March of Empire.* A Pageant, Los Angeles, California. George T. Miterber.

June 3–5. *Old Royal House Pageant.* Medford, Massachusetts. (D) Lotta A. Clark.

June 4, 5, 7, 8. *Historical Pageant of Newburgh-on-Hudson.* Newburgh, New York. (D) Margaret MacLaren Eager.

June 4, 5. *Pageant at Lincoln.* Nebraska. Robert D. Scott.

June 5. *Pageant of the Year and May Festival.* Chicago, Illinois. (D) Sidney A. Teller.

June 9. *Historical and Symbolic Pageant.* Washburn College, Topeka, Kansas.

June 12. *Pageant of Southampton.* (275th Anniversary), Southampton, New York.

June 17. *A Pageant of World Peace.* Somerville, Massachusetts. Rev. Frederick A. Wilmot.

June 18. *Peace Pageant.* Yankton College Campus, Yankton, South Dakota. (D) Cora Mel Patton.

June 19. *Bridgewater Normal School Pageant.* Bridgewater, Massachusetts. (D) Lotta A. Clark.

June 20, 21, 24. *Centennial Pageant at Allegheny College.* Meadville, Pennsylvania. (D) George P. Baker.

June 21. *Universal Peace Pageant.* State Normal School, Clarion, Pennsylvania. (D) L. Guy Carson.

June 21–23. *The Pageant of Lexington.* Lexington, Massachusetts. (A) F. Willard Hayden, Jr. (C) Chalmer Clifton.

June 24. *Pageant at Ridgewood.* New Jersey. (Given by school children.) (D) Mrs. Frances G. Wood.

July. *Pageant of American Independence.* North Chillicothe, Illinois. (D) Constance D'Arcy MacKay.

July 3–5. *The Festival of the Hills.* Conway, Massachusetts. Margaret MacLaren Eager.

July 3–5. *Saugus Centennial Pageant.* Saugus, Massachusetts. (D) Esther Willard Bates.

July 3–5. *Somerville Pageant of World Peace.* Somerville, Massachusetts (postponed from June 17). (D) Frederick A. Wilmot.

July 4–5. *Pageant in Celebration of the 200th Anniversary of the Settlement of Caldwell.* Caldwell, New Jersey. Vechten Waring.

July 17. *A Pageant of the Odyssey.* Casco Bay, Maine. Virginia Tanner.

July 28. *A Pageant of Education.* University of Wisconsin, Madison, Wisconsin. Class in Pageantry & Peter W. Dykema.

August 2. "Father Penn," A Pageant, Penn State College. (D) Mary Wood Hinman.

August 6. "The Victory of Peace," Normal School, Minot, North Dakota. (D) J. H. Patton.

August 7. Bohemian Club Grove Play, "Apollo." (A) Frank Pixley. (C) Edward F. Schneider. (D) Frank L. Mathieu.

August 10, 11. *Mid-Summer Festival.* "Robin of Sherwood," Dartmouth College, Hanover, New Hampshire. Jack Randall Crawford.

August 27, 28. *Historical Pageant of Freeport.* Freeport, Illinois. (D) Ethel T. Rockwell.

September 3. *Roxbury Pageant.* Roxbury, New York. (A) (D) Margaret MacLaren Eager. (C) Charles M. Beckford.

September 23. "Endymion," The Greek Pageant, Fort Fairfield, Maine. (D) Margaret MacLaren Eager.

October 11–16. *Pageant of Austin.* Austin, Texas (postponed from April 26–29). William Chauncy Langdon.

October 13. *The Pageant of Athens.* Vassar College, (D) Hazel MacKaye.

November 20. *A Pageant of Fellowship.* (D) Mrs. Laura Palmer Ingalls and Isabelle Fiske Conant.

December 13. "The Pageant of Susan B. Anthony," Convention Hall, Washington, D.C. (D) Hazel MacKaye.

December 24. *Charles Pageant.* Outdoors. Weymouth, Massachusetts. (D) Harriet Harris.

Festivals, Masques, etc.

April 8. "Every Child." A Masque of Youth. Greenfield, Massachusetts. (D) Margaret MacLaren Eager.

April 9. "The Queen's Masque." Fourth Partheneia. University of California, Berkeley, California. (A) Mary Van Orden. (C) Charles Louis Seeger. (D) Porter Garnett.

May 15. *Symbolical Festival, A Story of Springtime.* Landsdowns, Pennsylvania. (D) George N. Braden.

May 22. *May Festival, A Woodland Myth.* Repeated June 15. Wheaton College, Norton, Massachusetts. Irene U. Telford & Lillian Keith.

June 9. *A Symbolic Masque for Class Day.* St. Johnsbury Academy, St. Johnsbury, Vermont. (D) Madeline T. Randall.

July 17. *Music, A Fountain of Poetry and Dance.* Outdoor fete. Ravinia, Illinois. (D) Ruth Coffin Collins.

July 28. Masque of "Endymion," Rockport, Massachusetts. Virginia Tanner.

August 19. A Repetition of the "Partheneia" (see April 9).

August 25, 26. *Masque of the Nations in Wilmerding.* Wilmerding, Pennsylvania. (A) (D) Thomas Wood Stevens.

October 20–22. "Merrie England," Gloucester, Massachusetts.

The Pageants of 1916

January 6. Twelfth Night Revels. "Twelfth Night in Italy." Written by one of the students at the University of North Dakota.

February 1. *Pageant of the City History Club of New York.* (A) (D) John F. Parker.

February 17, 18. *Heroines of Literature, A Pageant.* Worcester, Massachusetts. (D) Annie Russell Marble.

February 18, 19. *Shakespeare Festival.* Teachers College, Columbia University, New York City.

February 23, 24. *Pageant of the Y.M.C.A.* Boston, Massachusetts. (C) Albert M. Kanrich (D) Lotta A. Clark.

February 25. "The Portals of Light," Jubilee Celebration, Y.W.C.A., New York City, New York. Hazel MacKaye.

April 7. *The Partheneia.* Berkeley, California. (D) Porter Garnett.

April 26. *In Honor of Shakespeare.* Bloomington, Indiana. (A) (D) William Chauncy Langdon.

May. *Shakespearean Pageant.* Paducah, Kentucky. (D) Anne Lisle Booth.

May. *A Pageant and Masque for the Shakespeare Tercentenary.* Atlanta, Georgia. (C) Mrs. Annie May Bell Carroll. (D) Mrs. W.C. Jarnagin.

May. *Pageant of the Southern Highlands.* Berry School, Mt. Berry, Georgia. Isabel N. Rawn.

May 1. *Pageant of the School of Social Science.* Buffalo, New York. (D) Julia W. Pratt.

May 1. *An Old English May Day Festival.* Greenville, Mississippi. Anne Hamilton.

May 12. *Shakespeare Pageant.* Iowa City, Iowa. (D) Glenn N. Merry.

May 13. *Shakespeare Masque by the Town of Wellesley.* Massachusetts. Mrs. Laura Palmer Ingalls.

May 16. *Procession of the Drama—Shakespeare Celebration.* Ward Belmont, Nashville, Tennessee. (A) (D) Pauline Sherwood Townsend.

May 16–18. *Pageant of Bloomington and Indiana University.* Bloomington, Indiana. (C) Charles Diven Campbell, (A) (D) William Chauncy Langdon.

May 20. *The Mountain Maid.* (A) (D) Emily F. A. Hoag.

May 20. Children's Community Pageant, " A Fair Day in the Time of Shakespeare." Hudson Park, New York. (C) (D) Evelyne Hilliard.

May 22. *Shakespeare Pageant.* Denton, Texas. (D) S. Justina Smith.

May 23–27. Shakespeare Tercentenary Masque *Caliban, by the Yellow Sands,* New York City, New York. Percy MacKaye & Richard Ordynski.

Pageant at Newark, Newark, New Jersey, 1916
Poster.
(Courtesy Brown University Library)

May 30, 31, June 1, 2. *Pageant at Newark.* New Jersey. (C) Henry C. Hadley. (A) (D) Thomas Wood Stevens.

May 31. *An Old English May Day.* Normal School, Fort Hays, Kansas. (D) Althea H. Brown and Elsie Macintosh.

June. *A Pageant of Fellowship.* Pittsfield, Massachusetts. (D) Mrs. Laura Palmer Ingalls, (A) Isabelle Fiske Conant.

June 2. *A Pageant, Julius Caesar.* Greenville, Mississippi. (D) Ella T. Darling.

June 2, 3. *The Pageant of Corydon, the Pioneer Capital.* Corydon, Indiana. (C) Charles Diven Campbell. (A) (D) William Chauncy Langdon.

June 2, 3. *Pageant at Beloit.* Wisconsin. (D) Ethel T. Rockwell.

June 3. Shakespeare Pageant, "William of Stratford," Baltimore, Maryland. Constance D'Arcy MacKay.

June 6. *Greek Pageant.* Kirkwood, Missouri. (D) Nina B. Lamkin.

June 6. *Pageant of the Peddie Institution and the Community of Hightstown.* New Jersey. (A) (D) Jack Randall Crawford.

June 7–9. *Fort Wayne Historical Pageant.* Fort Wayne, Indiana. Wallace Rice, Kenneth Sawyer Goodman, & Donald Robertson.

June 7–9. *The Rochester Shakespeare Pageant.* Rochester, New York. (A) (D) Margaret MacLaren Eager.

June 10, 13. *The Technology Pageant and Masque.* Cambridge, Massachusetts. (A) Ralph Adams Cram. (C) James Ecker. (D) Virginia Tanner.

June 11, 12. Shakespeare Tercentenary Masque, *Shakespeare the Playmaker,* Given by Students of University of North Dakota, Grand Forks, North Dakota. (D) Frederick H. Koch.

June 13. Pageant, "In Quest of Freedom," Earlham College, Richmond, Indiana. (A) W.C. Woodward. (D) Mary H. Flanner.

June 13, 14. *Pageant of Montgomery County and Crawfordsville.* Crawfordsville, Indiana. (C) Frank Davis, (D) Daniel D. Hains.

June 14. *A Peace Masque.* St. Johnsbury, Vermont. (A) (D) Madelaine Randall.

June 14–16. "The Pageant of Yankton, the Ultimate City," Yankton, South Dakota. (A) Joseph Mills Hanson. (D) Zinita Barbara Graf.

June 14, 16, 19. "Cupid and Psyche," a Masque given at the Yale School of Fine Arts, New Haven, Connecticut. (A) John Jay Chapman, (C) Horatio Parker, (D) Jack Randall Crawford.

June 17, 19. *The Pageant of Hope.* Holland, Michigan. (A) Adreana S. Kolyn, (D) Arthur C. Cloetingh.

June 19. *Shakespeare Pageant.* Galena, Illinois. (D) Nina N. Lamkin.

June 22. *Punahou 75th Anniversary Pageant.* Oahu College, Honolulu, Hawaii. (A) Ethel M. Damon, (D) L. Young Correthers.

June 26. *Shakespeare Festival, Twelfth Annual Pageant.* Clarion State Normal School, Clarion, Pennsylvania. (D) L. Guy Carson.

June 26, 27. *Dedicatory Masque.* Greek Theatre "Cranbrook," Bloomfield Hills, Birmingham, Michigan. (A) Sidney Coe Howard. (D) Sam Hume.

June 29. "The New Vision," a Masque of Modern Industry, Buffalo, New York. (C) John Lund. (A) (D) Hazel MacKaye.

July 4. *Pageant of Industries.* Tacoma, Washington. (A) (D) Maude J. Jackson.

July 4. *Shakespeare Tercentenary Civic Festival.* Boston, Massachusetts. (D) Lotta A. Clark.

July 8. *Shakespeare Pageant.* Hinfield, Kansas. (D) Nina B. Lamkin.

July 10. *Historical Pageant.* Port Allegheny, Pennsylvania. (A) (D) Lyle W. Holden.

July 15. *Shakespeare Pageant.* Hirthington, Minnesota. (D) Nina B. Lamkin.

July 27–29. *The Pageant of Lake Minnetonka.* Excelsior, Minnesota. (A) Willard Dillman, (D) Mary E. Cutler.

July 28. *Historical Pageant.* Traverse City, Michigan. (D) Nina B. and Grace M. Lamkin.

August 5. *Shakespeare Pageant.* Fort Fairfield, Maine. (D) Nina B. Lamkin.

August 8–10. *Centennial Pageant.* Fort Fairfield, Maine. (D) Eva Winnifred Scates.

August 10. *Mid-Summer Festival.* "Chlorida," A Masque, Dartmouth College. (A) Ben Jonson. (D) Jack Randall Crawford.

August 11, 12, 14, 15. *Pageant of Old Deerfield.* Deerfield, Massachusetts. (C) Charles M. Beckford, (A) (D) Margaret MacLaren Eager.

August 12. *Park County Centennial Pageant.* Rockville, Indiana. (D) D. D. Hamins.

August 12. *Shakespeare Pageant.* Shellyville, Indiana. (D) Grace M. Lamkin.

August 26. *Shakespeare Pageant.* Coudersport, Pennsylvania. (D) Lyle W. Holden.

August 28. *Pageant at Hollis.* New Hampshire. (A) (D) Lotta A. Clark.

September 1. *Agricultural Pageant.* St. Louis, Missouri. (C) Charles P. Seymour, (A) Frank E. Goodwin & Joseph Solari, (D) Joseph Solari and W. E. Babb.

September 2, 4. *The Masque and Pageant of Play.* Northampton, Massachusetts. (A) (D) Margaret MacLaren Eager.

September 15, 16. *Civic Masque.* Duquesne, Pennsylvania. (D) Thomas Wood Stevens.

September 16. *Pageant of Palos.* Palos Park, Illinois. (A) Hattie S. Pashley and Eleanor Reese Dunn.

September 21–23. "Kennet," an Historical Pageant, Kennett Square, Pennsylvania. (A) (D) L. Eastwood Seibold.

October 2–7. *The Pageant of Indiana.* Indianapolis, Indiana. (C) Charles Diven Campbell. (A) (D) William Chauncy Langdon.

October 3–5. *Historic Pageant of St. Joseph County.* South Bend, Indiana. (C) (D) Henry B. Raney.

October 12. *Christopher Columbus, A Masque Pageant.* San Francisco, California. (A) Mrs. D. E. F. Easton.

October 13. *The Cornell Pageant.* Ithaca, New York. (A) Marjorie Barstow, (D) Margaret MacLaren Eager.

October 18, 19. *Pageant of the Church.* St. Louis, Missouri. (A) Arthur E. Bostwick. (D) Rev. George Long.

October 21. *Pageant at Yale University.* New Haven, Connecticut. (D) Frank Markoe and Jack Randall Crawford.

December 20. *Historical Pageant of Revere.* Revere, Massachusetts. (A) (D) Mrs. Belle R. Fish.

December 23, 24. *Christmas Mystery.* Duquesne, Pennsylvania. (A) (D) Thomas Wood Stevens.

December 24. *Municipal Christmas Eve Pageant.* San Francisco, California. (D) Ralph Rincus.

The Pageants of 1917

January 29. *The Spirit of South County.* Shannock, Rhode Island. (A) (D) Susan Sharp Adams.

March 1, 2. *Community Pageant.* East Boston, Massachusetts. (D) Mrs. Pearl M. Keating.

April 13. *Youth's Adventure, A Masque.* (Partheneia). Berkeley, California. (A) Mariquita de Laguna, (C) Sarah Unna and Ruth Cornell, (D) Porter Garnett.

April 21. *Pageant of Womanhood.* Boston Arena, Boston, Massachusetts. (D) Marie Ware Laughton.

May 3. *Cartoons of Dress.* Atlantic City, New Jersey. (A) (D) Mrs. Lansing P. Wood.

May 7. *Historical Pageant of Florida.* Tallahassee, Florida. (A) Thomas Wood Stevens. (D) Du Bois Elder.

May 14–19. *Masque of American Drama.* University of Pennsylvania, Philadelphia, Pennsylvania. (D) Leicester B. Holland. (A) Albert E. Trombley. (C) Reginald DeKoven.

The Pageant of Indiana, Indianapolis, 1916
Poster.
(Courtesy Brown University Library)

May 16. *The Pageant of Fairmont.* Sylvania Park, Fairmont, Minnesota. (A) Miss Bernice Cone and Miss Helen Currier.

May 18, 19. *The Cornell Pageant.* Ithaca, New York. (A) Marjorie Barstow. (D) Margaret MacLaren Eager.

June. *Y.W.C.A. Pageant at Fort Niagara.* New York. (D) Dorothy Smith.

June. *Pageant of Dover.* Delaware.

June 1, 2. *San Jose Pageant.* Luna Park, Santa Clara County, San Jose, California. (A) Helen Stocking. (D) Garnet Holme.

June 2. *Pageant of the Dunes.* Indiana Dunes. (A) Thomas Wood Stevens. (D) Donald Robertson.

June 4. *A Pageant of Education.* Valley City Normal School, North Dakota. (D) Martha Dewey.

June 5. "The Drawing of the Sword," a War Masque, Carnegie Institute of Technology, Pittsburgh, Pennsylvania. (A) Thomas Wood Stevens. (D) B. Iden Payne.

June 28–July 21. "Caliban, by the Yellow Sands," a Masque, Boston, Massachusetts. (C) Arthur Farwell. (A) Percy MacKaye, (D) Frederick Stanhope.

August 9–11. *The Pageant of Twinsburg.* Twinsburg, Ohio. (A) (D) S. Gertrude Hadlow.

August 11. Fifth Annual Mid-Summer Festival. "The Dance of Youth." Hanover, New Hampshire. (A) Julia Cooley. (D) Jack Randall Crawford.

August 18. "The Torchbearers." U.S. War Camp Pageant. Peterborough, New Hampshire. (A) (D) Lotta A. Clark.

October 5. *American Red Cross Masque.* Huntington, Louisiana. (A) Joseph Lindon Smith and Thomas Wood Stevens, (D) Thomas Wood Stevens.

October 31. *Semi-Centennial Pageant.* Drew Theological Seminary. Madison, New Jersey. (D) Marie Moore Forrest.

Appendix B

English Pageants, 1905–1911

1905

The Sherbourne Pageant—Louis N. Parker

1906

The Warwick Pageant—Louis N. Parker

1907

The St. Edmundsbury Pageant—Louis N. Parker
A Masque of Life: The Royal Fete at Claremont (the development of the
    Smith family)—Louis N. Parker
The Liverpool Pageant—a procession—D'Arcy de Ferrara
The Oxford Historical Pageant—Frank Lascelles
The Porchester Pageant
Romsey Millenary Celebration—F.R. Benson
The St. Albans Pageant—Herbert Jarman & Philip Carr
The Isle of Wight Pageant

1908

The Chelsea Historical Pageant—J. Harry Irvine
The Dover Pageant—Louis N. Parker
The Kings Lynn Pageant
Winchester National Pageant—F.R. Benson
Gloucester Historical Pageant—George P. Hawtrey
The Quebec (North America) Tercentenary Celebration—Frank Lascelles

1909

The Colchester Pageant—Louis N. Parker
The Bath Historical Pageant—E. Baring
The English Church Pageant—Hugh Moss
Stepney Children's Pageant at London—Louis N. Parker & F. J. Harvey Darton
The National Pageant of Wales at Cardiff—George P. Hawtrey
The York Pageant—Louis N. Parker

1910

The Army Pageant at London—F. R. Benson
The Chester Historical Pageant—George P. Hawtrey
The Ilford Children's Pageant—Leonard C. F. Robson
The Pageant of South Africa at Cape Town—Frank Lascelles

1911

The Pageant of London—Frank Lascelles
The West Dorset Historical Pageant at Bradpole—Edward Lloyd
Mid-Gloucestershire Historical Pageant of Progress—Miss May E. Cull

Appendix C

Bohemian Club Festivals, 1904–1914

The pageant literature makes references to the Bohemian Club festivals. The following explanation and list is taken from APA Bulletin No. 8, October 15, 1914.

Since 1878 the Bohemian Club of San Francisco has held each year in one of the redwood groves of California a dramatic and musical festival known as the "Midsummer High Jinks" which—particularly in recent years—partakes of the pageant character. Prior to 1902 the jinks were composite entertainments to which the various participants contributed their own parts, which were fitted into a general scheme prepared by "the sire." In that year, and since then, the festivals have been in the form of dramas with music and called "grove plays." They are witnessed only by the members of the club, those holding visitors' privileges, and a few invited guests. During the past ten years three of the plays have been produced by Mr. Porter Garnett; the remaining seven have been directed by Mr. Frank L. Mathieu.

August 20, 1904. *The Hamadryads, A Masque of Apollo,* by Will Irwin. Music by W. H. McCoy. Sire: J. Wilson Shiels. Direction and costumes: Porter Garnett. Stage and properties: George Lyon. Lighting: Edward J. Duffey.

August 12, 1905. *The Quest of the Gorgon,* by Newton J. Tharp. Music by Theodor Vogt. Sire: Newton H. Tharp. Direction: Frank L. Mathieu. Costumes: Newton J. Tharp. Scene: George Lyon. Lighting: Edward J. Duffey.

August 4, 1906. *The Owl and Care,* by Charles K. Field. Music by Humphrey J. Stewart. Sire: Charles K. Field. Direction: Frank L. Mathieu. Scene: George Lyon. Lighting: Edward J. Duffey.

July 27, 1907. *The Triumph of Bohemia,* by George Sterling. Music by Edward F. Schneider. Sire: George Sterling. Direction and costumes: Porter Garnett. Lighting: Edward J. Duffey.

August 8, 1908. *The Sons of Baldur,* by Herman Scheffauer. Music by Arthur Weiss. Sire: Herman Scheffauer. Scene: George Lyon. Lighting: Edward J. Duffey.

August 7, 1909. *St. Patrick at Tara,* by H. Morse Stephens. Music by Wallace A. Sabin. Sire: H. Morse Stephens. Direction: Frank L. Mathieu. Costumes: Porter Garnett. Scene: George Lyon. Lighting: Edward J. Duffey.

August 6, 1910. *The Cave Man,* by Charles K. Field. Music by W. J. McCoy. Sire: Charles K. Field. Direction: Frank L. Mathieu. Costumes: Haig Patigan. Scene: George Lyon. Lighting: Edward J. Duffey.

August 12, 1911. *The Green Knight, A Vision,* by Porter Garnett. Music by Edward G. Stricklen. Sire: Porter Garnett. Direction and costumes: Porter Garnett. Lighting: Edward J. Duffey.

August 10, 1912. *The Atonement of Pan,* by Joseph D. Redding. Music by Henry Hadley. Sire: Joseph D. Redding. Direction: Frank L. Mathieu. Scene: Willis Polk, Clarence Ward, Earl Cummings, George Lyon. Lighting: Edward J. Duffey.

August 9, 1913. *The Fall of Ug, a Masque of Fear,* by Rufus Steele. Music by Herman Perlet. Sire: Rufus Steele. Direction: Frank L. Mathieu. Costumes: Frank Can Sloun. Scene: Douglass Tilden, William Bryant. Lighting: Edward J. Duffey.

August 8, 1914. *Nec-Netama,* by J. Wilson Shiels. Music by Uda Waldrop. Direction: Frank L. Mathieu. Costumes: Amedee Joullin. Scene: George Lyon. Lighting: Edward J. Duffey.

Appendix D

Articles in APA Bulletins

Bulletins on Pageant Nomenclature and Directors

A Set of Tentative Definitions of Principal Types of Modern Community Celebrations. Bulletin No. 53. December 1, 1917.

List of Active Members of the American Pageant Association. Bulletin No. 23. August 1, 1915.

Some General Explanatory Bulletins

Fundamental Essentials of Successful Pageantry. Mary Porter Beegle. Bulletin No. 7. September 15, 1914.

Development of American Pageantry. Lotta A. Clark. Bulletin No. 9. November 1, 1914.

The Building of the Pageant, Margaret MacLaren Eager. Bulletin No. 25. September 1, 1915.

The Purpose of Pageantry, Charles S. Stephens. Bulletin No. 19. June 1, 1915.

Bulletins Giving Suggestions as to Pageant Opportunities

Pageantry and the New Country Life. President Kenyon L. Butterfield. Bulletin No. 49. October 1, 1914.

The Pageant as a Form of Dramatic Literature. Francis Howard Williams. Bulletin No. 17. May 1, 1915.

The Spirit of Pageantry. Violet Oakley. Bulletin No. 39. September 1, 1916.

Pageantry as a Means of Improving American Standards of Dramatic Art. Frank Chouteau Brown. Bulletin No. 45. July 15, 1917.

Possibilities of the Lyric and Ode in Modern Pageantry. Francis Howard Williams. Bulletin No. 20. June 15, 1915.

Educational Dramatic Work in Providence, R.I. Sarah Minchen Barker. Bulletin No. 60. September 1, 1919.

The "Mayflower Tercentenary." Rev. D. MacFadyen. Bulletin No. 63. October 15, 1919.

Pageantry in Americanization Work. Thomas Wood Stevens. Bulletin No. 65. November 15, 1919.

Bulletins Dealing with "The Production of the Pageant"

Importance of the Site in Determining Dramatic Form. Bulletin No. 51. November 1, 1917.

Determining the Stage and the Episodes. Bulletin No. 54. December 15, 1917.

Resources of the Pageant Stage, Distances and Entrances. Bulletin No. 56. June 15, 1918.

Resources of the Outdoor Stage, Making Use of Levels and Properties. Bulletin No. 57. June 15, 1918.

Bulletins Containing Specific and Technical Information

Necessity of Originality in Pageant Work. William Chauncy Langdon. Bulletin No. 40. September 15, 1916.

Pageant Grounds and Their Technical Requirements. William Chauncy Langdon. Bulletin No. 11. December 1, 1914.

The Spoken Word in Pageantry. Thomas Wood Stevens. Bulletin No. 23. August 1, 1915.

Problems of Color and Costume in Pageantry. Vesper L. George. Bulletin No. 21. July 1, 1915.

Pageant Dancing. Mary Porter Beegle. Bulletin No. 34. June 1, 1916.

Pageant Music. Arthur Farwell. Bulletin No. 43. December 1, 1916.

Importance of Movement Tones in Pageantry. George M. Browne. Bulletin No. 55. January 1, 1917.

The Dances of American Pageantry. Virginia Tanner. Bulletin No. 64. November 1, 1919.

Books on Dancing, a Working Bibliography for the Pageant Director. Virginia Tanner. Bulletin No. 66. December 1, 1919.

Two Supplements

Graphic Chart of Pageant Organization Scheme. Supplement A to Bulletin No. 11.

Graphic Time Analysis of Three Typical Pageants. Supplement B to Bulletin No. 19.

Notes

Chapter 1

1. Percy MacKaye, "The Gospel of Community Drama," *Blue Triangle News* 96 (1920). Published by the War Work Council of the National Board of the Young Women's Christian Association. Edited by Kathlene Burnett Winter.

2. Louis Napoleon Parker, *Several of My Lives* (London: Chapman and Hall, 1928), p. 278.

3. Ibid., p. 95.

4. Parker wrote five more pageants after *Sherbourne*, finishing his pageant career by 1909. He wrote pageants for the towns of Warwick, Bury St. Edmonds, Dover, Colchester, and York. Among his professional playwright credits were *Joseph and His Brethren, The Vagabond King, The Mayflower,* and *Disraeli.* He began his career in London as an organist, pianist, and conductor. In 1873 he began teaching music at the Sherbourne School, where he worked for nineteen years. Wagner's ideas about the purpose of art to unify the people influenced Parker, but was never mentioned by any American pageant leaders and so has not been discussed here. Key selections from Richard Wagner's "The Art Work of the Future" (1849) are reprinted in Bernard Dukore, *Dramatic Theory and Criticism: Greeks to Grotowski* (New York: Holt, 1974), pp. 777–94.

5. The cover page for this masque is in the MacKaye Collection of the Special Collections at Dartmouth College Library.

6. The numerous pageants and masques of this era are best categorized by identifying the sponsoring group: political pageants sponsored by groups with agendas for social change; institutional pageants produced by colleges and universities; and civic pageants sponsored by a town, city, or village. This is the first time these three categories have been put forward as a way of organizing the diverse material that characterizes pageants and masques. This author feels other forms of organization are confusing and unclear, having set up categories which are not distinct. Frederick G. Walsh, in an unpublished dissertation, *Outdoor Commemorative Drama in the U.S., 1900–1950* (Western Reserve, 1952), sets up many categories, but they serve to confuse rather than illuminate. They are as follows:

   (1) The Historical Pageant: a) major city historical pageant, b) smaller community historical pageant, c) rural historical pageant;
   (2) The Masque: a) the neighborhood masque, b) the masque on a large scale;

(3) Historical Pageant-Masque;
(4) Patriotic holiday pageant;
(5) Processional Pageant;
(6) Pageant in honor of individual;
(7) Pageant in honor of institutions;
(8) Pageants of progress.

Sidney Martin Tackel's unpublished dissertation, *Women and American Pageantry, 1908–1918* (City College of New York, 1982), establishes four categories: Historical Pageant, Pageant of Ideas, Pageant of the Arts, Pageant of the American Spirit.

7. Arthur S. Link and Richard L. McCormick, *Progressivism* (Arlington Heights, Ill.: Harlan Davidson, 1983), p. 2.

8. Ibid., pp. 12–13.

9. Ibid., pp. 110–11.

Chapter 2

1. Lincoln Steffens, "Tweed Days in St. Louis," *McLure's* 19 (October 1902): 577–86; "The Shamelessness of St. Louis," *McLure's* 20 (March 1903): 545–60.

2. Charlotte Rumbold, *The Survey*, July 4, 1914, p. 373.

3. All the materials cited regarding *The Pageant and Masque of St. Louis Pageant* are in the extensive Langdon Collection in the Special Collections of the John Hay Library at Brown University Library. This quote is from an article by George E. Kessler in *The Pageant and Masque of St. Louis*, Bulletin No. 2.

4. Eugene Wilson, *The Pageant and Masque of St. Louis*, Bulletin No. 2.

5. Charlotte Rumbold, *The Survey*, July 4, 1914, p. 373.

6. Smith's comments are quoted in Percy MacKaye, *A Substitute for War*, pp. 49–51.

7. Ibid., p. 373. The remainder of Rumbold's comments are from the same article.

8. Mayor Henry W. Kiel, "Educational Value of Pageant and Masque One of Its Most Impressive Features," *The Pageant and Masque of St.Louis*, Bulletin No. 2. This and other documents pertaining to "Conference of Cities" are in Brown University Library.

Chapter 3

1. All documents relating to Boston-1915 are in the Langdon Collection, John Hay Library, at Brown University Library. The collection has reprints of *New Boston*, a magazine founded for Boston-1915.

2. *New Boston*, 1910, Langdon Collection, Brown University Library.

3. The text of the pageant and all related materials are in the collection cited above.

4. Some pageants used Roman numerals to identify episodes and some did not. Numbers are listed as found in original pageant text.

5. John Dewey, *The School and Society, Being Three Lectures by John Dewey, Supplemented by a Statement of the University Elementary School* (Chicago: The University of Chicago Press, 1900), p. 21.

6. Ibid., pp. 31–32.

7. Ibid., p. 45.

8. Ibid., pp. 72–73.

9. Jane Addams, "Hull House, Chicago: An Effort toward Sound Democracy," *Forum* 14 (October 1892): 226.

10. G. Stanley Hall, "Moral Education and Will Training," *Pedagogical Seminary* 2 (1892): 75.

11. G. Stanley Hall, *Adolescence* (New York: Appleton, 1904).

12. Luther Gulick, "The Playground Association of America: Purpose," *Playground* 4 (1910): 73.

13. Unsigned article in *New Boston* (1910): 299–300.

14. William Chauncy Langdon, *The Pageant of Thetford*, August 12, 14, 15, 1911 (*The Vermonter Press*). His comment is in the foreword to the published script.

15. Langdon, *Vermonter* (July 1911).

16. Brown University Library.

17. Hazel MacKaye wrote several important suffrage pageants, among them *Six Periods of American Life*, April 17, 1914 (produced under the auspices of the Men's League for Woman's Suffrage in collaboration with the Equal Franchise Society at New York's 71 Regiment Armory); *Suffrage Allegory*, May 13, 1913 (on Treasury Steps, Washington, D.C., commissioned by the National Women's Suffrage Association); and *Pageant of Susan B. Anthony*, December 13, 1915 (Washington's Convention Hall, commissioned by the National Women's Party).

18. The music was listed separately as being arranged by William Kraft; among the selections used were a combination of pieces from the standard repertory as well as original compositions by American composers. William Kraft was credited with three pieces: "The Dance of Fire," "Minuet," and "Columbian Labor Song." Selections from Victor Herbert's opera *Natoma* were used, as were several Indian songs "acquired from native Indians." Franklin Bishop and Frederick H. Cowen, two American composers, contributed "The Steam Dance" and "Rustic Dance" respectively. Other music used was Wagner's "Spinning Song" from *The Flying Dutchman;* a minuet by Boccherini; the first movement of Schubert's *Unfinished Symphony;* a waltz by Strauss; and Mendelssohn's "The March of the Priests" from *Athalia.* Several southern plantation songs arranged by J. B. Lampe were used, including "Dandy Jim of Caroline" and "Peter Go Ring them Bells." *The Romance of Work* pageant script is in the Brown University Library.

19. Martin Green, *New York 1913. The Armory Show and the Paterson Strike Pageant* (New York: Charles Scribner's Sons, 1988). Green's book contains good bibliographic material and notes illuminating older and more recent articles, biographies, and autobiographies relating to the strike and the pageant.

Chapter 4

1. Romain Rolland, *The People's Theatre*, trans. Barret H. Clark (New York: Henry Holt & Co., 1918). All quotations in the section on Rolland are from this book.

2. There were many Hiawatha pageants written by different writers. The other legends mentioned appear in the following pageants and masques: Old Quail John—*The Thetford Pageant;* Cahókia—*The Pageant and Masque of St. Louis;* Sakakawea—*The Pageant of the North-West.*

3. A very important book written during the height of American pageantry surveys all aspects of the outdoor theatre, Sheldon Cheney, *Open Air Theatre* (New York: Mitchell Kennerly, 1918).

4. All of Craig's quotations are from *On the Art of the Theatre* (London: Heinemann, 1911) unless otherwise noted.

5. Craig, *Towards a New Theatre,* p. 7.

6. Craig, *On the Art of the Theatre,* p. 3.

7. Percy MacKaye, *The Playhouse and the Play and Other Addresses* (New York: Macmillan, 1909); *The Civic Theatre in Relation to the Redemption of Leisure: A Book of Suggestions* (New York: Mitchell Kennerly, 1912). All quotations are from these books unless otherwise noted.

8. Percy MacKaye, *A Substitute for War* (New York: Macmillan, 1915).

9. All materials cited in reference to the Boston production of *Caliban* are in the Dartmouth College Library, MacKaye Collection, housed in the Baker Library, Special Collections. This collection also houses a great deal of important material on the first production of *Caliban,* which took place in New York in 1916. There is an excellent article on this production by Mel Gordon, "Percy MacKaye's Masque of Caliban," *Tulane Drama Review* 70 (1976). Hazel and Percy MacKaye were involved with both productions but they had different individuals assisting them in each city.

    The New York performance ran from May 24 through June 6, 1916. Among the professionals working with MacKaye in New York were the Viennese-born artist and producer Joseph Urban; the director Richard Ordynski from Max Reinhardt's Deutsches Theater; the composer Arthur Farwell; the designer and artist Robert Edmond Jones; and the author and director Garnet Holme, who organized the community interludes and later wrote the *Ramona Pageant,* still given annually in Hemet, California. Also assisting MacKaye were Alice and Irene Lewisohn, who worked on the Egyptian Interlude with participants from the Neighborhood Playhouse; Cecil Sharp, who directed the Elizabethan Interlude; and John Collier of the People's Institute and the School for Community Centre Workers. The 1917 Boston production was directed by Frederick Stanhope with Irving Pichel as stage manager and Virginia Tanner as dance director.

10. Steele MacKaye (1842–94) was the father of Percy and Hazel, and an important theatrical figure of the nineteenth century. Percy MacKaye wrote a two-volume biography of his father, *Epoch: The Life of Steele MacKaye, Genius of the Theatre* (Boni and Liveright, 1927), which contains all the information about the elder MacKaye's theatrical innovations and his work with Francois Delsarte. Hazel MacKaye (1880–1944) remained active in pageantry through the 1920s. The other MacKaye siblings were Benton, James Medbury, William Payson, and Harold. For detailed information on the entire family see Edwin

Osgood Grover, ed., *Annals of an Era: Percy MacKaye and the MacKaye Family, 1826–1932*, published under the auspices of Dartmouth College, The Pioneer Press, Washington, D.C., 1932.

11. In the New York production Miranda was played by Edith Wynn Mathison. Some of the other professionals who had parts in the New York production were Allan Ross Madougall, Emmanuel and Hedwig Reicher, Augustin Duncan, Margaret Wycherly, Clara Tree Major, Mary Lawton, and John Drew.

12. In a script available in Dartmouth's MacKaye Collection, from the Harvard Stadium performance, Shakespeare does not appear in the epilogue. It is not clear whether MacKaye actually deviated from the published script or merely printed a condensed version for the Boston audience. The script shows Caliban saying, "Lady of the Yellow Sands," then offering homage to Prospero, and ending with the following as all the participants kneel:

> Glory and serenity,
>> Splendor of desire
> Kindle where the dreams of Man
>> Lift their Master's lyre:
>> Dreams of the world:—behold
> How they glister the night with their cloth of gold
> Where the spirits dance on the yellow sands
> And the children of earth clasp hands!

Chapter 5

1. Lotta A. Clark, "Pageantry in America," *The English Journal* 3, no. 3 (March 1914): 6.

2. In May 1914 the American Pageant Association issued a small booklet, "Who's Who in Pageantry." In that year Frank Chouteau Brown was president; Mary Porter Beegle, secretary; and H. H. Davenport, treasurer. The directors were L. H. Behymer, Frank H. Brooks, Percival Chubb, Lotta A. Clark, Peter W. Dykema, Margaret MacLaren Eager, Arthur Farwell, Peter Garnett, Vesper Lincoln George, George F. Kunz, William Chauncy Langdon, Mrs. E. A. MacDowell, Percy MacKaye, Ellis B. Oberholtzer, Thomas Wood Stevens, and Virginia Tanner. The booklet is in the files of the American Pageant Association at the Library of Congress and also in Brown University Library and the Boston Public Library. Clark lists many of the same people for the APA directors in her article in *The English Journal*, describing the formation of the organization.

3. Frank Chouteau Brown, "The American Pageant Association—A New Force Working for the Future of Pageantry in America," *Drama* 9 (February 1913): 178–91.

4. APA bulletins and conference reports are housed in the Library of Congress. Unless otherwise noted, references to APA activities and policies, and comments of members are from these documents.

5. George Pierce Baker is discussed extensively in chapter 6." There is very little information on Lotta Clark, but an unpublished manuscript with details of her pageant career is in the Pageant Collection of the Boston Public Library.
    William Chauncy Langdon's career is extensively documented in the William Chauncy Langdon Papers in the John Hay Library at Brown University. Langdon (1871–1947) had

several careers, as historian, teacher, writer, and pageanteer. His father founded the American Episcopal Church and worked as founder of the YMCA. After graduating from Brown in 1892, he taught English there while studying for his master of arts degree. During the last two years of his teaching career (1903–5) he was instructor of history at the Boy's School of Pratt Institute under Luther Halsey Gulick. During this time he organized the Juvenile City League of New York. From 1906 to 1909 he held two different positions; first as executive secretary of the Red Cross in New York and then as secretary to the District Attorney of New York County. After his pageant career (1911–21) he worked until 1936 as historical librarian for the American Telephone and Telegraph Company. In 1937 he left his library to Brown University, and that same year wrote *Everyday Things in American Life*, Volume I, followed by Volume II in 1941, and published by Scribner's.

6. "Margaret Olivia Slocum Sage," *Dictionary of American Biography* (New York: Charles Scribner's Sons, 1935), p. 291.

7. All correspondence between Langdon and Baker cited in this chapter is in the Langdon Collection, Brown University Library.

8. This information is included in the Langdon Collection in the files on Boston-1915.

9. Although religious pageants were produced by several pageant masters, the APA was a secular organization. Given the tradition of puritan ambivalence toward dramatic production, the relationship of American pageantry to the church is an interesting one. Holding a conference on theatrical spectacles in a church with ministers participating was a way of making a bold statement about the pageant's role in society.

10. Mary Porter Beegle's work in pageantry is discussed in great detail in chapter 7.

11. All correspondence and comments cited about this pageant are from the MacKaye Collection in the Dartmouth College Library.

12. Stevens, one of the most important pageant masters, is discussed briefly in chapter 6. All his correspondence is in the University of Arizona Library, Special Collections.

13. The John B. Rogers Company moved to Pittsburgh in 1977. An extensive collection of pageant-related material is still in their former headquarters in Fostoria, Ohio.

14. Thomas H. Dickinson, *The Case of American Drama* (Boston and New York: Houghton-Mifflin Company, 1915), p. 181.

15. "A Letter from Percy MacKaye," *Theatre Arts* 34 (July 1950): 52.

Chapter 6

1. The George Pierce Baker Collection in the Harvard Theatre Library has Baker's notes for public lectures, among them the following: 1895, "The American Drama Today"; 1898, "The Drama of the Century"; 1900, "The Drama of the Next Decade" and "The Theatre as a Social Force."

2. Baker's articles written as a result of his European sabbatical include the following: " 'Iris': Pinero's New Play: A Review and a Criticism," *Boston Evening Transcript* (October 12, 1901): 18; "The Young French Dramatist: His Public as Contrasted with the American," *B.E.T.* (April 9, 1902): 16; "The American Public and the Theatre: An Attempt to Analyze Public Taste," *B.E.T.* (June 7, 1902): 19; "A Subsidized Theatre: Professor Baker Renews

an Urgent Plea; Why Should Our Public Be Denied the Beauties of Foreign and Old English Drama Simply Because They Will Not Pay?—The Volks-Theater of Vienna as an Example for Boston—Arguments and Objections Examined," *B.E.T.* (September 10, 1902): 16.

3. *Peterborough Memorial Pageant* (Peterborough, N.H.: MacDowell Memorial Association, 1910), p. 4.

4. "The Peterborough Pageant: As the Producer Saw It," *New Boston* 1 (October 1910): 256–61.

5. Neither one of these pageants materialized. The correspondence concerning these is in the Harvard Theatre Library.

6. Baker kept a journal of his 1912 continental theatre tour, housed in the Harvard Theatre Library, Baker Collection.

7. Ibid.

8. Ibid.

9. Ibid.

10. *A Pageant of Hollis Hall, 1763–1913* (Cambridge, Mass.: University Press, 1913).

11. Baker to Arthur Lord, a member of the Pilgrim Tercentenary Commission, letter dated January 5, 1917, and available at Harvard Theatre Library.

12. All correspondence and articles about *The Pilgrim Pageant* are in the Harvard Theatre Library.

13. An early undated sheet labeled "estimate of costs of Pilgrim Tercentenary Pageant" showed a budget of $176,852.46. A budget sheet dated April 1, 1921, provided a revised estimate—$138,992.76. Baker's salary was $5,000, authorized fairly early in 1920. Authorization for composers and poets did not occur until January and a letter dated January 5 authorized Baker to spend $2,000 on composers and $500 on poets.

14. The notes for this lecture are in the Harvard Theatre Library, written on the stationery of a local hotel. Baker was involved in plans for a civic theatre in Cambridge during 1909. Lecture notes on this topic from 1909 through 1911 are also in the Harvard Library. *The Drama in Adult Education*, London: H. M. Stationery Office, 1926, states on page 111 that the success of the Little Theatre Movement in America was due largely to Baker's efforts. Correspondence concerning lectures on pageantry during the period 1909 through 1911 is also in the Harvard Library, and these lectures coincide with the lectures on the civic theatre.

15. Thomas Dickinson, *The Insurgent Theatre* (New York: B. W. Huebsch, 1917), pp. 9–10. Dickinson wrote an earlier book analyzing the state of American theatre, *The Case of American Drama* (Boston and New York: Houghton Mifflin Company, 1915).

16. *The Insurgent Theatre*, p. 199.

17. Kenneth MacGowan, *Footlights across America: Towards a National Theater* (New York: Harcourt, Brace & Company, 1929). This map is also in the Harvard Theatre Library.

18. Hume studied with Craig in Florence before he came to Harvard in 1913. At the end of October of that year the 47 Workshop presented a wordless fantasy by Hume reminiscent of Reinhardt's *Sumurun*. In 1915 he went to Detroit to direct the opening production in

an open-air theatre built on the Cranbrook estate of George C. Booth. He then developed an association with the Detroit Society of Arts and Crafts and out of this association developed a little theatre seating about two hundred. In 1914–15 Hume was largely responsible for bringing to New York an exhibition of scene design and theatre models, and later in Detroit he founded *Theatre Arts Magazine.*

19. Wisner Payne Kinne in his book *George Pierce Baker and the American Theatre* (Cambridge: Harvard University Press, 1954), has a detailed discussion of Baker's problems at Harvard and his move to Yale. Edward S. Harkness provided an endowment for both a department of drama and a theatre and Yale was Baker's base of operations until he passed away.

20. Frederick Henry Koch, *The Dakota Playmakers.* Reprinted as a booklet from the *Quarterly Journal of the University of North Dakota* 9, no. 1 (October 1918): 15–16.

21. Ibid., p. 16.

22. Ibid., p. 16.

23. Frederick Koch, "American Drama in the Making," *Carolina Play-Book* (Special feature edition, 30th Anniversary of Folk Playmaking), p. 82.

24. Frederick H. Koch, "An Interpretation of the Rural Community Drama, A New Form," introduction to *The New Day,* by Margaret Plank-Ganssle (1918), pp. 5–6.

25. F. Samuel Selden, *Frederick Henry Koch: Pioneer Playmaker* (Chapel Hill: The University of North Carolina, 1954), p. 14.

26. Ibid., p. 17.

27. Paul Green, *Dramatic Heritage* (New York: Samuel French, 1953), p. 45.

28. Ibid., p. 46.

29. Ibid., p. 18.

30. From 1923 to 1927 Koch's choice for state representative for the Bureau of Community Drama was Ethel Rockwell, who had been heavily involved in the American Pageantry Movement from 1913 to 1921, as writer, teacher, producer.

31. Joseph Wesley Zeigler, *Regional Theatre, the Revolutionary Stage* (Minneapolis: University of Minnesota Press, 1973), p. 8.

32. Frederick McConnell, who assumed leadership of the Cleveland Playhouse in 1921, is credited with making it a successful little theatre. McConnell was a student of one of the leading pageant masters, Thomas Wood Stevens (1880–1942), who wrote and/or directed over fifty pageants and masques in twenty states and in Europe, beginning with 1909. Stevens had a long and distinguished career in the theatre. He taught at the Chicago Art Institute, the Universities of Wisconsin, Michigan, and Arizona, Stanford University, and the State University of Iowa. He lectured and wrote on a variety of subjects. He helped form theatres in Pittsburgh, Kansas City, Boston, Denver, and Philadelphia, and Shakespearean Globe Theatres in Chicago, San Diego, Dallas, and Cleveland. Stevens was the director of the central region of the Federal Theatre Project and served as president of the APA intermittently from 1914 through 1924. At the height of the American Pageantry Movement, and concurrent with his own pageant work, Stevens created the first four-year undergraduate drama program in the United States, at the Carnegie Institute of Technol-

ogy in 1914. In 1925 he became the first director of the newly opened Kenneth Sawyer Goodman Memorial Theatre in Chicago.

33. Zeigler, p. 12.

Chapter 7

1. *The Black Crook* premiered September 12, 1866, at Niblo's Garden, New York. It was a popular spectacle all over America for forty years. With elaborate scenery and well-endowed dancers doing clever routines, the production was a flashy melodrama with a silly story. For many dancers of the early twentieth century, it came to represent everything they were against—rampant commercialism, meaningless and routine movement, dance as a commodity rather than an art.

2. Isadora Duncan (1878–1927) had her first contract to dance in a public theatre in 1903 (Urania Theatre, Budapest). She had an important public debut at Kroll Opera House, Berlin, in 1904, and during the next years performed in Russia and the Scandinavian countries, and opened her own school.

   Ruth St. Denis (1877–1968) made her debut in an Indian dance, a 1905 Progressive Stage Society production of *Sakundala,* at Madison Square theatre, New York. In 1906 she performed her first concert as a professional dance soloist. She performed *Incense, The Cobras,* and *Radha.* In 1906–7 she made a successful tour of Europe, appearing in places such as London, Berlin, Prague, Vienna, Hamburg, Brussels, and Budapest.

3. All the information about the courses at Teachers College, Columbia University, comes from the bulletins housed in the Teachers College Library.

4. *The Pageant of Schenectady,* written by Constance D'Arcy MacKay, was presented May 30 and 31 and June 1, 1912, in Schenectady, New York. MacKay was one of the leaders of American pageantry.

5. In May 1913 *The Conflict,* subtitled *A Health Masque in Pantomime,* was presented by the Department of Physical Education. Gertrude Colby recreated it in 1920 and in her introduction to the 1921 printed edition (New York: A. S. Barnes & Co., p. 5) she wrote that the original production "was a memorable one. Art values seemed to have been considered and expressed in choice and quality of music, in color and design of costume, as well as in arrangement and adaptation of pantomime and dance with the rest of the movements utilized. And then the entire appeal to the mind, the emotions and the ethical sense was so effective." A list of the characters is instructive: Pandora (Humanity), Wisdom, Enlightenment, and Spirits of Fresh Air, Water, Sunshine, and Exercise. Several dances are specifically detailed with steps and spatial instructions: Dance of the Athletes, Dance of the Three Graces, Dance of Evils and Disease, and March of the Evils—Commanded by Ignorance. A variety of composers were used for musical accompaniment: Delibes, Beethoven, Schumann, Tchaikovsky.

6. The pageant was produced on August 2 in connection with a summer session at the school.

7. All the information about the Dartmouth summer courses is housed in the Special Collections of the Dartmouth College Library.

8. The Ethical Culture Schools were part of the Ethical Culture Society, an international movement begun in 1876 by Felix Adler. The emphasis was on the affirmation of the worth of every human being as a common basis for life and faith, and not a belief in God.

The Ethical Culture Schools in New York were leaders in educational reform, and many of the directors and faculty were involved in the pageant movement. One of the early books on pageantry, *Festivals and Plays in Schools and Elsewhere,* was published in 1912 and written by Percival Chubb, who had been with the Ethical Culture School in New York.

9. According to Nancy Ruyter, in *Reformers and Visionaries* (New York: Dance Horizons, 1979), p. 111, "The first to launch a modern educational dance course was Gertrude Colby. This was in 1913 at Speyer School, the demonstration school connected with Columbia University's Teachers College. After the Speyer School was dismantled in 1916, Colby became an instructor at Teachers College. It was there that she developed a course called "Natural Dance" for college women, which was offered under her direction from 1918 through 1931."

10. By 1913 the Pageant Movement was intertwined with the playground and settlement-house movements and material on pageants was of great interest to social workers, physical educators, teachers, and those interested in various problems of society as well as those in the arts. Settlement houses became strong forces in the community in the first decade of the century. The first meeting of the National Recreation Congress was in 1907 and the first meeting on the issue of public recreational facilities took place in 1910. Concerns intersected and a place such as Teachers College remained embedded in the wider aspects of education. Lillian Wald, director of Henry Street Settlement, was adjunct teaching faculty at Teachers College. John Dewey had been on the board of Hull House in Chicago and was on the board of Henry Street Settlement House in New York. It was in 1913 that Henry Street Settlement House tried its first outdoor pageant with great success. In Alice Lewisohn Crowley's book, *The Neighborhood Playhouse,* she talked about the pageant (p. 13). "The first episode presented the purchase of Manhattan, followed by episodes showing a glimpse of succeeding generations and types of the various people who had inherited the neighborhood. . . . It was planned for a cast of five hundred. . . . A glimpse of contemporary history was suggested in the last scene by more recent comers to the neighborhood from Russia, Poland, Italy, Ireland, wearing their characteristic dress."

11. Bulletins of the American Pageant Association (housed in the Library of Congress and the Boston Library) list two pageants that Crawford created at Yale: one given on October 21, 1916, with Frank Markoe, listed as *Pageant at Yale* and the other on June 14, 15, and 16, *Cupid and Psyche,* given at the Yale School of Fine Arts (John Jay Chapman, author; Horatio Parker, composer; Crawford, director).

12. The UCLA Archives in Powell College Library have all the bulletins for UCLA—as a State Normal School and as the University of California, Los Angeles.

13. The Berkeley Archives have complete information on the *Partheneia* productions.

14. Information on the summer pageant courses comes from the University of Wisconsin—Madison Archives. Under the auspices of the Education Department Peter Dykema taught the following in 1914: "The School Festival Introductory" (2 credits) and "The Festival Movement: Advanced" (2 credits); Lotta Clark in 1915 taught "Dramatics and the School Festival" (2 credits) and "The Festival and Pageant Movement" (2 credits).

15. Percival Chubb, ed., *Festivals and Plays in Schools and Elsewhere* (New York/London: Harper & Brothers, 1912), pp. 261–62.

16. Mary Porter Beegle and Jack Randall Crawford, *Community Drama and Pageantry* (New Haven: Yale University Press, 1916). All quotations are from chapter IX, "The Dance," pp. 190–233.

17. Mary Porter Beegle directed The Riverdale Summer School of Pageantry in Riverdale, New York, in 1916. The school was held at the Riverdale Country School for Boys, 253 Street and Albany Post Road. Listed under the heading "Advisory Board and Special Lectures" were Frank C. Brown, Jack Randall Crawford, Arthur Farwell, Luther Halsey Gulick, Robert Edmond Jones, Percy MacKaye, Richard Ordinsky, Thomas Ward Stevens, Joseph Urban, Thomas D. Wood, and Josephine Beiderhase. Beegle taught "Pageants and Festivals" and "Pageant Dancing"; Helen Van Alst Smith taught "Costume Design"; Edith Eloise James taught "Technique of the Dance." "Pageant Dancing" involved the study of "Plot Dances, Illustrative Dances, and Symbolic or Decorative Dances." "Technique of the Dance" included "body control, poise, rhythm, expression of ideas."

18. Norma Gould's notes for the pageant course were among a large number of items found in Los Angeles by another dancer, Karoun Toutikian, when Gould was put in a nursing home. For more information on Norma Gould see Naima Prevots, *Dancing in the Sun: Hollywood Choreographers, 1915–1937* (Ann Arbor, Mich.: UMI Research Press, 1987).

19. This correspondence is housed in the Baker Collection, Harvard Theatre Library.

20. The Barnard College Archives have all the information on the Greek Games.

21. Christena L. Schlundt, *The Professional Appearances of Ruth St. Denis and Ted Shawn* (New York: The New York Public Library, 1962).

22. The complete text and program of the pageant is housed in the Berkeley Archives.

23. On July 29, 1911, a *California Pageant* was presented at Berkeley's Greek Theatre. On July 24, 1915, the Physical Education Department presented a "Dance and Music Demonstration." Mark Allen Wardrip compiled a list of Greek Theatre activities in a 1984 dissertation, *A Western Portal of Culture: The Hearst Greek Theatre of the University of California.* The Greek Theatre was opened in 1903.

24. Suzanne Shelton, *Divine Dancer: A Biography of Ruth St. Denis* (New York: Doubleday & Co., 1981), p. 134.

25. Ted Shawn, *Dance We Must*, 1946, p. 42.

26. *New York Herald*, May 25, 1916.

27. The letter is in the MacKaye Collection, Dartmouth College Library, Special Collections.

28. Marcia Siegel, *Days on Earth* (New Haven/London: Yale University Press, 1987), p. 28.

29. Selma Jeanne Cohen, *Doris Humphrey: An Artist First* (Middletown, Conn.: Wesleyan University Press, 1972), p. 28.

30. For greater detail on Horton's pageant, see Prevots, *Dancing in the Sun*.

31. Sheldon Cheney, *Isadora Duncan: The Art of the Dance* (New York: Theatre Arts Books, 1977), pp. 47–50.

Chapter 8

1. All correspondence about *The Pilgrim Pageant* is in the Baker Collection at the Harvard Theatre Library.

2. There is discussion of the dates for the Wa-Wan Press in Edgar Lee Kirk's unpublished dissertation, "Toward American Music: A Study of the Life and Music of Arthur George

Farwell" (Eastman School of Music, 1958), and in Evelyn Johnson Davis' unpublished dissertation, "The Significance of Arthur Farwell as an American Music Educator" (The University of Maryland, 1972). Kirk states that Farwell stopped publishing in 1910, although it was not until 1912 that he sold the plates to G. Schirmer. Davis maintains that Farwell kept the press active through December 1912, and bases her information on Farwell's article in *Musical America*, "An Eleven Year Adventure," October 14, 1912. The nine women composers published were: Gena Branscombe, Natalie Curtis, Julia Damon, Eleanor Everest Freer, Alice Getty, Katherine Ruth Heyman, Virginia Roper, Caroline Holme Walker, and Louise Drake Wright.

3.   Brice Farwell, ed., *A Guide to the Music of Arthur Farwell and to the Microfilm Collection of His Work, a Centennial Commemoration Prepared by His Children* (Briarcliff Manor, New York: 1972), p. 78. Evelyn Davis Culbertson is currently finishing a biography of Arthur Farwell to be published by Scarecrow Press which will contain definitive material on Farwell. Culbertson's recent article, "Arthur Farwell's Early Efforts on Behalf of American Music," *American Music* 5, no. 2 (Summer 1987), contains importantupdated information on Farwell.

4.   Ibid., p. 73.

5.   Arthur Farwell, "Pageant and Masque of St. Louis," *Review of Reviews* 1 (1914): 187.

6.   Ibid., p. 192.

7.   Kenneth S. Clark, *Musical America* 24, no. 21.

8.   All of the information on the formation of the Hollywood Bowl comes from archives in Los Angeles at the Hollywood Bowl Museum. For more information on this history see *A Vision for Music*. Hollywood Bowl Museum, Opening Exhibit, 1984. Available from Hollywood Bowl Museum, 2301 North Highland Avenue, Los Angeles, California 90078.

9.   In reviewing all the documents on the Theatre Arts Alliance there is no other mention of a man named Charles Farwell. Since careful research has revealed numerous errors in their record-keeping and in the translation of these records by later authors, it seems a safe assumption that Charles Farwell and Arthur Farwell are one and the same person.

10.   Farwell lived in California until 1927. He taught music at the University of California, Berkeley in 1918–19 and was elected president of the San Francisco Music Teachers Association. In March 1919 he organized the Berkeley Municipal Community Chorus which he also conducted. While in Berkeley he also produced *California*, a masque of song which was given in the Greek Theatre on the campus. He was instrumental in founding the Santa Barbara Community School for the Arts and a community chorus. In Los Angeles he composed the music for *The Pilgrim Spirit*. First produced in 1921, this was a very successful pageant production (funded by Christine Wetherill Stevenson) which ran for many years in an outdoor amphitheatre across the road from the Hollywood Bowl. In 1921 Farwell was awarded the first composer's fellowship by the Pasadena Music and Art Association and held it for four years. Farwell also did some private teaching and his most illustrious pupil was the American composer Roy Harris, who studied with him from 1922–24. Farwell's last project in California was the establishment in 1925 of an outdoor theatre for music and drama at Fawnskin on Big Bear Lake. He called it the Theatre of the Stars and wrote a new masque, *The March of Man*, for its dedication. Many concerts were presented and reviews were good. In 1927 the financial backers withdrew support as they wanted to develop a resort. The theatre was closed and Farwell left California to teach at Michigan State University, where he was to remain until 1937.

Bibliography

A great deal of the primary material upon which this book is based can be found only in special collections and archives: pageant scripts; pictures; articles written by the pageant leaders and their supporters; APA bulletins; personal correspondence and notes.

Pageant scripts examined by the author are in two categories: those in the Library of Congress (under the heading of "pageants") and those in other libraries. In a few cases pageants are included which have not been located but about which there is some information. In many cases, the same pageant was given slightly different titles. As a result, listings in the APA bulletins may not be identical with Library of Congress or other special collections' catalogue identification.

Primary Sources

Pageants—Documents at the Library of Congress

The following pageants can be found in the Library of Congress under the heading "pageants" in the card catalogue located in the main reading room; this bibliographic listing follows the library's format. Pageants from the period 1905–25 as well as later ones are included.

Adams, Frances Duer. *The Home Triumphant, A Pageant.* Kansas City: The Raymond Youmans Publishing Company, 1931.

Alabama. Anthropological Society Montgomery, 1922.

Alexander, Hartley Burr. *The Pageant of Lincoln.* Lincoln, Nebr.: State Printing Co., 1915.

———. *Pageant of Lincoln, 1916 "The Gate City."* Lincoln, Nebr.: Woodruff Press, 1916.

———. *The Pageant of Lincoln MCMXVII "Nebraska."* Lincoln, Nebr.: 1917.

America, a Patriotic Pioneer Pageant Play. Chicago: Young America Publishing Co., 1918.

Americans All, Immigrants All. New York, Chicago: Silver Burdett Co., 1941.

Anderson, Marion C. *Children of Peace, a Pageant for Children and Young People.* Los Angeles: Pageant Publishers, 1931.

Andrew, Mrs. Marietta Minnigerode. *The Cross Triumphant, a Pageant of the Church in England & America.* Washington, D.C.: Columbian Printing Co., 1921.

———. *Many Waters, a George Washington Pageant.* Music arrangement by Lyman McCrary. Washington, D.C.: United States George Washington Bicentennial Commission, 1931.

Armstrong, Florence J. *The House on the Rock, a Pageant for Sunday School or Church.* Denver, Colo.: Eldridge Entertainment House, 1939.

Armstrong, Louis Oliver. *The Book of the Play of Hiawatha*. Lake Champlain, 1909.

Armstrong, Louise Van Voorhis. *The Old History Book, an Americanization Pageant*. New York: Longmans, Green & Company, 1928.

Arthur, Elizabeth L. *With Silvery Gleam*. Syracuse, N.Y.: The Willis N. Bugbee Company, 1933.

Atwater, Helen Woodard, and Charles Ford Langworthy. *America's Gift to the Old World; a Pageant or Masque for Home Economics Students*. Baltimore: Waverly Press, 1915.

Averill, Mrs. Esther (Cunningham), and Lawrence Augustus Averill. *A George Washington Pageant*. Washington, D.C.: United States George Washington Bicentennial Commission, 1931.

Averill, Mrs. Ester (Cunningham). *The Word, a Pageant of the Books of the Holy Bible*. Indianapolis, Ind.: Meigs Publishing Company, 1931.

Avery, Frances Jane. *The Flag Makers, a Vocational Pageant*. Chicago: Lindquist Printing Company, 1918.

Ayers, Samuel Gardiner. *Troy Conference Centennial Pageant, 1832–1932*. Printed by order of the Conference presented April 10, 1932, Saratoga Spring, New York by the Department of Dramatics, Green Mountain Junior College. New York: Methodist Book Concern, 1932.

Bailey, Ruth O. *Making the Summer*. Los Angeles: Pageant Publishers, 1932.

Baird, George M. *The Pageant & Masque of Freedom*. Pittsburgh, 1916.

Baker, George Pierce. *The Pilgrim Spirit*. Boston: Southgate Press, 1921.

_____. *Control, a Pageant of Engineering Progress*. New York: The American Society of Mechanical Engineers, 1930.

Bates, Carroll Lund. *Democracy Saving the World*. Hobart, Ind.: The Parish Leaflet Company, 1918.

Bates, Esther Willard. *George Washington of Young America*. Boston: Walter H. Baker Company, 1931.

_____. *A Pageant of Pilgrims*. Boston, Chicago: The Pilgrim Press, 1920.

_____. *A Pageant of Pilgrims*. Boston, Los Angeles: Walter H. Baker Company, 1936.

_____. *A Pageant of the League of Free Nations*. Boston: Joint Committee for a League of Free Nations, 1919.

Bates, William Oscar. *The Indianapolis Centennial Pageant*. Indianapolis: H. B. Williams, 1920.

Beagle, Maude Stewart. *The Book Review, a Pageant for Children's Book Week*. New York: The H. W. Wilson Company, 1928.

Bibbins, Ruthella Bernard (Mory). *The Romance of Methodism, Building a Lovely Lane Around the World*. Richmond, Va: Methodist Publication House, 1934.

Bissell, Walter Lewis. *The Arch of Triumph, a Pageant for Commencement, Stressing the Seven Objectives of Education*. Cleveland, Ohio: W. C. Bissell, 1931.

_____. *The Builders, a Pageant for Commencement*. Cleveland, Ohio: W. L. Bissell, 1928.

_____. *The Tower of Memories, a Pageant for Commencement, Depicting the History of the High School*. Cleveland, Ohio: W. L. Bissell, 1938.

Bitner, Sarah E. *The Spirit of Christmas*. Philadelphia: The United Lutheran Publication House, 1934.

Block, Mrs. Marguerite. *The Pageant of Reading 175 Anniversary*. Reading, Pa.: 1923.

Bogard, Mrs. David. *The Coming of the Great Light*. Philadelphia: Hall–Meak Co., 1934.

Booth, Mrs. W. Harris. *Middlesex Historical Pageant*. Urbanna, Va: 1938.

Bowman, Harold Leonard. *Heroic Faith of Pioneers*. Portland, Ore., 1929.

Brewster, Sadie B. *America's Making*. Dansville, N.Y.: F. A. Owen Publishing Company, 1926.

Brownson, Mary Wilson, and Vanda E. Kerst. *Victory through Conflict.* Pittsburgh, 1920.

Bryce, Catherine Turner. *The Light, an Educational Pageant.* Boston: The Atlantic Monthly Press, 1920.

———. *To Arms for Liberty, a Pageant of the War for Schools and Societies.* Boston: C. C. Birchard & Co., 1918.

Bucks, Dorothy S. *The Torch Leads On.* Boston, Chicago: The Pilgrim Press, 1936.

Buffalo Public School 53. *The Nations of the World, a Pageant Designed to Show their Contribution to Civilization.* New York: A. S. Barnes Co., 1927.

Burleigh, Louise. *Signal Fires, a Masque of Service with a Pageant of the Lives of Florence Nightingale and Sadie Heath Cabaniss.* Charlottesville, Va.: The University of Virginia, 1924.

Burrell, Percy Jewett. *Pageant of New Brunswick.* Presented by People of New Brunswick & Vicinity. New Brunswick, N.J.: Blue Printing Co., 1930.

———. *Pageant of Gratitude—200 years of Blessing upon Lancaster County.* Lancaster, Pa.: Intelligence Printing Co., 1929.

———. *Pageant of Liberty.* Lancaster, Pa.: Lancaster Press, 1926.

———. *The Pageant of Hingham.* Boston: Buck Printing Co., 1935.

———. *For Freedom's Sake! A Pageant of the People in Three Actions: in Celebration of Victory; in Gratitude for Peace; in Consecration to Freedom.* Los Angeles: Baker's Plays, 1945.

Burrell, Percy Jewett, with Robert Ellsworth Will. *America's Making in Connecticut, a Pageant of the Races.* Hartford, Conn.: 1935.

Campbell, Thomas Beverly. *Liberty or Death, a Pageant Drama of the Life of Patrick Henry Presented on the Occasion of the Bi-Centennial of his Birth.* Virginia: The Herald-Progress, Printers, 1936.

Campbell, Thomas Beverly, and Howard Alexandria Southgate. *Alexandria Thy Sons.* Virginia, 1949.

Carlton, Mabel Mason and Henry Fisk Carlton. *The Spirit of Independence, a Patriotic Pageant.* New York, Chicago: C. Scribner's Sons, 1926.

Clausen, Bernard Chancellor, and Florence Lois Purington. *Pilgrim's Progress in Pageant.* New York: American Tract Society, 1928.

Coakley, Thomas Francis. *The Discovery of America.* Frank Meany Co., 1917.

Collins, Ruth Coffin. *The History of Chicago from 1613 to 1914 at Ravinia Park.* Chicago: Stearns Bros., 1914.

Conant, Mrs. Isabella (Fiske). *Persephone; Myth in Pageant Form.* San Diego, Calif.: Frye & Smith, 1914.

———. *Pageant of the Charles River.* Wellesley, Mass.: Maugus Printing Company, 1914.

Connecticut: *250 Anniversary of Founding.* Suffield, Conn.: 1920.

Connecticut: *Stonington. Battle Centennial.* Stonington Publishing Company, 1914.

Coontz, Kathleen Read. *St. Mary's Mother of Maryland.* Baltimore, Md.: Lord Baltimore Press, 1934.

———. *Living Pages from Washington's Diary.* United States George Washington Bicentennial Commission, 1931.

Copenhaver, Laura Scherer, and Katharine Scherer Cronk. *The Way: A Pageant of Japan.* Philadelphia, 1925.

Crider, Mary Elizabeth. *Texas through the Ages.* San Antonio, Tex.: Naylor Company, 1935.

Crumpton, Sara. *A Pageant of Superior.* 1916.

Dallin, Mrs. Colonna (Murray). *A Pageant of Progress.* Lawrence, Mass.: The Boothby Press, 1911.

_____ . *The Arlington Pageant to Commemorate the Dedication of the New Town Hall*. Boston: Stetson Press, 1913.

Davis, Dorothy Maril. *Wings over the World, Pageant of World Friendship and Youth*. Los Angeles: Pageant Publications, 1932.

Davison, Walter B. *Pageant for Semi-Centennial of River Falls State Normal School 1874–1929*. River Falls, Wis.: 1924.

Day, Anne Marjorie. *The Guiding Light, Pilgrim Tercentenary Pageant*. Boston: R. G. Badger, 1921.

Dickey, Jeston and Bessie Lee Dickey Roselle. *Pageants and Plays of Pioneers Commemorating Centennial of Texas*. San Antonio, Tex.: Carleton Company, 1935.

Doll, Florence K. *Pageant of Enlightenment*. East Orange, N.J.: East Orange Press, 1914. Presented by College Women's Club of Essex County, Weequahic Park, June 1914 to give publicity to the cause of a state college for women.

Dye, Charity. *Historical Pageant*. Closing Centennial Celebration June 6–13, 1914, of the founding of New Harmony, Ind. Indianapolis: Hollenbeck Press, 1914.

Dye, William Seddinger. *Father Penn*. Pageant presented by members of summer session at Pennsylvania State University August 2, 1915. (Master of Pageant, Mary Wood Hinman).

Eager, Margaret MacLaren. *Historical Pageant of Bennington, Vermont*. Troy, N.Y.: Troy Times Art Press, 1911.

Eastman, Fred. *A Pageant of Worship*. Written by class in pageant construction. Boston: Walter H. Baker, 1934.

Eastwood-Seibold, Lloyd. *An Historical Pageant in the Protestant Reformation*. Philadelphia: Westminster Press, 1917.

Eckert, Florence. *The Victory of Peace*. H. W. Wilson, 1932.

Ehrmann, Bess, and Virginia (Hicks) Ehrmann. *When Lincoln Went Flatboating from Rockport*. Rockport, Ind., 1930.

Elderdice, Dorothy. *The Sheathing of the Sword, Pageant of Peace*. Westminster, Md.: Times Printing Company, 1922.

Emerson, Elizabeth, and Gladys May Hunt. *Life of George Fox*. Tercentenary Committee of Meeting of Friends. Richmond, Ind., 1924.

Epstein, Max. *For All, Pageant on Democracy*. Chicago: Dramatic Publishing Company, 1941.

Erskine, John. *A Pageant of the 13 Century for the 700 Anniversary of Roger Bacon*. New York: Columbia University Press, 1914.

Florida, Jacksonville. *Florida Historical Pageant*. Jacksonville, Fla.: Tutewiler Press, 1922.

Forrest, Mrs. Marie Moore. *The Vision of George Washington*. U.S. Government Printing, 1932.

French, Allen. *The Drama of Concord*. Tercentenary Celebration, 1935.

Gaither, Frances O. Jones. *The Pageant of Columbus within a Masque of Industrial Institute and College*. Columbus, Miss., 1915.

_____ . *The Shadow of the Builder, Centennial Pageant*. University of Virginia, 1921.

Gardner, Flora Clark. *Famous Mothers and Daughters*. Lebanon, Ohio: March Bros., 1931.

Garnett, Porter. *A Pageant of May*. Walla Walla Union, 1914.

Georgia: *Augusta Bicentennial*. Phoenix Printing Company, 1935.

Gordon, Phyllis Galentine. *The Oaksmere Pageant*. New York: Schoen Printing Company, 1918.

Green, Mary Wolcott. *The Women Who Did*. Chicago: T. S. Denison, 1911.

Gruver, Suzanne Cary. *The Pageant of Stoughton, 1726–1926*. Stoughton, Mass.: 1926.

_____ . *The Pageant of Brockton*. Brockton, Mass.: Newsom & Toner, 1921.

Gross, Philip. *Victory Pageant*. New York: Civic Drama and Pageant Production Company, 1919.

Halsworth, Doris Campbell. *Pathways to the Light.* Windsor, Conn.: B. S. Carter, 1930.

———. *The Leaves of the Tree.* Participation by people of Wethersfield, Glastonberg, Newington, Rocky Hill, and Windsor, Conn., 1934.

Hare, Walter Ben. *A Pageant of History.* Boston: W. H. Baker, 1914.

———. *Progress, the Parent-Teacher Association Pageant.* Springfield, Mo.: W. B. Hare, 1922.

Herbst, Eva. *Ruth a Harvest Pageant.* Cincinnati, Ohio: Union of American Hebrew Congregations, 1921.

Hickman, Elmer W., and Roy Minet. *Titusville, Birthplace of Petroleum Industry.* 75 Anniversary of First Oil Well Drilling. Titusville, Pa.: Titusville Herald, 1935.

Hodgson, Gertrude Simms. *Thirteen as One.* Society of Friends, Richmond, Ind.: 1922.

Holbrock, Marion. *The Distaff, a Pageant Play of Women's Progress.* 1931.

Houson, Joseph Mills. *The Book of the Pageant of Yankton.* Yankton, S.Dak.: Yankton Printing Company, 1916.

Howard, Sidney Coe. *"Lexington" Pageant Drama of The American Freedom.* Lexington Historical Society, 1925.

Hurley, George O. *Pageantry for Iowa Communities.* State Historical Society of Iowa, 1923.

Hutchin, George. *Lost Paradise Regained.* Los Angeles: 1917.

Johnston, Mable. *A Pageant of Texas.* Dallas: 1935.

Jones, Mrs. Alice Archer (Sewall). *The Torch, A Pageant of Light, from the Early History of Urbana, Ohio.* Urbana, Ohio: Gaumer Publishing Co., 1922.

Kearns, John. *The Torch-Bearer.* Illinois Woman's College. Jacksonville, Ill.: 1921.

Keigwin, Albert Edwin. *Return of the Pilgrim Fathers.* 1920.

Kentucky: *Sesqui-Centennial Jubilee Celebration.* Citizens general committee. Lexington, Ky.: 1925.

Knoch, Nancy Jane. *Our Missouri.* Burton Publishing Co., 1949.

Koch, Frederick H., Supervisor. *A Pageant of the Lower Cape Fear.* Written in collaboration by citizens of Wilmington, North Carolina. Wilmington: NC Printing Co., 1921.

———. *A Pageant of the North-West.* Grand Forks, N.Dak.: Times-Herald Publishing Company, 1914.

Kolyn, Adriana S. *The Pageant of Hope.* Holland, Mich.: 1916.

Lafferty, Maude (Ward). *Pageant of Kentucky.* Louisville, Conn.: Dearing Printing Co., 1924.

Lamkin, Nina B. *America, Yesterday and Today.* Chicago: T. S. Denison, 1917.

Lamport, Mrs. Helen Rose (Morey). *The Historic Pageant of St. Joseph County.* South Bend, Ind.: C. P. Hardy, 1916.

Langdon, William Chauncy. *Pilgrim Tercentenary Pageant of Marietta, Ohio.* 1920.

———. *The Pageant of Meriden.* Hanover, N.H.: Dartmouth Press, 1913.

———. *Centennial Pageant of Auburn Theological Seminary 1818–1918.* Auburn: The Jacobs Press, 1918.

———. *The Pageant of Corydon, the Pioneer Capital of Indiana 1816–1916.* New Albany, Ind.: Baker Printing, 1916.

———. *The Pageant of Thetford.* Vermonter Press, 1911.

———. *The Pageant of St. Johnsbury.* Vermont: Caledonian Press, 1911.

———. *The Bronxville Christmas Mystery.* Bronxville, N.Y.: Christ Church, 1914.

———. *Illinois Day Celebration for the University of Illinois.* Champaign-Urbana, Ill., 1917.

———. *The Pageant of Indiana.* Indianapolis: Hollenbeck Press, 1916.

———. *The Centennial Pageant of Indiana University 1820- 1920.* Bloomington, Ind., 1920.

———. *The Pageant of Bloomington and Indiana University.* Bloomington, Ind., 1916.

———. *The Pageant of Cape Cod.* Boston: Blanchard Printing Co., 1914.

———. *The Pageant of Darien.* New York: Clover Press, 1913.

Lee, Henry Washington. *George Washington*. Chicago: The Calumet Record, 1932.

Lee, Rebecca Washington (Smith). *Following the Lone Star*. Fort Worth, Tex.: 1924.

Louisiana: *The Attakapas Trail*. Morgan City, La.: King-Hannaford Co., 1923.

MacKay, Constance D'Arcy. *America Triumphant*. New York: Appleton, 1926.

_____. *The Historical Pageant of Portland, Maine*. Portland: Southwirth Printing Co., 1913. (Director of Dances, Gertrude K. Colby; composer, Will C. Macfarlane).

_____. *Memorial Day Pageant*. New York and London: Harper Bros., 1916.

_____. *The Pageant of Schenectady*. Gazette Press, 1912.

MacKaye, Hazel. *The Quest of Youth, a Pageant for Schools*. Washington, D.C.: U.S. Government Printing Office, 1924.

MacKaye, Percy. *The New Citizenship; a Civic Ritual Devised for Places of Public Meeting in America*. New York: Macmillan Co., 1915.

_____. *The Roll Call, A Masque of the Red Cross for Community Acting and Singing*. Scene & costume designs by Robert Edmond Jones; cover design, Arnold Genthe; Director of initial production in Washington, Irving Pichel. National Headquarters of American Red Cross, Washington, D.C., 1918.

Mahan, Bruce Ellis. *The Pioneers, Pageant of Early Iowa*. Iowa State Historical Society, 1927.

_____. *The History of the Indian, a Pageant of Early Iowa*. Iowa City, Iowa, 1928.

Maine: *Historic Pageant of Fort Fairfield & Aroostock Valley*. Fort Fairfield, Maine: Review Press, 1916.

Marble, Mrs. Annie (Russell). *Pageant: Heroines of Literature*. Worcester, Mass.: Communications Press, 1915.

Massachusetts: *The Mohawk Trail*. North Adams, Mass.: Excelsior Printing Co., 1914.

Mather, Eleanne Price. *Thou Philadelphia, 250th Anniversary of 1st arrival of William Penn in 1682*. Philadelphia. John C. Winston Co., 1932.

McEnroe, Fanny Clapp. *Pageant of Craftsbury*. St. Johnsbury, Vt., 1929.

McGroarty, John Steven. *The Mission Play*. Los Angeles, 1911.

Messer, Nellie Stearns. *A Pageant Drama of Salem*. Salem, Mass.: Newcomb & Gauss, 1926.

Michigan: *The Pageant of Escanaba*. Escanaba, Mich., 1917.

Miller, Estelle. *Uncle Sam's S.O.S.* Boston, 1918.

Miller, Florence Maria. *Historical Pageants, State Normal School*. Fitchburg, Mass., 1911.

Minnesota: *Pageant of Minnesota History under auspices of St. Paul Institute of Art*. St. Paul, Minn., 1911.

Missouri, a Pageant and Masque. Columbia, Mo.: Press of Columbia Printing Co., 1920.

Munson, Harold, and Howard Munson. *Sibley Centennial Pageant*. St. Paul, Minn., 1934.

Murphy, Ethel Allen. *The Triumph of Humanity; a Pageant of Victory, Reconstruction and Democracy*. Women's Committee, Council of National Defense. Ky., 1919.

_____. *The Victory of the Gardens*. Written for U.S. School Garden Army Washington, D.C., 1919.

National Education Association of U.S. *The Drama of American Independence: Pageant Episodes for Schools and Colleges in Commemoration of 150 Anniversary of Signing of Declaration of Independence*. Washington, D.C.: NEA, 1926.

National Pageantry Corporation. *Grand Patriotic Pageant, The Glory of Old Glory*. Directed by the National Pageantry Corporation, Cedar Rapids, Iowa: The Torch Press, 1917.

Nettleton, George Henry. *The Book of the Yale Pageant*. New Haven, Conn.: Yale University Press, 1916.

Nevada: The Pageant of Nevada History, 1914.

New Hampshire: *The Durham Pageant*. Manchester, N.H.: Williams Printing Co., 1918.

New Jersey: State College Trenton. *Two Patriotic Pageants.* Planned and written by classes in the English and Historical Departments of N. J. State Normal School. Boston: Baker & Co., 1921.

New Jersey: *Pageant for 200 Anniversary of Settlement of Haddenfield, N. J.* Haddenfield Publishing Co., 1913.

New Jersey: *Program of the Pageant and Folk Dances in Celebration of the 225 Anniversary of the Settlement of Caldwell, N. J.* New York: Vechten Waring Co., 1915.

New York: *Pageant for 275 Anniversary.* Founding of Southhampton, N.J., 1640–1915. Sag Harbor, N.Y.: J. H. Hunt, 1915.

Oakley, Violet. *The Book of Words. Westchester County Historical Pageant.* Philadelphia, 1909.

Ohio: *The Reformation, a Pageant by the Students of the College of Wooster in Commemoration of 400 Anniversary of Protestant Reformation.* 1917.

Oregon: *An Historical Pageant of Milwaukie.* Compiled by the writer's program of the WPA in the state of Oregon. 1941.

Oregon: *Salem Centennial Pageant.* WPA in Oregon, sponsored by Salem Centennial Committee. 1940.

Owen, Grace Arlington. *The Wonderful Story of Illinois.* Illinois Centennial Committee. 1918.

Oxnard, Henry E. *Anawan Rock Pageant. The Atonement of Anawan, a Tercentenary Drama from the Indian Point of View.* Rehobeth, Mass. Boston, Chicago: Pilgrim Press, 1921.

Park, James Stanton. *The Pageant of Old Detroit.* Detroit: Speaker-Hines Press, 1915.

Parker, Mrs. Maude May. *Louisiana, a Pageant of Yesterday and Today.* New Orleans: Hauser Printing Co., 1917.

Pashley, Hattie Sinnard, and Eleanor Reese Dunn. *Pageant of Palos.* Presented by people, Palos Township Chicago: Hildman Printing Co., 1916.

Patten, Cora Mel, and Elma Ehrlich. *A Peace Pageant for Children and Young People.* Chicago, 1915.

Payne, Fanny Ursula. *Plays and Pageants of Democracy.* New York and London: Harper, 1919.

Pearce, Haywood Jefferson. *King Cotton, an Allegorical Pageant.* Atlanta: Johnson & Dallis Printing Co., 1920.

Pearson-Spellman, Margaret. *Pageant of Oklahoma 40 Anniversary of Chilocco Indian School.* Chilocco: The Indian Print Shop, 1924.

Penrose, Stephen Beasley Linnard. *How The West Was Won,* with Percy Jewett Burrell. Walla Walla, Wash.: Bulletin Printing Co., 1923.

Poler, Nora. *The Pageant of Southhampton.* Westfield, Mass.: W. F. Leitch & Co., 1930.

Rice, Wallace de Groot Cecil. *The Masque of Illinois.* Springfield, Ill.: Jefferson Printing Co., 1918.

———. *The Pageant of the Illinois Country.* Illinois State Journal Co., 1918.

———. *Primavera, the Masque of Santa Barbara.* Santa Barbara, Calif., 1920.

Riley, Mrs. Alice Cushing (Donaldson). *The Brotherhood of Man; a Pageant of International Peace for Pageantry Class Institute of 1921.* Drama League of America. New York: A. S. Barnes, 1924.

Rockwell, Ethel Theodora. *Children of Old Wisconsin.* Madison Bureau of Dramatic Activities, University Extension Division, 1935.

———. *Children of Old Carolina, Historical Pageant.* Chapel Hill, N.C.: University of North Carolina Press, 1925.

———. *Star Spangled Banner Pageant.* Madison, Wis., 1914.

———. *The Freeport Pageant of the Black Hawk Country.* Wisconsin, 1915.

———. *The Pageant of William Woods College.* Fulton, Mo., 1915.

Samuels, Maurice Victor. *A Pageant of the Strong.* New York: Jarvis Maxwell, 1923.

Scales, Caroline Lydia Greenleaf. *The Olden Time and the New*. Pageant for Commencement and Dedication of New Buildings at State Normal & Training School. New York: Oswego Normal School Press, 1914.

Schulz, William Eben. *Cantonia: A Historical Pageant in Commemoration of the One-Hundredth Anniversary of the Founding of the Town of Carlton, Missouri*. 1930.

Sexton, Ethelyn. *March on Michigan: a Pageant of the Making of a State*. Galesburg, Mich.: Ayers Press, 1934.

Shumway, Mrs. Lucy C. *The Grange in the Community*. Towanda, Pa.: Towanda Printing Co., 1923.

Smith, Henry Augustine. *The City Beautiful*. New York City Centenary Conservation Committee, 1919.

Spear, Samuel W. *Washington and Genet: An Historical Pageant*. New York: Hamilton Printing Company, 1932.

Spencer, Mrs. Lillian White. *Pageant of Colorado*. Music by Charles Wakefield Cadman. Denver, Colo.: Welch-Haffner Printing Co., 1927.

Stalker, Clara Inglis. *The Student's Dream*. Commemorative for 100 Years of Statehood. Chicago: F. W. Black, 1918.

Stevens, Augusta. *Romantic Indiana*. Indianapolis: Bobbs-Merrill, 1916.

Stevens, Thomas Wood. *Pageant of Virginia*. Richmond, Va.: The Virginia Historical Pageant Association, 1922.

_____ . *Yorktown Sesquicentennial Pageants*. Washington, D.C.: U.S. Government Printing Office, 1933.

_____ . *Magna Carta, A Pageant Drama*. Seattle Association, American Bar Association, in Chicago, 1930. Yale University Press, 1930.

_____ . *The Drawing of the Sword Together with the Text of the Red Cross Pageant*. Boston: CC Birchard & Co., 1918. Prepared for celebration at Carnegie Institute of Technology, 1917.

_____ . *Book of Words, the Pageant of Newark*. Newark, the Committee of One Hundred, 1916.

_____ . *The Dunes under Four Flags; an Historical Pageant of the Dunes of Indiana*. 1917.

_____ . *"Fighting for Freedom," Independence Day Pageant*. St. Louis: Britt Printing Co., 1918.

_____ . *The Books of Words of the Pageant and Masque of Saint Louis*. The words of the pageant by Thomas Wood Stevens; the words of the masque by Percy MacKaye. St. Louis: Nixon-Jones Printing Co., 1914.

_____ . *The Historical Pageant of Madison County*. Illinois, 1912.

Sutton, Vida Ravenscroft. *A Pageant of Women of the Sixteenth Century*. New York: The Woman's Press, 1927.

Taft, Linwood. *An English May Festival*. New York: A. S. Barnes, 1929.

Tanner, Virginia. *The Pageant of the Little Town of X*. Boston: A. T. Bliss, 1914.

_____ . *Albany's Tercentenary 1624–1924, "The Founding of the City of Albany."* Albany, N.Y.: J. B. Lyon, 1924.

_____ . *A Pageant of Quincy*. Concord, N.H.: Rumford Press, 1925.

_____ . *A Pageant of Portsmouth*. Concord, N.H.: Rumford Press, 1923.

_____ . *Pageant at Bennington Vermont*. Concord, N.H.: Rumford Press, 1927.

_____ . *A Pageant of the State of Maine*. 1928.

Tobey, Francis, and Nellie Margaret Statler. *Two Community Entertainments*. Colorado State College, Greely, 1917.

Wallace, Florence Magill. *The Seven Ages of Giving*. New York: S. French, 1910.

Warner, Estelle Damon. *The Story of the Grange*. Williamsburg, Mass., 1922.

Watson, Mrs. Annah. *The Path of Progress, 1620–1920*. Memphis Pilgrim Tercentenary Association, 1920.

Weyrauch, Martin H. *The Pageant of Brooklyn*. 1915.

White, Jeanette (Morris). *Louisiana in Song and Story*. Lake Charles, La.: 1924.

Williams, Francis Howard. *Philadelphia, Historic Pageant*. Notes and adaptations by Ellis Paxson Oberholtzer, Master of the Pageant. Philadelphia Historical Pageant Committee, 1912.

Wisconsin: *A Pageant of the University*. Written and directed by class in pageantry. Madison, Wis.: F. C. Blied & Co., 1914.

Wisconsin: *A Pageant of Education*. Written by class in pageantry. Madison, Wis.: F. C. Blied & Co., 1915.

Wood, Frances Gilchrist. *Pageant of Ridgewood, N. J.* Paterson Press Print, 1915.

Woodward, Walter Carleton. *The Pageant of Earlham College: in Quest of Freedom*. Richmond, Ind.: Nicholson Press, 1922.

Wright, Theodore Lyman, and Marion Hawthorne Hedges. *The Beloit Pageant*. Beloit: Beloit Daily News Printing Co., 1916.

Wyndham, Margaret. *Historical Pageant of the University of Tulsa*. Oklahoma, 1928.

Young, Cecila Mary. *The Illini Trail*. Chicago: C. M. Young, 1918.

Pageants—Other Collections

Each library identified in this list has a special collection where pageants can be found, as detailed under the bibliographic heading "Archives and Special Collections." Only dates are provided here, since publication information is not necessary to locate the material.

Baker, George Pierce. *Allegheny Centennial Pageant*. 1915, Brown University Library.

———. *A Pageant of Engineering Progress*. 1930, UCLA Library.

———. *A Pageant of Hollis Hall, 1763–1913*. 1913, Brown University Library.

———. *Peterborough Memorial Pageant*. 1910, Harvard University Library.

Barber, Lucia Gale, with Laura Palmer Ingalls. *The Pageant of the Tree*. For the benefit of the Child Welfare Work of the Fathers and Mothers Club. 1916, Boston Public Library.

Bates, Esther. *Springfield Colonial Pageant*. 1908. Reprinted in *Pageants and Pageantry*, Boston: Ginn & Company, 1912.

Beegle, Mary Porter, and Jack Randall Crawford. *Pageant of Elizabeth*. 1914, Boston Public Library.

———. *The Romance of Work*. Given for the Convention of the National League of Women Workers by the New York Association. 1914, Brown University Library.

Carman, Bliss, and M. P. King. *Daughter of Dawn*. 1913. (not located)

Clark, Lotta. *Cave Life to City Life, Pageant of the Perfect City*. 1910, Brown University Library.

———. *Charlestown Pageant*. 1910, 1912, Boston Public Library.

———. *Torchbearers*. 1917, 1918, Boston Public Library.

Copeland, Jennie Freeman. *Pageant of Boston*. 1916, Boston Public Library.

Crawford, Jack Randall. *Robin of Sherwood*. 1915, Dartmouth College Library.

———. *Dante, A Pageant*. 1921, New York.

Cumer, Helen. *The Pageant of Fairmont*. 1916, Harvard University Library.

Dallin, Mrs. Cyrus E. (Vittoria); with Lotta A. Clark, Lucia Gale Barber, Vesper L. George, and Grant Drake. *Pageant of Education*. 1908, Boston Public Library.

Dance—Pageant of Egypt, Greece, and India. 1916, Berkeley Greek Theatre, University of California, Berkeley Archives.

Eager, Margaret MacLaren. *Brattleboro Pageant.* 1912, Pocumtuck Valley Memorial Association Library, Deerfield, Mass.

_____. *Bennington Pageant.* 1911. Pocumtuck Valley Memorial Association Library, Deerfield, Mass.

_____. *Duxbury Days.* 1909. Pocumtuck Valley Memorial Association Library, Deerfield, Mass.

_____. *Hartford Pageant.* 1911. Pocumtuck Valley Memorial Association Library, Deerfield, Mass.

_____. *Ipswich Pageant.* 1910. Pocumtuck Valley Memorial Association Library, Deerfield, Mass.

_____. *Pageant of Northampton.* 1911. Pocumtuck Valley Memorial Association Library, Deerfield, Mass.

_____. *Pageant of Plattsburgh.* 1914. Pocumtuck Valley Memorial Association Library, Deerfield, Mass.

_____. *Pageant of Old Deerfield.* 1910, 1913, 1916. Pocumtuck Valley Memorial Association Library, Deerfield, Mass.

_____. *Pageant of Salem.* 1913. Pocumtuck Valley Memorial Association Library, Deerfield, Mass.

_____. *Pageant of Utica.* 1914. Pocumtuck Valley Memorial Association Library, Deerfield, Mass.

_____. *Rochester Shakespeare Pageant.* 1916. Pocumtuck Valley Memorial Association Library, Deerfield, Mass.

Ganssle, Margaret Plank. *The New Day.* 1918. UCLA Library.

Gould, Norma. Several pageants in Naima Prevots' private collection.

Grimball, Elizabeth. *The Hope of the World.* 1918.

Gruver, Suzanne Cary. *Daughters of Wisdom, Pageant of Famous Women.* 1917. Boston Public Library.

Hadlow, S. Gertrude. *The Pageant of Twinsburg.* 1917. Boston Public Library.

Hayden, J. Willard, Jr. *The Pageant of Lexington.* 1915. Harvard University Library.

Jackson, Maude M. *Pageant of Industries.* 1916. Harvard University Library.

Knickerbocker, Vera, and Miriam Thurman. *A Pageant of Wichita.* 1915. Boston Public Library.

Lewisohn, Alice and Irene. *Jephthah's Daughter.* 1915. Dance Collection. New York Public Library at Lincoln Center.

_____. *Pageant in Celebration of Twentieth Anniversary of Henry Street Settlement House.* 1913 (not located).

Light of Asia. 1918. Information and pictures in UCLA Library.

MacKay, Constance D'Arcy. "Hawthorne Pageant." In *Patriotic Plays and Pageants for Young People.* New York: Holt, 1912.

_____. "Pageant of Patriots, 1911." In *Patriotic Plays and Pageants for Young People.* New York: Holt, 1912.

_____. *Pageant of Sunshine and Shadow.* 1916. Theatre Collection, New York Public Library at Lincoln Center.

_____. *The Pilgrims.* Springfield, Ohio, 1920. Boston Public Library.

MacKaye, Hazel. *The Awakening.* 1916. Dartmouth College Library.

_____. *The New Vision, A Masque of Modern Industry.* 1916. Dartmouth College Library.

_____. *Pageant of Athena.* 1915. Dartmouth College Library.

_____. *Pageant of Susan B. Anthony.* 1915. Dartmouth College Library.

_____. *The Portals of Light.* 1916. Dartmouth College Library.

———— . *Six Patriots of American Life, A Woman's Suffrage Pageant.* 1914. Dartmouth College Library.

———— . *Suffrage Allegory.* 1913. Dartmouth College Library.

———— . *Uncle Sam's Birthday Pageant.* 1913. Dartmouth College Library.

MacKaye, Hazel, and Mrs. Christian D. Hemmick. *A Pageant for Peace.* 1915. Dartmouth College Library.

MacKaye, Percy. *Caliban By the Yellow Sands.* 1916. Dartmouth College Library.

———— . *The Evergreen Tree, A Masque of Christmas Time for Community Singing and Acting.* Music by Arthur Farwell; scenes and costume design by Robert Edmond Jones. 1917. Dartmouth College Library.

———— . *George Washington.* Scene design by Robert Edmond Jones, note on production by Walter Hampden. 1920. Dartmouth College Library.

———— . *The Gloucester Pageant.* Based on Percy MacKaye's *The Canterbury Pilgrims,* arranged as a dramatic pageant; directed by Eric Pope, music by Walter Damrosch, dances by Virginia Tanner. 1909. Dartmouth College Library.

———— . *Sanctuary, A Bird Masque.* Meriden, N.H. Directed by Joseph Lindon Smith, original music by Frederick S. Converse and Arthur Farwell. 1913. Dartmouth College Library.

Massachusetts: *Pageant of Old Salem.* 1913. Boston Public Library.

Massachusetts: *Womanhood, A Pageant Portraying the Progress of Women.* 1917. Brown University Library.

New York: *Plattsburgh Centennial Celebration.* 1914. Harvard University Library.

A Pageant of Nations. 1914. Brown University.

A Pageant of the Melting Pot. 1914. Brown University Library.

Parker, Louis N. *The Bury Saint Edmund's Pageant.* 1907. Harvard University Library. (Listed as *The St. Edmundsbury Pageant* in the APA Bulletin.)

———— . *The Sherbourne Pageant.* 1905. Brown University Library.

———— . *The York Pageant.* 1909. Harvard University Library.

Reed, John. *Paterson Silk Strike Pageant.* 1913. Boston Public Library.

Rice, Wallace, and Kenneth Sawyer Goodman. *The Glorious Gateway of the West.* 1916. UCLA Library.

Seward, Edith de Charms, and Azubah J. Latham. *The Masque of Joy or Drudgery Transformed.* 1914. Teachers College Archives, Columbia University.

Smith, Joseph Lindon, and Henry Copley Greene. *A Pageant of Boston and the Old South Church.* 1913. Harvard University Library.

Steele, Evelyn Agnes. *The Partheneia: A Masque.* 1914. University of California, Berkeley Archives.

Stevens, Thomas Wood. *Adventure, A Pageant-Drama of Life and Chance.* New York: National Bureau of Causality & Surety Underwriters, 1923. University of Arizona Library, Tucson.

———— . *Book of Words, An Historical Pageant of Illinois.* 1909. University of Arizona Library, Tucson.

———— . *The Book of Words of Saint Clair County Pageant.* 1914. University of Arizona Library, Tucson.

———— . *The Centennial Pageant of Rensselaer Polytechnic Institute.* 1925. University of Arizona Library, Tucson.

———— . *The Entrada of Coronado.* 1945. University of Arizona Library, Tucson.

———— . *Joan of Arc.* 1932. University of Arizona Library, Tucson.

———— . *Missouri 110 Years Ago.* 1921. University of Arizona Library, Tucson.

———— . *The Pageant Drama of Old Fort Niagara.* 1934. University of Arizona Library, Tucson.

———— . *A Pageant of the Italian Renaissance.* 1909. University of Arizona Library, Tucson.

———— . *A Pageant of the Old Northwest.* 1911. University of Arizona Library, Tucson.

_____ . *A Pageant of Victory and Peace.* 1919. University of Arizona Library, Tucson.

Stevens, Thomas Wood, and Kenneth Sawyer Goodman. *Masque of East and West.* Includes *A Pageant of Independence Day.* 1914. Boston Public Library.

Tanner, Virginia. *Historical Masque of Rockport.* 1914. Boston Public Library.

_____ . *Pageant of the Machias Valley.* 1913. Boston Public Library.

Tanner, Virginia, and Thomas Wood Stevens. *The Technology Pageant and The Masque of Power.* 1916. Harvard University Library.

Teachers College, Columbia University: *The Conflict.* First presented in 1913 by the Department of Physical Education by Anne M. Thornton, Jesse F. Williams, Eva Alberti. Presented again in 1921 by Gertrude K. Colby at Teachers College. Teachers College Library, Columbia University.

_____ . *A Festival of the Flag of Stars.* 1919. Teachers College Archives.

_____ . *A Festival of Gifts.* 1918. Teachers College Archives.

_____ . *The Light of the Jewel.* 1919. Teachers College Archives.

_____ . *The Spirit of the East.* 1920. Teachers College Archives.

_____ . *The Trouveur.* 1915. Teachers College Archives.

Thorp, Josephine. *The Road to Tomorrow.* 1920, Boston Public Library.

Van Leehuwen, Nora. *Festival and Pageant of Nations.* 1914. Theatre Collection, New York Public Library at Lincoln Center.

Secondary Sources

Books

Addams, Jane. *The Second Twenty Years at Hull House.* New York: Macmillan Co., 1930.

_____ . *The Spirit of Youth and the City Streets.* New York: Macmillan Co., 1909.

_____ . *Twenty Years at Hull House.* New York: Macmillan Co., 1910.

Ainsworth, Dorothy S. *The History of Physical Education in College for Women.* New York: A. S. Barnes & Co., 1930.

Altschuler, Glenn C. *Race, Ethnicity, and Class in American Social Thought 1865–1919.* Arlington Heights, Ill.: Harlan Davidson, Inc., 1982.

Amberg, George. *Ballet, The Emergence of an American Art.* New York: New American Library, 1949.

American Pageant Association "Who's Who" in pageantry, issued by the American Pageant Association (founded at Boston, 1913) in the endeavor to establish a uniform standard for pageants and pageantry in America. New York: American Pageant Association, 1914.

Angell, Emmet. *Play.* Boston: Little, 1910.

Appia, Adolphe. *Music and the Art of the Theatre.* Translated by Robert W. Corrigan and Mary Douglas Dirks. Edited by Barnard Hewitt. Coral Gables, Fla.: University of Miami Press, 1962.

_____ . *The Work of Living Art; a Theory of the Theatre; and Man Is the Measure of All Things.* Trans. H. D. Albright and Barnard Hewitt, resp. Coral Gables, Fla.: University of Miami Press, 1960.

Appleton, Lilla. *A Comparative Study of the Play Activities of Adult Savages and Civilized Children: An Adult Investigation of the Scientific Basis of Education.* Chicago: University of Chicago Press, 1910.

Archambault, Reginald D., ed. *John Dewey on Education, Selected Writings.* New York: The Modern Library, 1964.

Atkinson, Carroll, and Eugene T. Maleska. *The Story of Education.* Philadelphia: Chilton Co. Book Division, 1962.

Bailey, L. H. *The Country-Life Movement in the United States.* New York: Macmillan Co., 1911.

Baker, Blanche Merritt. *Theatre and Allied Arts; A Guide to Books Dealing with the History, Criticism and Technique of the Drama and Theatre and Related Arts and Crafts.* New York: Wilson, 1952.

Baker, George Pierce. *The Development of Shakespeare as a Dramatist.* New York: Macmillan Co., 1907.

_____. *Dramatic Technique.* Boston: Houghton Mifflin Company, 1919.

_____. *The Principles of Argumentation.* Boston: Ginn & Company, 1895.

Baldwin, James Mark. *Social and Ethical Interpretations in Mental Development: A Study in Social Psychology.* New York: Macmillan Co., 1897.

Bancroft, Jessie. *Games for the Playground, Home, School and Gymnasium.* New York: Macmillan Co., 1909.

Barnum, Madalene Demarest. *American Festivals for Elementary Schools.* Prepared under the auspices of the New York Center of the Drama League of America. New York: Samuel French, 1916.

Bates, Esther Willard. *The Art of Producing Pageants.* Boston: Walter H. Baker Company, 1925.

_____. *How to Produce a Pageant in Honor of George Washington.* Written for the bicentennial celebration in 1932. Washington, D.C.: United States George Washington Bicentennial Commission, 1931.

_____. *Pageants and Pageantry.* With an Introduction by William Orr. Boston: Ginn & Company, 1912.

Beegle, Mary Porter, and Jack Randall Crawford. *Community Drama and Pageantry.* New Haven, Conn.: Yale University Press, 1916. Contains very extensive bibliography indicating the wide sources utilized by pageant masters. This book is in the UCLA and Teachers College Libraries.

Beegle, Mary Porter. *The Shakespeare Tercentenary. Suggestions for School and College Celebrations.* Prepared by Drama League of America by Percival Chubb, Mary P. Beegle, Mary Wood Hinman, William E. Bohm. Washington, D.C., 1916.

Bender, Thomas. *Community and Social Change in America.* New Brunswick, N.J.: Rutgers University Press, 1978.

Bentley, Joanne. *Hallie Flanagan, A Life in the American Theatre.* New York: Alfred A. Knopf, 1988.

Bergeron, David Moore. *English Civic Pageantry 1558–1642.* Columbia: University of South Carolina Press, 1971.

Best, A. S. *The Drama League.* Chicago: Doubleday, 1914.

Bestor, Arthur Eugene, Jr. *An Historical and Bibliographical Guide.* Chautauqua, N.Y.: Chautauqua Press, 1934.

Bitney, Mayme. *Pageants and Plays for Holidays.* Dayton, Ohio: Paine, 1926.

Boris, Eileen. *Art and Labor: Ruskin, Morris and the Craftsman Ideal in America.* Philadelphia: Temple University Press, 1986.

Bowers, William L. *The Country Life Movement in America 1900–1920.* Port Washington, N.Y.: Kennikat Press, 1974.

Brilliant, Nathan, and Libbie Braverman. *Religious Pageants for the Jewish School.* Cincinnati, Ohio: Union of American, Hebrew Congregations, 1941.

Brockett, Oscar G., and Robert R. Findlay. *Century of Innovation: A History of European and American Theatre and Drama since 1870.* Englewood Cliffs, N.J.: Prentice-Hall, Inc., 1973.

Brockett, Oscar G. *History of the Theatre.* Boston: Allyn & Bacon, 1968.

Brooks, Van Wyck. *America's Coming of Age.* New York: Viking Press, 1915.

Burchenal, Elizabeth. *Folk-Dances and Singing Games: Dances of the People.* 3 vols. New York: G. Schirmer, 1909–22.

Burleigh, Louise. *The Community Theatre in Theory and Practice.* Boston: Little, Brown and Company, 1917.

Case, Victoria and Ormond, Robert. *We Called It Culture: The Story of Chautauqua.* New York: Doubleday, 1948.

Caughey, John. *Los Angeles: Biography of a City.* Berkeley, Calif.: University of California Press, 1976.

Cavallo, Dominick. *Muscles and Morals, Organized Playgrounds and Urban Reform, 1880–1920.* Philadelphia: University of Pennsylvania Press, 1981.

Chalif, Louis. *The Chalif Text Book of Dancing.* New York: Vol. 1, 1914. Vol. 2, 1915.

Chamberlain, Alexander. *The Child: A Study in the Evolution of Man.* London: W. Scott, 1900.

Cheney, Sheldon. *The Art Theatre: A Discussion of Its Ideals, Its Organization and Its Promise as a Corrective for Present Evils in the Commercial Theatre.* New York: Alfred A. Knopf, 1917.

———. *The New Movement in the Theatre.* New York: Mitchell Kennerly, 1914.

———. *The Open-Air Theatre.* New York: Mitchell Kennerly, 1918.

———, ed. *Isadora Duncan: The Art of the Dance.* New York: Theatre Arts Books, 1928.

Chubb, Percival. *Festivals and Plays in Schools and Elsewhere.* New York: Harper & Bros., 1912.

Clark, R. H., and C. M. Torrey. *California Play and Pageant.* Berkeley, Calif.: English Club, University of California, 1913.

Cohen, Selma Jeanne. *Doris Humphrey: An Artist First.* Middletown, Conn.: Wesleyan University Press, 1972.

Colby, Gertrude K. *Natural Rhythms and Dances.* New York: A. S. Barnes & Co., 1922.

Community Drama. Playground and Recreation Association, 1926.

Community Drama: Suggestions for a Community Wide Program of Dramatic Activities. New York: Community Service, 1921.

Corathel, Elisabeth. *Oberammergau and Its Passion Play.* Westminister, Md.: Newman Press, 1960.

Craig, Anne A. T. *The Dramatic Festival.* New York: G. P. Putnam's Sons, 1912.

Craig, Edward Gordon. *On the Art of the Theatre.* Chicago: Brownes' Bookstore, 1911.

———. *Towards a New Theatre.* London: J. M. Dent & Sons, 1913.

Cremin, Lawrence. *The Transformation of the School: Progressivism in American Education.* New York: Alfred A. Knopf, 1961.

Cremin, Lawrence, and Merle L. Borrowman. *Public Schools in Our Democracy.* New York: Macmillan Co., 1956.

Cremin, Lawrence A., David A. Shannon, and Mary Evelyn Townsend. *Teachers College, Columbia University.* New York: Columbia University Press, 1954.

Crowley, Alice Lewisohn. *The Neighborhood Playhouse: Leaves from a Theatre Scrapbook.* New York: Theatre Arts Books, 1959.

Crum, Mason. *A Guide to Religious Pageantry.* New York: Macmillan Co., 1923.

Curtis, Henry. *Education through Play.* New York: Macmillan Co., 1915.

Davis, Allen. *American Heroine: The Life and Legend of Jane Addams.* New York: Oxford University Press, 1973.

———. *Spearheads for Reform. The Social Settlements and the Progressive Movement 1890–1914.* New York: Oxford University Press, 1967. New edition with no major changes: Rutgers University Press, 1984.

Davis, Caroline Hill. *Pageants in Great Britain and the United States: A List of References.* New York Public Library, 1916.

Davol, Ralph. *A Handbook of American Pageantry*. Taunton, Mass.: Davol Publishing Company, 1914.

Day, Ernest Hermitage. *Ober-Ammergau and the Passion Play*. London: A. R. Mowbray and Company, Ltd.; Milwaukee: The Young Churchman Co., 1910.

De-Hart-Matthews, Jane. *The Federal Theatre Project 1935–1939: Plays, Relief and Politics*. Princeton: Princeton University Press, 1967.

Dewey, John. *Democracy and Education: An Introduction to the Philosophy of Education*. New York: Macmillan Co., 1916.

———. *The Educational Situation*. Chicago: University of Chicago Press, 1902.

———. *John Dewey on Education, Selected Writings*. New York: The Modern Library, 1964.

———. *The School and Society*. Chicago: University of Chicago Press, 1900.

Dewey, John, and Evelyn Dewey. *Schools of Tomorrow*. New York: Dutton, 1915.

Dickinson, Thomas Herbert. *The Case of American Drama*. Boston: Houghton, Mifflin Company, 1915.

———. *The Insurgent Theatre*. New York: B. W. Huebsch, 1917.

Dictionary of American Biography. New York: C. Scribner's Sons, 1937.

Dorjan, Ethel. *Luther Halsey Gulick*. New York: Teachers College, Columbia University, 1934.

The Drama in Adult Education. London: H. M. Stationary Office, 1926.

Drama League of America. *The Shakespeare Tercentenary: Suggestions for School and College Celebrations of the Tercentenary of Shakespeare's Death in 1616*. Prepared by the Drama League of America under the direction of Percival Chubb, Mary P. Beegle, Mary Wood Hinman, William E. Bohm. Washington, D.C.: National Press, 1916.

Dubofsky, Melvyn. *Industrialism and the American Worker, 1865–1920*. Arlington Heights, Ill.: AHM Publishing Corporation, 1975.

Duffus, Robert Luther. *The American Renaissance*. New York: Alfred A. Knopf, 1928.

Dulles, Foster R. *America Learns to Play: A History of Popular Recreation*. New York: Appleton-Century, 1940.

Dye, Charity. *Pageant Suggestions for the Indiana Statehood Centennial Celebration*. Indianapolis, 1916.

Earhart, Mary. *Frances Willard—From Prayers to Politics*. Chicago: University of Chicago Press, 1944.

Evans, Marshal Blakemore. *The Passion Play of Lucerne*. New York: The Modern Language Association of America, 1943.

Farwell, Brice, ed. *A Guide to the Music of Arthur Farwell and to the Microfilm Collection of His Work: A Centennial Commemoration Prepared by His Children*. Briarcliff Manor, N.Y.: B. Farwell, 1972.

Fisher, David James. *Romain Rolland and the Politics of Intellectual Engagement*. Berkeley, Calif.: University of California Press, 1988.

Flannagan, Hallie. *Arena*. New York: Limelight Editions, 1940.

Forbush, William. *The Boy Problem: A Study in Social Pedagogy*. Boston: Pilgrim Press, 1901.

Forty-seven Workshop. *Plays of the 47 Workshop*. New York: Brentano's, 1918, 1920, 1922, 1925.

Friedman, Saul S. *The Oberammergau Passion Play: A Lance against Civilization*. Carbondale: Southern Illinois University Press, 1984.

Gard, Robert Edward. *Grassroots Theatre: A Search for Regional Arts in America*. Madison: University of Wisconsin Press, 1955.

Geertz, Clifford. *The Interpretation of Cultures*. New York: Basic Books, 1973.

Goist, Park D. *From Main Street to State Street: Town, City, and Community in America*. Port Washington, N.Y.: Kennikat Press, 1977.

Gould, Joseph E. *The Chautauqua Movement*. New York: State University of New York, 1961.

Green, Martin. *New York 1913, The Armory Show and the Paterson Strike Pageant*. New York: Charles Scribner's Sons, 1988.

Green, Paul. *Dramatic Heritage*. New York: Samuel French, 1953.

Grover, Edwin Osgood, ed. *Annals of an Era: Percy MacKaye and the MacKaye Family, 1826–1932*. Washington, D.C.: Pioneer Press, 1932.

Gulick, Luther. *The Dynamic of Manhood*. New York: Association Press, 1917.

———. *The Healthful Art of Dancing*. New York: Doubleday, Page and Co., 1910.

———. *Mind and Work*. New York: Doubleday, 1908.

———. *A Philosophy of Play*. New York: C. Scribner's Sons, 1920.

Hall, G. Stanley. *Adolescence*. New York: D. Appleton and Company, 1904.

———. *Educational Problems*. New York: D. Appleton and Company, 1911.

———. *Life and Confessions of a Psychologist*. New York: D. Appleton and Company, 1923.

Harris, Herbert. *American Labor*. New Haven, Conn.: Yale University Press; London: H. Milford, Oxford University Press, 1938.

Harrison, Harry P. as told to Karl Detzer. *Culture under Canvas, The Story of Tent Chautauqua*. New York: Hastings House, 1958.

Harvard University Dramatic Club. *Plays of the Harvard Dramatic Club*. New York: Brentano's, 1918–19.

H'Doubler, Margaret. *The Dance*. New York: Harcourt, Brace & Co., 1925.

———. *Dance and Its Place in Education*. New York: Harcourt, Brace & Co., 1925.

———. *A Manual of Dancing*. Madison, Wis.: Tracey & Kilgore, 1921.

Henderson, Archibald., ed. *Pioneering a People's Theatre*. Chapel Hill: University of North Carolina Press, 1945.

Hobsbawm, Eric, and Terence Ranger, eds. *The Invention of Tradition*. New York: Cambridge University Press, 1983.

Hofstader, Richard. *The Age of Reform*. New York: Alfred A. Knopf, 1955.

———. *Social Darwinism in American Thought, 1860–1915*. Boston: Beacon Press, 1944.

Holt, Roland. *A List of Music for Plays and Pageants*. New York: D. Appleton and Company, 1925.

Hornblow, Arthur. *A History of the Theatre in America*. 2 vols. Philadelphia: J.B. Lippincott Company, 1919; Reprint ed. New York: Benjamin Blom, 1935.

Howe, Frederick. *The Modern City and Its Problems*. New York: C. Scribner's Sons, 1915.

Indiana State Library, Indianapolis. *List of Books on Pageants*. Indiana State Library. Indianapolis, 1915.

Irwin, Alfreda L. *Three Taps of the Gavel: Pledge to the Future: The Chautauqua Story*. Westfield, N.Y.: The Westfield Republican, 1970.

James, William. *The Principles of Psychology*. 2 vols. New York: Henry Holt & Company, 1899.

Johnson, George. *Education by Plays and Games*. Boston: Ginn and Company, 1907.

Kaplan, Wendy. *"The Art That Is Life": The Arts and Crafts Movement in America, 1875–1920*. Boston: Museum of Fine Arts, 1987.

Kammen, Michael. *A Season of Youth: The American Revolution and the Historical Imagination*. New York: Alfred A. Knopf, 1978.

Katz, Michael. *The Irony of Early School Reform*. Cambridge, Mass.: Harvard University Press, 1968.

Keeley, Mary. *How to Make a Pageant*. London: Putnam, 1936.

Kennedy, Marion, and Katharine Isabel Benis. *Special Day Pageants for Little People*. New York: A. S. Barnes & Co., 1927.

Kenney, Vincent S. *Paul Green*. New York: Twayne Publishers, Inc. 1971.

Keppel, Frederick P., and R. L. Duffus. *The Arts in American Life*. New York: McGraw-Hill Book Co., 1933.

Kinne, Wisner Payne. *George Pierce Baker and the American Theatre*. Cambridge: Harvard University Press, 1954.

Kinney, Troy, and Margaret Kinney. *The Dance, Its Place in Art and Life*. New York: Frederick A. Stokes, 1924.

Koch, Frederick Henry. *Amateur Values in Pageantry*. Ann Arbor, Mich.: Ann Arbor Press, 1915.

———. *The Dakota Playmakers*. Grand Forks, N.Dak.: University of North Dakota, 1918.

———. *Play Producing for School and Little Theatre Stages*. Chapel Hill, N. C.: University of North Carolina Press, 1935.

Kraut, Alan M. *The Huddled Masses, The Immigrant in American Society, 1880–1921*. Arlington Heights, Ill.: Harlan Davidson, Inc., 1982.

Langdon, William Chauncy. *The Celebration of the Fourth of July by Means of Pageantry*. With an article and notes on the music by Arthur Farwell. New York: Russell Sage Foundation, 1912.

———. *Everyday Things in American Life*. New York: C. Scribner's Sons, 1941.

Langner, Lawrence. *The Magic Curtain*. New York: E. P. Dutton, 1951.

Lasch, Christopher. *The New Radicalism in America 1889–1963: The Intellectual as a Social Type*. New York: Alfred A. Knopf, 1965.

Lears, T. J. Jackson. *No Place of Grace: Anti-Modernism and the Transformation of American Culture, 1880–1920*. New York: Pantheon Books, 1981.

Lee, Joseph. *Constructive and Preventive Philanthropy*. New York: Macmillan Co., 1902.

———. *Play in Education*. New York: Macmillan Co., 1915.

Leland, Arthur, and Lorna Leland, eds. *Playground Technique and Playcraft*. New York: Baker & Taylor Co., 1910.

Lewis, Benjamin. *Pageantry and the Pilgrim Tercentenary Celebration with Sample Pilgrim Pageants, Suggestions for Preparing Bibliographies for State of Utah*. Salt Lake City: University of Utah, 1920.

Link, Arthur S., and Richard L. McCormick. *Progressivism*. Arlington Heights, Ill.: Harlan Davidson, Inc., 1983.

Linnell, Adelaide. *The School Festival*. New York: C. Scribner's Sons, 1931.

Lower, Charles, and William Fee. *History into Drama, Case Book on The Lost Colony*. Odyssey, 1963.

Lynch, Kevin. *The Image of the City*. Cambridge, Mass: Technology Press, 1960.

Lynes, Russell. *The Lively Audience: A Social History of the Visual and Performing Arts in America, 1840–1950*. New York: Harper & Row, 1985.

MacCalmon, George, and Christian H. Moe. *Creating Historical Drama*. Carbondale, Ill.: Southern Illinois University Press, 1965.

MacGowan, Kenneth. *Footlights across America: Towards a National Theatre*. New York: Harcourt, Brace & Co., 1929.

MacKay, Constance D'Arcy. *The Little Theatre in the United States*. New York: Henry Holt & Company, 1917.

———. *Patriotic Drama in Your Town*. New York: Henry Holt & Company, 1918.

———. *Patriotic Plays and Pageants for Young People*. New York: Henry Holt & Company, 1912.

MacKaye, Percy. *The Canterbury Pilgrims*. New York: Macmillan, 1908.

———. *The Civic Theatre in Relation to the Redemption of Leisure*. New York: Mitchell Kennerly, 1912.

———. *Community Drama: Its Motive and Method of Neighborliness, An Interpretation.* Boston: Houghton Mifflin Company, 1917.

———. *Epoch, The Life of Steele MacKaye.* New York: Boni & Liveright, 1927.

———. *Jeanne d'Arc.* New York: Macmillan Co., 1906.

———. *Kentucky Mountain Fantasies.* New York: Longmans Green & Co., 1928.

———. *The Playhouse and the Play and Other Addresses.* New York: Greenwood Press, 1909.

———. *The Scarecrow.* New York: Macmillan Co., 1908.

———. *A Substitute for War.* New York: Macmillan Co., 1915.

———. *This Fine-pretty World, a Comedy of the Kentucky Mountains.* New York: Macmillan Co., 1924.

———. *Yankee Fantasies: Five One-Act Folk-Plays.* New York: Ouffield & Co., 1912.

Magriel, Paul. *Nijinsky, Pavlova, Duncan.* New York: Da Capo Press, 1977.

Marsh, Agnes L., and Lucile Marsh. *The Dance in Education.* New York: A. S. Barnes & Co., 1924.

McCullough, Jack W. *Living Pictures on the New York Stage.* Ann Arbor, Mich.: UMI Research Press, 1983.

McLaren, Gay. *Morally We Roll Along.* Boston: Little, Brown and Company, 1938.

McWilliams, Carey. *Southern California: An Island on the Land.* Santa Barbara, Calif.: Peregrine Smith, 1973.

Mero, Everett B., ed. *American Playgrounds.* New York: Baker, 1909.

Mickel, Jese C. *Footlights on the Prairie: The Story of the Repertory Tent Players in the Midwest.* St. Cloud, Minn.: North Star Press, 1974.

Mohl, Raymond A. *The New City: Urban America in the Industrial Age, 1860–1920.* Arlington Heights, Ill.: Harlan Davidson, 1985.

Moody, Aileen. *Pageants for School and College Use.* Minneapolis, Minn.: Burgess Pub. Co., 1937.

Moore, Sally F., and Barbara Myerhoff, eds. *Secular Ritual.* Assen: Van Gorcum, 1977.

Morrison, Theodore. *Chautauqua: A Center for Education, Religion and the Arts in America.* Chicago: University of Chicago Press, 1974.

Nagler, Alois Maria. *Theatre Festivals of the Medici, 1539–1637.* New Haven: Yale University Press, 1964.

Nash, Jay B. *The Organization and Administration of Playgrounds and Recreation.* New York: A. S. Barnes & Co., 1927.

National Council for Prevention of War. *List of Pageants and Plays for Children, Young People, Adults.* Washington, D.C.: Education Department National Council for Prevention of War, 1928.

National Recreation Association. *Community Drama.* New York: The Century Co., 1926.

Needham, Mary. *Folk Festivals: Their Growth and How to Give Them.* New York: B. W. Huebsch, 1912.

Nelson, Alan H. *The Medieval English Stage: Corpus Christi Pageant and Plays.* Chicago: University of Chicago Press, 1974.

Noffsinger, John F. *Correspondence Schools, Lyceums, Chautauquas.* New York: Macmillan Co., 1926.

Northcutt, John Orlando. *Magic Valley: The Story of the Hollywood Bowl.* Los Angeles: - Fushich Press, 1967.

Oetting, E. R., and Alice M. Oetting. *Pageants for High Schools.* Keokuk, Iowa: The Extra Curricular Publishing Co., 1940.

Osterweis, Rollin. *The Myth of The Lost Cause, 1865–1900.* Hamden, Conn.: Archin Books, 1973.

Parker, Anthony. *Pageants, Their Presentation and Production*. London: The Bodley Head, 1954.

Parker, Louis Napoleon. *Several of My Lives*. London: Chapman and Hall, 1928.

Perry, Clarence. *Wider Use of the School Plant*. New York: Charities Publication Committee, 1910.

Perry, Clarence Arthur. *The Work of the Little Theatres*. New York: Russell Sage Foundation, 1933.

Philanthropy and Social Progress: Essays by Jane Addams and Others. Originally a series of lectures delivered in 1893 for the School of Applied Ethics in Plymouth, Massachusetts. Montclair, N.J.: Paterson Smith, 1970.

Pierce, Bessie Louise. *Public Opinion and the Teaching of History in the United States*. New York: Alfred A. Knopf, 1926.

Poggi, Jack. *Theater in America: The Impact of Economic Forces, 1870–1967*. Ithaca, N.Y.: Cornell University Press, 1968.

Porter, Glenn. *The Rise of Big Business, 1860–1910*. Arlington Heights, Ill.: Harlan Davidson, Inc., 1973.

Prevots, Naima. *Dancing in the Sun: Hollywood Choreographers, 1915–1937*. Ann Arbor, Mich.: UMI Research Press, 1987.

Proceedings of the Conference on Drama in American Universities and Little Theatres. Pittsburgh: Carnegie Institute of Technology, 1915.

Putter, Joseph. *The Boy and His Gang*. Boston: Houghton-Mifflin Company, 1912.

Quandt, Jean. *From the Small Town to the Great Community: The Social Thought of Progressive Intellectuals*. New Brunswick, N.J.: Rutgers University Press, 1970.

Quinn, Arthur Hobson. *A History of the American Drama from the Civil War to the Present Day*. New York: Harper & Bros., 1927.

Rainwater, Clarence. *The Play Movement in the United States*. Chicago: University of Chicago Press, 1922.

Rath, Emil. *Aesthetic Dancing*. New York: A. S. Barnes & Co., 1914.

Ratner, L., and S. Cohen, eds. *The Development of an American Culture*. Englewood Cliffs, N.J.: Prentice-Hall, 1970.

Riis, Jacob Arthur. *The Battle with the Slum*. New York: Macmillan Co., 1912.

_____ . *How the Other Half Lives: Studies among the Tenements in New York*. New York: C. Scribner's Sons, 1890.

_____ . *The Making of an American*. New York: Macmillan Co., 1902.

Rockwell, Ethel Theodora. *Historical Pageantry: A Treatise and a Bibliography*. Madison, Wis., 1916.

Rolland, Romain. *The People's Theater*. New York: Henry Holt and Company, 1918. Translated from the French by Barrett H. Clark. Chapters originally appeared as articles in the *Revue d'art dramatique* between 1900 and 1903.

Rosenzweig, Roy. *Eight Hours for What We Will: Workers and Leisure in an Industrial City 1870–1920*. Cambridge: Cambridge University Press, 1983.

Ross, Dorothy. *G. Stanley Hall, The Psychologist as Prophet*. Chicago: University of Chicago Press, 1972.

Royce, Josiah. *Race Questions, Provincialism and Other American Problems*. New York: Macmillan Co., 1908.

Russell, Mary. *The Drama as a Factor in Social Education*. New York: George H. Doran Co., 1924.

_____ . *How to Produce Plays and Pageants*. New York: George H. Doran Co., 1923.

Ruyter, Nancy Lee Chalfa. *Reformers and Visionaries, The Americanization of the Art of Dance*. New York: Dance Horizons, 1979.

Sarlos, Robert Karoly. *Jig Cook and the Provincetown Players: Theatre in Ferment.* Amherst: The University of Massachusetts Press, 1982.

Saylor, Oliver M. *Our American Theatre.* New York: Brentano's, 1923.

————, ed. *Max Reinhardt and His Theatre.* Trans. Barret H. Clark. New York: Henry Holt & Company, 1918.

Schlundt, Christena L. *The Professional Appearances of Ruth St. Denis and Ted Shawn: A Chronology and Index of Dances, 1906–1932.* New York: New York Public Library, 1962.

A Second List of Plays and Pageants. YWCA Women's Press, 1921.

Selden, Samuel, ed. *The Carolina Play-Book.* 30th Anniversary of Playmaking. University of North Carolina, 1935.

————. *Organizing a Community Theatre.* Cleveland, Ohio: National Theatre Conference, 1945.

Selden, Samuel, and Mary Tom Sphangos. *Frederick Henry Koch: A Pioneer Playmaker.* Chapel Hill: The University of North Carolina Library, 1954.

Sharp, Cecil. *The Country Dance Book.* London: Novello & Co., 1909–27.

Shawn, Ted. *Dance We Must.* Great Britain: Dennis Dobson, 1946.

Shelton, Suzanne. *Divine Dancer: A Biography of Ruth St. Denis.* New York: Double day, 1969.

Short, Josephine Helena. *Oberammergau.* New York: T. Y. Crowell and Co., 1910.

Siegel, Marcia. *Days on Earth: The Dance of Doris Humphrey.* New Haven: Yale University Press, 1987.

Spearman, Walter, with the assistance of Samuel Selden. *The Carolina Playmakers, the First Fifty Years.* Chapel Hill: The University of North Carolina Press, 1970.

Spencer, Matthew Lyle. *Corpus Christi Pageants in England.* New York: The Baker & Taylor Company, 1911.

The Speyer School Curriculum. New York: Teachers College, Columbia University, 1913.

Stelzle, Charles. *Boys of the Street.* New York: F. H. Revell, 1904.

Stevens, Thomas Wood. *The Theatre From Athens to Broadway.* New York: D. Appleton and Company, 1932.

Strong, Roy C. *Splendor at Court: Renaissance Spectacle and Theater of Power.* Boston: Houghton Mifflin Company, 1973.

Swift, Edgar. *Learning and Doing.* Indianapolis, Ind.: Bobbs-Merrill Co., 1914.

————. *Mind in the Making.* New York: C. Scribner's Sons, 1908.

————. *Youth and the Race.* New York: C. Scribner's Sons, 1912.

Taft, Linwood. *Pageants with a Purpose.* New York: A. S. Barnes & Co., 1924.

————. *The Technique of Pageantry.* New York: A. S. Barnes & Co., 1921.

Tarbell, Ida. *All in the Day's Work.* New York: Macmillan Co., 1939.

Taylor, Loren E. *Pageants and Festivals.* Minneapolis, Minn.: Burgess Publishing Co., 1965.

Terry, Walter. *Miss Ruth: The "More Living Life" of Ruth St. Denis.* New York: Dodd Mead, 1969.

————. *Ted Shawn, Father of American Dance.* New York: Dial Press, 1976.

Thorndike, Edward L. *Education: A First Book.* New York: Macmillan Co., 1912.

————. *Educational Psychology.* Vol. 1. New York: Teachers College, Columbia University, 1913–14.

————. *Notes on Child Study.* New York: Macmillan Co., 1901.

Torrence, Bruce. *Hollywood: The First 100 Years.* Hollywood, Calif.: Hollywood Chamber of Commerce, 1979.

Tripp, Anne Huber. *The IWW and the Paterson Silk Strike of 1913.* Urbana, Ill.: University of Illinois Press, 1987.

United States Country Life Commission. *Report of the Commission on Country Life.* New York: Sturgis and Walton, 1911.

A Vision for Music. Opening Exhibit, Summer 1984. Los Angeles: Hollywood Bowl Museum, 1985.

Wald, Lillian. *Windows on Henry Street.* Boston: Little, Brown and Company, 1934.

Wallace, Florence Magill. *Pageant Building.* Published by Illinois Centennial Commission. Springfield, Ill.: Schnepp Barnes State Printers, 1918.

Warren, Larry. *Lester Horton: Modern Dance Pioneer.* New York: Marcel Dekker, 1977.

Weingartner, Fannia, ed. *Ravinia: The Festival at Its Half Century.* Highland Park, Ill.: Ravinia Festival Association in conjunction with Rand McNally & Company, 1985.

Wells, Jeannette L. *A History of the Music Festival at Chautauqua Institution, 1874–1957.* Washington, D.C.: The Catholic University of America Press, 1958.

White, Morton. *Social Thought in America: The Revolt against Formalism.* New York: Viking Press, 1949.

Wiebe, Robert. *The Search for Order, 1877–1920.* New York: Hill and Wang, 1967.

_____. *The Segmented Society: An Introduction to the Meaning of America.* New York: Oxford, 1975.

Wilson, Richard Guy, Dianne H. Pilgrim and Dickran Tashjian. *The Machine Age in America, 1918–1941.* The Brooklyn Museum in association with Harry N. Abrams, Inc., Publishers, New York, 1987.

Wilson, R. Jackson. *In Quest of Community: Social Philosophy in the United States, 1860–1920.* New York: Wiley, 1968.

Withington, Robert. *English Pageantry.* 2 vols., Cambridge, Mass.: Harvard University Press, 1918–20.

_____. *A Manual of Pageantry.* Bloomington, Ind., 1915.

Witmer, Eleanor Montgomery. *Introducing Teachers College: Some Notes and Recollections.* New York: Bureau of Publications, Teachers College, Columbia University, 1948.

Young Women's Christian Association, U.S. National Board, Bureau of Pageantry. *A Second List of Pageants and Plays.* New York: The Women's Press, 1921.

Zeigler, Joseph Wesley. *Regional Theatre: The Revolutionary Stage.* Minneapolis: University of Minnesota Press, 1973.

Zenderland, Leila. *Recycling the Past: Popular Uses of American History.* Philadelphia: University of Pennsylvania Press, 1978.

Zueblin, Charles. *American Municipal Progress.* New York: Macmillan Co., 1916.

Articles, Journals, Periodicals

Addams, Jane. "Hull House, Chicago: An Effort Toward Sound Democracy." *Forum* (October 1892).

Appia, Adolphe. "The Future of Production." *Theatre Arts Anthology.* New York: Theatre Arts Books, 1950, pp. 519–32.

Baker, George Pierce. "The 47 Workshop." *Century* (February 1921): 417–25.

_____. "The 47 Workshop." *Quarterly Journal of Speech Education* (May 1919): 185–95.

_____. "The Hollis Hall Pageant." *Harvard Graduates Magazine* (September 1913): 214–17.

_____. "Pageantry." *Art and Progress* (1913): 831–35.

_____. "Pageantry." *New Boston* (November 1910): 295–96.

_____. "The Peterborough Memorial Pageant as the Producer Saw It." *New Boston* (October 1910): 256–61.

_____. "The Pageant and Masque of Saint Louis." *World's Work* (August 1914): 389–94.

_____. "Proposal Building for the Drama." *Harvard Alumni Bulletin* (May 1914): 512–15.

_____ . "The Theatre and the University." *Theatre Arts Monthly* (February 1925): 98–108.

_____ . "What the Theatre Can Do for the School." *Ladies Home Journal* (January 1913): 47.

Baltz, Trudy. "Pageantry and Mural Painting: Community Rituals in Allegorical Form." *Winterthur Portfolio* (1980): 211–28.

Beard, Adelia Belle. "The American Pageant." *American Homes and Gardens* (July 1912).

Becht, J. George. "A Normal School Commencement." *The Playground* (February 1911): 363–68.

Bjorkman, Frances. "A Nation Learning to Play." *World's Work* (September 1909): 12038–45.

Brown, Frank Chouteau. "The American Pageant Association—A New Force Working for the Future of Pageantry in America." *The Drama* (February 1913): 178–91.

_____ . "The Book of the Pageant and Its Development." *The Drama* (May 1915): 269–93.

_____ . "Boston Sees the First American Civic Pageants." *Theatre* (February 1911): 45–50.

_____ . "Directing a Pageant." *Boston Common Magazine* (1910): 10–11.

_____ . "The Peterborough Pageant as a Spectator Saw It." *New Boston* (1910).

Brown, John Mason. "The Four Georges; G. P. Baker at Work." *Theatre Arts Anthology*. New York: Theatre Arts Books, 1950, pp. 481–89.

Brown, Rollo Walter. "George Pierce Baker." *The Atlantic Monthly* (February 1948): 66–70.

Brownell, Edith. "The Pageant of Thetford: The Development of a Rural Community through Pageantry." *New Boston* (August 1911): 142–44.

Burbage, F. C. "An Old Historic Town." *Vermonter* (June 1909): 175–80.

Cheney, Sheldon. "Gordon Craig: The Theatre's Chief Revolutionary." *Theatre Arts Anthology*. New York: Theatre Arts Books, 1950, pp. 379–85.

Clark, Lotta A. "Pageantry in America." *English Journal* (March 1914): 146–53.

Collier, John. "The Lantern Bearers—XI. Caliban of the Yellow Sands." *The Survey* (July 1916): 343–50.

Cowan, Gertrude. "The Peterborough Pageant." *Musical Courier* (August 1910): 24–25.

Crawford, Jack Randall. "Pageant Technique." *Quarterly Journal of Speech Education* (1920): 76–78.

_____ . "Pageantry—Study Course." *Drama League Monthly* (1916): 226–36.

Culbertson, Evelyn Davis. "Arthur Farwell." *American Music* (Summer 1987).

Davol, Ralph. "Two Mountain Holidays: A Pageant of Rural Progress and a Festival of Music." *Congregationalist and Christian World* (August 1911): 293.

Dickinson, Thomas. "The Pageant." *Playbook* (September 1914): 4–31.

Dudley, Pendleton. "The New England Playground Institute." *The Playground* (February 1911): 387–92.

Duerr, Edwin. "Teaching Theatre." *Theatre Arts Anthology*. New York: Theatre Arts Books, 1950, pp. 497–501.

Durand, E. Dana. "Our Immigrants and the Future." *The World's Work* (February 1912): 431–43.

Dykema, Peter W. "Paper by Professor Dykema." *School Music* (September 1912): 5–13.

Eaton, Walter Prichard. "Baker's Method of Making Playwrights." *Bookman* (June 1919): 478–80.

Eberele, Louise. "The Lady of the Pageants." *Today's Magazine* (April 1914): 10–11.

Edlund, Roscoe C. "Pageant of Saint Johnsbury." *Survey* (September 1912): 771–72.

Farwell, Arthur. "Pageant and Masque of Saint Louis." *American Review of Reviews* (August 1914): 187–93.

_____ . "St. Johnsbury's Past Retold in Noble Pageant." *Musical America* (September 1912).

Fisher, David James. "Romain Rolland and the French People's Theatre." *Tulane Drama Review* 73 (1977).

Flanagan, Hallie. "Federal Theatre Project." *Theatre Arts Anthology*. New York: Theatre Arts Books, 1950, pp. 96–98.

Glassberg, David. "History and the Public: Legacies of the Progressive Era." *Journal of American History* (March 1987): 957–80.

Gordon, Mel. "Percy MacKaye's Masque of Caliban." *Tulane Drama Review* 70 (1976).

Green, Paul. "Drama and the Weather." *Theatre Arts Anthology*. New York: Theatre Arts Books, 1950, pp. 105–11.

Gulick, Luther. "The New and More Glorious Fourth." *World's Work* (1909): 11784–87.

———. "The Playground Association of America: Purpose." *The Playground* (1910).

Hagedorn, Hermann. "The Pageant at Plymouth." *Outlook* (1921): 699.

"Indiana University's Centenary Pageant." *American Review of Reviews* (June 1916): 683–85.

"Indiana's Patriotism Stirred by Pageant." *Musical America* (June 1916): 32–33.

Isaacs, Edith J. R. "Paul Green: A Case in Point." *Theatre Arts Anthology*. New York: Theatre Arts Books, 1950, pp. 490–96.

Jones, Robert Edmond. "The Gloves of Isadora." *Theatre Arts Anthology*. New York: Theatre Arts Books, 1950, pp. 184–92.

Keppel, Frederick P. "The Arts in Social Life." *Presidents Committee on Recent Social Trends*. New York: McGraw-Hill Book Company, 1933.

Koch, Frederick. "Folk-Play Making in Dakota and Carolina." *Playground* (January 1925): 599–600.

———. "The New Art of Pageantry." *Current Opinion* (September 1914): 178–79.

Kunz, George Frederick. "Historical Pageantry in America: A Brief Review of Its Developments, Tendencies and Requirements." In *American Scenic and Historic Preservation Society 21 Annual Report* (1916).

Langdon, William Chauncy. "The Composing of the Hymn to Indiana." *Indiana University Alumni Quarterly* (1920).

———. "The Deerfield Pageant." *The Playground* (March 1911): 417–28.

———. "Historical Pageants in America." *City Club Bulletin* (November 1913).

———. "Ideas for Civic Education from the Juvenile City League." *Chautauquan* (June 1906).

———. "Music in Pageantry." *The Drama* (1918): 494–504.

———. "The New Pageants." *The Playground* (February 1911): 383–86.

———. "The Pageant in America." *The American Monthly Magazine* (March 1911): 99–103.

———. "The Pageant of Meriden, New Hampshire." *American City* (April 1914): 355–61.

———. "The Pageant of Saint Johnsbury: Pageantry as a Constructive Force in Community Betterment." *American City* (May 1913): 481–87.

———. "The Pageant of the Perfect City." *The Playground* (April 1911): 2–16.

———. "Pageant of Thetford." *National Municipal Review* (January 1912): 76–77.

———. "Pageant of Thetford." *The Playground* (December 1911): 302–18.

———. "Pageant of Thetford." *Vermonter* (July 1911).

———. "The Philadelphia Historical Pageant." *The Survey*. (November 1912): 215–18.

Levine, Henry. "American Composers Provide Music for Pilgrim Pageant." *Musical America* (July 1921): 1, 2, 4.

Lord, Katherine. "How to Conduct a Village Pageant: Peculiar Fitness of the Small Town Setting for the Revival of the Ancient Out-door Drama." *Suburban Life* (November 1911).

MacKay, Constance D'Arcy. "The American Folk Festival." *The Drama* (April 1913): 341–44.

———. "The Rebirth of American Pageantry." *American Magazine of Art* 17 (1925): 303–4.

MacKaye, Hazel. "Art and the Women's Movement." *Forum* (June 1913): 680–84.

———. "The Art of the Theatre in a New Form." *Vassar Quarterly* (1916).

———. "The Future of Pageantry in the Life of the People." *The Drama* (Winter 1913).

_____ . "Outdoor Plays and Pageants, a Sketch of the Movement in America." *The Indepen-dent* (1910): 1227–34.

_____ . "The Peterborough Pageant." *The Drama* (1910): 136–47.

MacKaye, Percy. "The Drama of Democracy." *Columbia University Quarterly* (March 1908): 173–83.

_____ . "Professor of Dramatic Literature at Harvard." *American Magazine* (December 1911): 180–82.

MacGowan, Kenneth. "Little Theatre Backgrounds." *Theatre Arts Anthology.* New York: Theatre Arts Books, 1950, pp. 473–80.

McCandless, Stanley. "A Map of These United States Showing the Influence of the Work of George Pierce Baker (1890–1924)." *Theatre Arts Monthly* (February 1925): 106–8.

McNamara, Brooks. "The Pageant Era." *Theatre Crafts* (September 1975): 10–13.

_____ . "The Paterson Strike Pageant." *Tulane Drama Review* 51 (1971).

McReynolds, George. "The Centennial Pageant for Indiana: Suggestions for Its Performance." *Indiana Magazine of History* (September 1915).

"The Meriden Pageant." *The Playground* (June 1913): 129.

Mitchell, Roy. "The New Pageantry." *Theatre Arts Monthly* (August 1930): 695–702.

Morton, D. M. "Yale University Department of Drama." *Theatre Arts Monthly* (April 1926): 254–61.

Nochlin, Linda. "The Paterson Strike Pageant of 1913." *Art in America* 62 (May–June 1974).

Oberholtzer, Ellis Paxon. "Historical Pageants in England and America." *Century Magazine* (July 1910): 416–27.

Orr, William. "An American Holiday." *Atlantic Monthly* 103 (1909): 782–89.

Oster, Donald Bright. "Nights of Fantasy: The Saint Louis Pageant and Masque of 1914." *Bulletin of the Missouri Historical Society* 13 (April 1975): 175–205.

"A Pageant at Knoxville, Tennessee." *The Playground* (February 1911): 369.

"The Pageant of Thetford." *Vermonter* (1911): 191–194.

"The Pageant of Illinois." *Outlook* (January 1910): 185.

"The Pageant of the Mohawk Trail." *Outlook* (July 1919).

"The Pageant of Nations." *Survey* (May 1914): 209.

Parker, Louis N. "What Is a Pageant." *New Boston* (1910): 296–98.

"The Paterson Strike Pageant." *Outlook* (June 1913): 352.

Pierce, Lucy. "The Secessionists in the Arena." *The Drama* (August 1913): 127–37.

Pollock, Arthur. "Woman in the Theatre." *Harper's Weekly* (September 1915): 237–38.

Porter, Elizabeth. "A Pageant of Progress." *Outlook* (November 1912): 653–58.

Quinn, John. "Lady Gregory and the Abbey Theater." *Outlook* (1911): 915–20.

"Report of the Committee on Festivals." *The Playground* (February 1911): 372–82.

Riggs, Lynn. "A Credo for the Tributary Theatre." *Theatre Arts Anthology.* New York: Theatre Arts Books, 1950, pp. 502–4.

Roberts, Mary. "The Civic Theatre." *Craftsman* (May 1914): 140–41.

_____ . "How the Red Cross Mobilized." *Touchstone* (November 1917): 116–25.

_____ . "The Value of Outdoor Plays to America." *Craftsman* (August 1909): 491–506.

Rockwell, Ethel. "Pageantry in Wisconsin." *The Wisconsin Alumni Magazine* (February 1915).

Rumbold, Charlotte. "Shakespeare Pageant in Saint Louis." *Journal of Education* (May 1916): 551–52.

_____ . "The Saint Louis Pageant and Masque." *The Survey* (July 1919): 372–75.

Saylor, Oliver M. "The Return of the Pilgrims." *New Republic* (August 1921): 303.

Slade, Rev. and Mrs. William. "The Pageant of Thetford." *Vermonter* (1912): 476–90.

Smith, Ethel. "The Independence Day Pageant at Washington." *The Drama* (February 1914): 118–30.

Sumner, Mark. "Staging History Outdoors." *Theatre Crafts* (September 1975): 4–5.

Taintor, J. F. "An Historical Pageant in a Small Town." *The Playground* (February 1911): 357–62.

Tanner, Virginia. "The Dances of American Pageantry." *The Radcliffe Quarterly* 4 (1920): 46–49.

"The Thetford Pageant." *American Lumberman* (July 1911).

"Two New England Festivals of Note." *Musical America* (August 1912).

"Vermont Villages Co-Operate in Historical Pageant." *American Lumberman* (August 1911): 32–33.

Wagner, Richard. "The Art Work of the Future." Bernard Dukok, *Dramatic Theory and Criticism, Greeks to Grotowski*. New York: Holt, 1974, pp. 777–94.

Woodley, Ruth. "Conference on the National Shakespeare Pageant." *The Playground* (April 1915): 14–15.

Dissertations & Theses

Curry, Jane Kathleen. "William Chauncy Langdon and American Historical Pageantry." Brown University, 1985. (Thesis).

Davis, Evelyn Johnson. "The Significance of Arthur Farwell as an American Music Educator." The University of Maryland, 1972. (Dissertation).

Dierolf, C. E. "The Pageant Drama and American Pageantry 1905–1952." University of Pennsylvania, 1952. (Dissertation).

Glassberg, David Harold. "American Civic Pageantry and the Image of the Community, 1900–1932." The Johns Hopkins University, 1982. (Dissertation).

Kirk, Edgar Lee. "Toward American Music: A Study of the Life and Music of Arthur George Farwell." Eastman School of Music, 1958. (Dissertation).

Leggette, L. Poe. "Festival Drama." Teachers College, Columbia University, 1956. (Dissertation).

Mallery, Mary Louise. "A Thesis in Support of Increased Pageant Drama Production; Based upon the Consideration of 'The Lost Colony' by Paul Green; 'Toward the Western Sky' by Lynn Riggs; 'The Enduring Game' by Edward Percy; and 'William Tell' by Frederick Schiller." Syracuse University, 1952. (Thesis).

Moe, Christian H. "From History to Drama: A Study of the Influence of the Pageant, the Outdoor Epic Drama and the Historical Stage Play upon the Dramatization of Three American Historical Figures." Cornell University, 1958. (Dissertation).

Rambin, William Robert, Jr. "Thomas Wood Stevens: American Pageant Master." Louisiana State University, 1977. (Dissertation).

Shea, Ann Marie. "Community Pageants in Massachusetts, 1908–1932." New York University, 1984. (Dissertation).

Tackel, Martin Sidney. "Women and American Pageantry: 1908 to 1918." City College of New York, 1982. (Dissertation).

Treat, Donald R. "Paul Green's Concept of Symphonic Drama and Its Application to His Outdoor Plays." University of Denver, 1963. (Dissertation).

Tryon, Virginia Vaughn. "The 47 Workshop: Its History and Significance." University of Southern California, 1933. (Thesis).

Walsh, Frederick G. "Outdoor Commemorative Drama in the United States, 1900–1950." Case Western Reserve University, 1952. (Dissertation).

Wardrip, Mark Allen. "A Western Portal of Culture: The Hearst Greek Theatre of the University of California, 1903–1984." University of California, Berkeley, 1984. (Dissertation).

Weston, Pearl Ott. "Pageantry in the United States." Duquesne University, 1934. (Dissertation).
Zellers, Parker. "A Survey of American Pageantry from 1753 to 1955." Indiana University, 1956. (Thesis).

Archives & Special Collections

Baker & Pageant Collections, Harvard Theatre Collection, Harvard University.
Barnard Archives, Barnard College, New York.
Jack Randall Crawford Papers, Manuscripts and Archives. Yale University Library.
Federal Theatre Project, Special Collections, George Mason University, Virginia.
Norma Gould. Unpublished notes for pageantry course at the University of Southern California, 1924–1925. Dance collection of Naima Prevots, Washington, D.C.
Langdon & Harris Collections, John Hay Library, Brown University Library.
MacKaye Family Collection, Baker Library, Dartmouth College.
Pageant Collection, Boston Public Library.
Smithsonian Institution: Archives; Division of Community Life. Both in the National Museum of American History.
Stevens Collection, Special Collections, University of Arizona, Tucson, Arizona.
Teachers College Archives, Teachers College, Columbia University.

Index